SANDSTONE WAY

HIKING CEDAR MESA

Jim Beard

"Sandstone Way" by Jim Beard. ISBN 1-58939-358-9.

Published 2003 by Virtualbookworm.com Publishing Inc., P.O. Box 9949, College Station, TX , 77842, US.

Manufactured in the United States of America

To those who understand.

CONTENTS

FIRST LEDGE

of Anasazically acceptable realm. Not so much that I would no longer need a map, but that every corner I turn gives me an "Ahah! I am home, I know you, you know me." I wish for some level of familiarity of landscape; that I am welcomed in some nameless gully at any time of season, for any lack of reasons.

I know this kind of acceptance only comes with time, not miles traveled but rest breaks in ubiquitous places, pauses to reflect and soak up a vista, corners turned out of curiosity, and stumbles endured because I had to be looking around in awe; yes in awe at perceived magnificence and sublime beauty. I never met an archaeologist yet who could admit that beauty even more than some other whiteman's rationale could have drawn Anasazi to this land, to build their homes where they did, and to draw as they did on rock faces.

I wish I could turn back some imaginary clock, using my time-machine, as a young man go to school and become first archaeologist who is shunned by his fellows for excavating some ruin merely for purpose of finding beauty, for finding proof of appreciation of beauty in Anasazi, above and beyond their other considerations. To find a shard which showed conclusively that beauty was in their souls, under their soles, and that when it ended is partly why they had to leave.

I have seen rock art, I have seen ruins with much inherent beauty; well, how to define beauty, is that not a question for another session(?); I could only stand in awe and know that here is represented love: of land, of their lifeway, and of each other. It was not forever, this appreciation, and when it ended, they left.

As such an archaeologist, I would travel to strange lands with prior civilizations and pontificate endlessly on meaning to prehistoric residents of beauty. I would have to write lengthy papers, well-annotated and bibliographied, on significance of such and such a site, or glyph. And as I came upon a new and strange-to-me feature, artifact, or element, whether sieved or not, I would know it was but one more piece of a puzzle, only locked into my inner being, waiting to spring forth and amaze our world.

But, amazement from this world is not always easy, some require proof, some require a gps to show their way. Some cannot imagine an answer before they know a question. Some cannot see a ruin for rocks inherent in it.

I suppose what I am coming to is admitting that I am in love with a landscape, bounded on all sides by some sort of imaginary barrier, wherein a people once roamed, lived, farmed, hunted, loved each other and died, were reborn and lived again in another form. They could not know how to finally leave this land until there was no choice. Their religion was land, sun, moon, planting, resident animals, perceived powers of animals and plants; there were no tv's, no books, no entertainment to divert and detract.

Whatever luck they found had to come from inside, had to come from an appreciation of forces which shaped their lives, dreams and fellows. Without a sure knowledge of seasons, weather, and fertility of soils, microclimes of best farming lands, best places to build and store their corn and food, there could be no living here in a semi-desert.

I have read many books and articles written by explorers and archaeologists, but did they show me a way, did they get me to know where to look, what to think, and ease my sore feet by a proper place to rest? Was there any specific helper, or leader who showed me what to look for? I think perhaps so, but he was imaginary, somewhere deep in unknown recesses of my brain, perhaps, or in some other realm besides one I currently reside in. He shaped my life, directed my footsteps towards this place, and this time in my life, reached out into space and time and tweaked chance, using whatever grossly needful tools lay at hand.

Perhaps it was really a she, but one thing for sure, he or

she does not respond to a misnomer of a white man's god, or idea; no, we are talking of some other wholly different kind of guide,. of some kind of helper not always recognized in what we see as a rational world. There is no name for what I am talking about, thinking of, and I cannot really say what I feel, when next I launch out there for a hike, and entrenchment of my understanding.

There is no specific site or rock art element, or even vue which stands for idea of what I mean by a helper of my path, a guide to my knowledge enlargement, or put another way, to totality of my change. There is nobody but myself who puts one foot in front of other, and decides to explore such and such a place. There is some call I get to go there or here, now rather than later, but without some convenient label or name, can I convince you of anything more than that I am crazy? Perhaps, perhaps not.

Sometimes late at nite, just before going to sleep, I long to be such a person who could follow someone else, who could be lead by a leash to find a way, to not suffer momentary nightmares of stumbling or falling one time too many, to enjoy an easy hike full of pleasures and joy. But I know better, I know it is only by my constant desire to turn every corner, to open myself to possibilities, to listen to some indefinable call from some imaginary source to go look, that I have evolved and am evolving.

How I wish I could be as a child again, with loving parents helping me at every step. But no such dream ever happened anyway, so it is as a self-responsible adult I explore, accept my mistakes, forgive my lapses of judgment, and persist. I know, finally, that around some corner is what I am looking for, what I have been shaped to find, to know, and perhaps even to understand. Where and what that is, is for another time not yet come, I am not yet ready. 'Why' is better left to a philosopher, and you see I do not have my diploma, but I do have curiosity, persistence, and joy. I have two faithful companions, four-legged tho they are, who are always ready to hike with me, who sometimes need help at cliffs, who never argue tho they will hesitate, and who keep me grounded.

And by grounded, I mean that they keep me from being stupid, from thinking I am a better climber than I am, or from taking chances when I am alone and there is nobody with any idea where I am, or even cares. This comes with a real, and sometimes bitter, taste of being a solo-hiker. I have read a few hiking guide books by other solo hikers, but I am not same as they, have other goals in mind besides covering as many miles as possible only to write and sell books, or to find artifacts in places nobody would think of going. No, I am after more, and less than that.

I am basically a solo-hiker because there are no other ways to find what I must seek out, and my dogs keep me from escaping into some esoteric belief in my own invincibility, or some nihilistic desire to lose myself in some nameless canyon. There is a responsibility to live inherent in having small fellow-hikers along, who rely on me for fun, water, safety, and an eventual return home for dinner.

And, if I lock myself into all-too-brief encounters of outdoors by an inclination for only doing dayhikes, little snippets of experience, I make up for it by keeping after it, in persisting, in returning as soon as I can. I can edit my life to reflect my best, hiking, and leave out remainder.

For it is while hiking, alone with my dogs and meeting nobody for months, comes to me a gradual understanding, a base for my evolution, and a furthering possibility for discovery that defines me. And I am not a leader, nor a follower, simply a solo-hiker, and long after I am absorbed by this landscape someone else will come along to explore himself and think he merely explores a terrain.

He will know what I know, tho not in same way.

CHAPTER 7
SOLO HIKING

Hiking alone is not for everyone, but many people try it sometime or another. We cannot all find our perfect mate, who also loves to hike, or can put aside everyday living chores and go off for a hike.

I live alone, and I hike alone a hi percentage of time. Of course I also hike with two of my three dogs, other is crippled by a long ago car driver who did not stop, did not care.

Perhaps single biggest advantage of hiking alone is freedom towards spontaneity, both in choice of where to go, how fast to hike, and what changes to make or not make as I hike. I do not have to question, argue, or deny.

For some years I rafted some rivers in Southwestern US, my longest trips were thru Grand Canyon. I rafted mostly with one family, usually just parents. Sometimes just three of us, or one other passenger for my raft would be in Grand Canyon for 2 or 3 weeks. Usually my passenger would be someone not well known by us, and it did happen my passenger would decide to hike out early. Too often a romantic idea of "river trip thru Grand Canyon" clashed with reality--dirt, danger, and disagreements.

I started to evolve towards wanting to shorten trips, when my companions wanted to lengthen our trip. I wound up being more satisfied as trip leader, which was not always fair towards my companions.

What happened is that I started doing river trips on milder rivers totally by myself in a raft, and could not afford to pay for a car shuttle, so I would have to hitchhike with a dog.

More than anything, I started wanting solitude more than I wanted to be rafting Grand Canyon. Kayaking or canoeing did not seem to work for me, either.

It took awhile, but I stopped rafting, and stopped doing outback trips with other people, and hiking was easiest activity to do solo. Even mountain biking became less satisfying, for there are very many places to explore where you cannot go with a mountain bike.

When I moved to SE Utah, I began hiking more and more, and for years exclusively alone. I have hiked alone for so many hours and miles, it seems more natural to me than occasional times I hike with someone.

Once, long ago, I hitched a ride on a commercial raft trip in Grand Canyon. I was asked if I would like to stay overnite with them, going further downcanyon than originally I needed. My original plan was to merely get a ride from confluence of Little Colorado down to Tanner Trail. Since I had hitchhiked to Grand Canyon from Flagstaff, it did not really matter where I got out, and I had no job to return to, so I accepted.

Two women school teachers 'adopted' me, loaned me an extra blanket [it tends to get cold next to Colorado river, even in summer, at nite] and became friends. One question everyone wanted to know, but I could not quite satisfy, was how could I hike alone in "such a forbidding and wild place?"

But, I had already been hiking Grand Canyon alone every chance I could for a year or so. I used Harvey Butchart's early books as guides, not always following his routes exactly.

I made a few mistakes in those days, but I never got hurt, or in need of rescue, tho I did get lost once, and self-rescued myself. I learned and began to prefer to hike alone. Sometimes I would stop for a meal and sleep only when it was too dark to hike, and just plop down in or next to trail if nothing better offered itself.

Later, I stopped getting permits, and was never caught, or even questioned. I even camped right above Indian Gardens on Bright Angel trail one nite, watching happy campers below, perhaps feeling as some ancient enemy scout. My backpack became my only home, and I even hitched across country for a few years.

There is then a certain practice to art of hiking alone, it just takes time and miles, and little experiences which shape me into a solo-hiker. I am certainly not only one, nor most accomplished, but since I am not in any competition, who cares.

* * *

As I start off on a hike I try to take in my surroundings, and for awhile I look back behind me to memorize vue for when I return later. Usually I am hiking across jp flats to get to a canyon, and start out fast.

It is when I get to a canyon rim, whether I am going to descend or rimwalk, that I have to start vista-absorbing, using my binocs and moving along only to stop frequently. If I am dropping down into a canyon, I will often stop to scout my route, and check for sites, ruins or rock art.

Usually, I find that descending or ascending slickrock slopes is easier than using talus/jp slopes, but often it is a combination that works. And sometimes a faint deer trail helps, or even a faint human track. My way to descend into a canyon is to take it easy, to scout continually and know where I am going so as to avoid surprises such as a sudden cliff below me, or ice on a slope. And as simple as it sounds: every single footstep counts, so I try to avoid losing control or hurrying. There are times I seem to be doing a mad-cap dance of an out-of-balance idiot, it happens to us all.

In scouting an in/out route, almost always doing so from below is easier than from above, and quite often hiking any route is easier from below. In my progression as a solo-hiker, in/out routes have become so much an integral part of my spatial map, and focus of my efforts that as I hike a canyon and/or rimwalk, I am constantly looking for more of them.

When I see one, I scout it visually with and without binocs, as sometimes one way will reveal a key to a route better than another. Sometimes neither helps but to give it a try, and hidden keys reveal themselves only later. Sometimes part of a route will go easily, and then I contour endlessly to find cliff band breaks. I rarely get started on a route only to find it does not go. And if it goes, it is marked on my paper map. Whenever I find in/out routes with Anasazi Steps, rarely or never used by hikers, I know I am following Anasazi Way and I have obtained yet another key to entrenchment.

To a certain extent I seek to lose myself to white-man's way; not to become an Anasazi but to better grasp what they saw, felt, and dreamed. Perhaps someone once dreamed of me--thus I had to come about to answer her question. To fulfill her vision. I have often felt I am only a figment of her imagination, and my task is to interpret her dreams. Who is 'she'? That answer waits for another session.

* * *

My hiking pace nowadays is slower than years ago, not only because I am older, but I am looking more intensively than before. And I may make fewer miles because I am involved in a stop-and-go sort of hike, tho I still do "making-miles" hikes.

I am not looking for sites because I want to find artifacts, most often I am looking for rock art, and finding a ruin is mainly a potential art site. Some ruins, of course, are quite scenic or meaningful in their layout, revealing their purpose and use they served. And all ruins, no matter how insignificant or dilapidated are another piece to an ever-enlarging puzzle.

Rock art, and some people hesitate to label it 'art', means more to me. I soon came to realize that a house or granary ruin is where people slept when weather was bad/cold, but drawings and etchings were what they felt, or thot, or dreamed. It is a "window to their souls" if you wish. Most of time Anasazi worked and played outside in front of their dwellings, or on a nearby slickrock flat, sheltered from wind perhaps. Their houses were for storing material goods, and cold-weather sleeping, or for a slow fire and close company/conversations. Some archaeologists prefer to think that all or most kivas served ceremonial purposes, and perhaps this is so, tho I tend to agree with Lekson[1].

I will spend more time and energy looking for rock art and getting a reasonably fair photo than for any 3 ruins. Sometimes I have to sit near art and try to understand it, or even sit with my back to it and see what anthros and zoomorphs see, not of course that they are animate. Or are they?

So far I have only found one burial, one historic metal pan which could be very recently deposited, a pot which is relatively well-known, many miscellaneous artifacts such as shards and lithic flakes or metates/manos, a few arrowheads, a bag with historic cans [perhaps], and other odds and ends. I put little to no energy into a search for artifacts, and I have long ago passed a newbie's stage of wanting to pocket any and all shards or arrowheads for my own collection.

I have come around more to Fred Blackburn's [and others'] idea of an outdoor museum, well supported by overall site stewards BLM, and prefer to know that there are still artifacts out there I have not found, and may some day, left *in situ* for other visitors.

And as I hike, I am scouting for sites, trying to figure out how to access some ledgy sites if possible, evaluating my time remaining for a safe turnaround or a loop in/out further away, watching my dogs, watching for footprints and animal tracks, stopping to rest whenever I want to, usually with a vue of some sort and often in front of a site.

I have evolved to a rhythm of doing first part of my hike slowly, intensively looking around, and as I have decided to leave I usually get into a narrow-focus mood, mostly wanting to get to my pickup. Of course it all depends on whether I am returning to my access route, time remaining before sunset, weather, and my energy level, or where my return route takes me that might be new.

Four things I tend to look for, more than any others: rock art sites no matter how insignificant; scenic vues preferably from a canyon rim or even first or second ledge; ruins, large or small; and routes aka in/outs. I will go out of my way to contour along first or second ledge, even third ledge if better, whichever is easier and more continuous, when going into or out of a canyon. It serves as a finale or introduction to my hike, a way to soak in more ambiance.

Then, as I leave most canyons, I am going to cross a mile or more of jp and sage flats, where vues are open but not as satisfying, my feet are sore, dogs are tired, it is cooling off in winter, maybe even clouding up, I am ready for a hot shower and dinner, some reading or a good movie on my vcr/tv. My thots turn away, and ahead, but there is still a recap of my hike, sometimes I laugh for joy at some vue, some accomplishment, some connecting-dots route, or some rock art I found.

What I have done is go where I wanted, when and how I wanted, with only dogs for company, stopped when and where I wanted, taken as long as I wanted, and hurried when I wanted. I made decisions on my own, helped by a need to protect my dogs, I saw what I was able to, missed what I will try to come back for. I experienced my own stress, joys, and trepidation blues. What I did not have is someone to share with, to experience moments with, to converse with, or even to love this place with. But we all have to do our own hikes, whether with someone or not, because it is you as an individ, or I in this case, who puts one foot in front of other, safely, and survives to tell about it.

And I know I will be back.

CHAPTER 8
GETTING TO KNOW YOU

I do not pretend to be a geologist, nor a botanist, so do not expect me to go on about plants or rock layers. I could not tell you a Navajo sandstone from a Wingate. I do know a bit about Cedar Mesa sandstone, but not from any book.

It is rather miles logged, hours spent, and problems solved in getting thru it and up or down it, that bring me familiarity. I know how it feels under my boots, on my butt while slithering down a slope too steep for standing up, or on my elbow while I lounge around admiring vues.

One hike I came to an end of first ledge, I wanted a nearby way to get rimtop. I actually voiced this desire to my dogs, saying "We need a nice little Anasazi staircase." I walked about 150 feet further, around a hidden corner which was only place it could have hidden from my vue, and there was exactly what I asked for--as if I had wished it into place, or somehow known it would be there, yet I had never been to this small canyon as a white man, in this lifetime. It was a 3 foot-wide crack between a separated boulder block and cliff, filled with flat stones a bit larger than size Anasazi used in their houses. They were not arranged as a man-made staircase, but Sandstone-Way had very nearly done so by herself, and it was an easy ascent.

In another small canyon, on Comb Ridge, I once found a set of Anasazi Steps down a moderately steep slickrock slope--one which could be climbed without steps, but much easier with. This ramp got me down and enlarged my hike, from somewhat frustrating to joyful.

Plants are too often just something to get thru. Some seem

like friends to me, such as yucca, which also often is right where I need to step and prevents my dogs from following in my exact footsteps. Junipers and piñon pine [jp's] are everywhere and often I break off a clump of needles and squeeze their odor onto my fingers, I do this with sage sometimes too.

I am acquainted with prickly pear, from my earlier days living in NE Montana and near Tucson, plus more cacti that do not even grow on Cedar Mesa. Once I ran into some cholla while riding on a motorcycle, so yes I know some cacti well.

There are plants and geologic strata that help me, and some that hinder my progress, but it seems only fair, and all one and same. I am not lazy enuf to hope for completely easy hiking, perfect sets of boulder breaks whenever or wherever I choose to hike. I would say it is more up to me to accommodate myself to terrain and plant life than vice versa; perhaps a feeling or knowledge of serendipity will assist me.

I suppose it is really not so much serendipity, as *sandstonicity* [see Appendix] that gets me thru and up or down around on slickrock. For my variety of slickrock is not same as found around Moab, and so popular. Nor is it kind you might look for deep in some slot canyon, where your swimming and rock climbing skills see you safely thru.

I wish I could define sandstonicity, or find it in my Slickrock Dictionary, but mine is too new. I think it has something to do with finding my way up and down and along many contour flats. I prefer to think of many Cedar Mesa ledges as *first, second, third ledges*; [see Appendix] usually below these, ledges are not very continuous. So, it is connections between these 3 ledge systems, placed carefully where they are, and only waiting my coming along needfully, that I think of as sandstonicity. Also, a random-seeming placement of alcoves, canyon springs, sunlight exposure, ledges for access and denial of access, routes above to farm land, routes down to water, barriers to ingress against migrants, smooth rock faces patinated correctly for rock art, secret places to hide granaries, slickrock flats for unseen trails, ways for deer and bighorn to get about and hunters to lie in waiting, even underlying sandstone which form clay-loam hills with microclimes for growing or perfect niches for pithouse sites are all facets of sandstonicity--that complicity of nature to provide a sheltering and friendly landscape for a people to survive, thrive, and find happiness at times.

I believe sandstonicity applied to Anasazi also, tho they probably did not think in those terms. There must have been some understanding Anasazi had that it was up to them to adapt to sandstone and slickrock, and those 3 ledges, and if they could do this, they could make a home. Not just any home, also a happy home, for a time anyway.

One little hike that I like to repeat has zigzag sloping ramps thru sandstone, well placed to help me get up or down, and even a few jp's tastefully located to lend a bit of friendliness. Plus there are signs it is well-liked by other hikers, tho not in any guide books nor on any maps.

I already know that I have moved beyond those limitations, in getting to know Cedar Mesa. For it is only thru efforts of my feet, legs, and mind that I come to know a place, not by any maps or cute tools. I cannot follow any hiking guide book, because authors might not have been where I want to go, and I want to go everywhere; or had time to see much, and I want to see everything.

If some hiking author tried to write a book to completely cover all those places on Cedar Mesa I would like to see, he would have to hike a lifetime, and would be very old and could no longer hike. His book would be so thick I would have to build a library to house it, certainly I could not take it with me on a hike.

His map would be so weighty, and so well scribbled I doubt I could read it. But there are no such books, nor maps, so I am stuck with my own energy and curiosity. I do not think I will write such a book or draw such a map either because I would hope all other hikers desire to find their own way.

I suppose if I was lazy, or smart, I would hire some guide to show me secret places, then I could know his version of what to see, what to think, and where to go or not to go. But, too often, I do not know where I want to go until I hike where I do not want to go. And even worse, it seems I do not really care to put such limitations on my desire to know Cedar Mesa.

Sandstonicity, it seems, is a desire to know you, and help I receive from you. Well, in this case 'you' is not you as reader, but 'you' as in Cedar Mesa. I sometimes forget I am dealing with a landscape, full of variety, not some person.

I enjoy hiking along, not knowing what is around a corner on second or third ledge, and as I turn each corner a new vista opens up. Some will have only more artfully arranged boulders, jp's, cryptograms scribbled on soil, little water courses thru these hieroglyphs, all in some pre-fractal design. Some ledges will end, insisting I either climb up or down to another ledge. Some ledges will run for miles, undulating to some musical score I have not quite read yet.

One hike I did in new-to-me terrain, I was following along third ledge, nice and wide. Dusty went up a small talus/jp slope to second ledge, and Browny and I continued below. I saw her above, and called her down to us, she came reluctantly. We went on around a corner for another quarter mile, and I could see that there were no more breaks in cliff band for a half mile and ledge eventually ended. I did not want to return, and finally found another last break which we managed to get up. Somehow, Dusty had known we needed to go up where she did, and I ignored her--it has to do with her knowledge of Coyote Way.

Coyote Way is a very real subset of Sandstone Way. Coyote, deer and bighorn came to this land before man and found paths, water, and safety. Early Man followed these trails, Anasazi came along and followed these paths then I came along and tried to follow their footsteps. I got better at finding them, at ignoring white-man's path, and I know there is no understanding Anasazi without following their trails. Just as there is plenty of understanding I garner from reading white-man's footprints. Of course there are many other aspects of Coyote Way I cannot follow, perhaps Anasazi were better at this task than I.

There is a certain knowledge remnant out there in Anasazi-land--I have seen and felt some of it. One small corner of it is sandstonicity, one is Sandstone Way, one is Coyote Way, another is Anasazi Way. Somewhere in this mix I hike along waiting without waiting to turn some final corner where enuf is revealed to show me what lies *behind and beyond*'.

* * *

Sandstonicity is some totality I know is there, I just have not gone far enough yet. And perhaps it is some part inside me, some part awaiting an opening, a potential if you insist. What this makes me, is not for me to guess.

CHAPTER 9
HOZHO, OR WHY I HIKE

If I was Navajo, Hozho would have a certain meaning, one gained by hundreds or thousands of years of understanding. If I was some bright-eyed New Ager, I am sure I could expound on what it signifies. However, I am neither of these extremes; instead I will explain how it applies to my explorations of Cedar Mesa, or why I use such a term.

I see a certain affinity for beauty in some locations of Anasazi house sites, and in their rock art. There is a harmony expressed in some layouts of rooms, use of ledges, and scenic vues from some sites. Whether my appreciation is merely subjective, and not objectively proven does not matter. And whether Anasazi felt same way as Navajo, or had a word such as Hozho, is unclear. Not being an ethnologist specializing in Hopi and other Pueblo ideology, I could not say.

In some ways, even though modern Puebloans are descended from Anasazi [perhaps from Mogollon, Fremont, and others as well], there is not much connection between them. Time, space, and a weakening of traditional Puebloan culture has led them down a path probably not envisioned by Anasazi. Or perhaps some medicine man or shaman did envision his people's future [casinos and coal].

* * *

When I hike and explore Cedar Mesa it is usually on Saturday, sometimes on extra off-work days, from September thru May. My dayhike comes at end of a week of working in a oftentimes stressful job. Sometimes I cannot really focus on my plans for a coming-up hike due to my job. Sometimes I can. Always in my mind, tho, are memories of past hikes and places I have visited. These memories seem to help alleviate stress, give me a dream-world to hold up to "reality" as a shield, one perhaps graced with a pattern I once saw on a rock art panel.

But I have been working on myself for years, and trying not to let much of my job, or bad parts of it even come close to getting to me. It is not so much my current job, but any job, any situation where I am not in control of circumstances. I hold in my mind an image of a hike, of a ruin, or a rock art panel deep inside where I really reside. My outer self deals with a "real" world. Inside, tho, is a hiking-exploring self who does not care about everyday life, only wants to finish every week and go for another hike.

As I start on my hike, and leave my pickup behind, I morph into another sort of being, one who tunes into outside air, smells and vues. A being who is only going to get somewhere by putting one foot in front of another and keep doing it for hours. But process of hiking does not involve me mentally, That is all taken care of by another corner of my brain, perhaps my 'lizard brain.' What does involve me is my route, detours I must take, changes in my route, and what I see.

Then, too, there is a certain grin to myself, happy to be started on a hike again.

I quickly acclimatize to my surroundings and ambiance of Anasazi world. Civilized world falls behind, is momentarily forgotten. I move forward and focus on what is ahead, behind, to both sides, and above me. I realize this is an invocation from Navajo Beauty Way, but I merely intend by it that I become alert to full 3 dimensionality, or Anasazi-dimensionality.

I am looking ahead, thinking of where I am going, I am looking down to watch my footing and to look for signs of

Anasazi presence, such as shards, lithic flakes, or even trails. I am looking up to notice weather; I am looking to sides and even behind me to take in my landscape. Or to look for sites.

Often I stop and use my binocs to look closer at some distant feature, some shadow or some imagined home. If I am walking across Cedar Mesa's jp flats, I am in one sort of Anasazi world, one that is fully connected to their other worlds, but one that seems somehow different to me. Perhaps it is unlimited vues, intensity of lite, and a brand of openness unnerving to some.

When I get to my canyon and begin to rimwalk or drop down inside, things change. My focused attention has more to notice, my binocs come into increased play, and of course my path needs more attention. Whether I have done this route many times, or never, things change and I need sure footing. I often stop to admire and soak up a vista, even an ambiance. It becomes instantly another world, one with more vegetation, more water sometimes, more people or their trails, and usually more sites of scenic value. And certainly more slickrock of varying shapes, flavors, and colors.

As I am hiking down in a canyon, or rimwalking, unless I notice jet-trails overhead and a constant rumbling of jet engines, I tune out a previous world of job, money, stress. Now I have become an Anasazi hiker involved in a different world. What I notice, what I think or feel, and what I wonder about are not civilized issues. Perhaps some charm or grace comes from a simpler sphere of thot.

Any fear, stress or trepidation now comes from trying a little cliff face and scampering on knees and hands along some skinny ledge while dogs wait behind. Or perhaps from trying an in/out route that I do not know will go, cannot fully scout from above or below with binocs, when I may be close to running out of daylite. But these stresses, these issues are manageable, are part of my choosing to hike, and usually not overly significant.

When I find a new rock art panel, or a new Anasazi house ruin, have done with my photographing, and begin to lounge I tune out much of 'outside world' and soak up ambiance--Anasazi ambiance.

One strange aspect of my hiking and exploring of Cedar Mesa is my intensely, almost perfect, solitude. I regularly go for months without seeing another hiker, and usually thru a fall-winter-spring season of hiking may only see a handful; of course when spring break comes I will often run into more in popular places. This is strange because I see footprints and know other hikers have been out there recently, but usually get no 'feel' for their thots, activities, or wishes. Sometimes I step in their footprints for a distance, thinking thus to 'read' them.

This solitude helps me de-tune civilization, and float along in a haze of Anasazi reality. When I enter a house or granary site, I begin to look at surroundings, its access route, nearness to water, where farm land was, how a nearby arroyo has since cut so deeply, how winter sun heats an alcove, how well it is sheltered from rain and snow, how rooms take advantage of micro-terrain, how in front there is space to work and play, how shards reflect a certain period of occupation or hiatus, how smoke stains on an alcove roof even with no walls indicates a dwelling rather than a storage structure, and what kind of vue is offered up.

I want to finish my photography and sit for awhile, sometimes in front of a room, sometimes several hundred yards away, at a higher level. I want to get a feel for how life was at this site, how happy it was to live here, and where kids played, women ground their grain, young men climbed to draw their art, men sharpened their rock axes, how they hammered out steps to get into their home. I want to listen for sounds of lives lived to fullest, of cycles of living, dying, new birth. Even of sickness, death, and fear.

I noticed, for instance, that in and around one ruin, there are not any large rock art panels, there are not any improbably hi panels although in same area there are other panels. Upper level was at one time accessed probably via a tower, or by using a ladder off a lower house's roof. Some sites do have large art panels and signs that young men climbed up onto hi ledges for various reasons, perhaps to impress young women. Sometimes people may not realize that because a ruin is still standing, while nearby another is nothing but rubble, does not imply that one remaining was more important to Anasazi. Often there are few signs of relative importance to a site. Sometimes a large or multiple granaries does signify a need for massive food storage, even tho nearby may be no dwellings.

There is one place on Cedar Mesa where impressively interesting rock art elements are locationally combined with extensive panels, but dwellings seem only rubble, or few. Water is nearby, as are easy in/out routes to farming or gathering landscapes. Large figures on one panel seem to indicate a welcome to returning farmers and hunter-gatherers. There are many lovingly depicted scenes of animals, many seemingly done by one artist. There was a significance in this area for Anasazi, or its people had much time on their hands; perhaps it was a gathering place for other nearby resident Anasazi, for some purpose.

I wonder about such aspects of Anasazi sites as I approach them, and sit in them. I have heard that some people get a certain feeling for areas of Cedar Mesa, or of greater Anasazi world. Whether a 'bad' feeling of unhappiness or tragedy, or of uneasiness, it seems rarely do people express a good feeling, or a liking for a certain place. I have never gotten any 'bad' feelings from any Anasazi place, on Cedar Mesa or in greater Four Corners--only a very few seem unhomelike.

I have visited places that spoke to me of some ambiance not scribed in rock art, on remaining walls, or in any excavation article. These kinds of imaginings are subtle and often I only realize them much later, while doing something else. I have often thot I am engaged in a search for something on Cedar Mesa, not of a rare pot or basket, or of an unknown rock art panel. I do not know shape of this 'goal', I do know I will recognize it when I see it. I even know what it will probably look like.

Why this is so, I could only imagine; why me I do not know. But, as I hike on Cedar Mesa I am not thinking this to myself, hoping this will be "that hike" or that I would "better look over there," or I might miss it. I have gotten lately to be a sort of slickrock hiker who often does not really care where I go specifically, just pick some general area to hike, with or without a descent into a canyon, as long as it is on some slickrock, near where Anasazi lived and played and dreamed. I often take breaks in nondescript places with no particular vue, sometimes with a vue no more vast than 200 feet, a small pool, and slickrock to lounge on, a few plants, a kind of closed space bounded above by sky. An Anasazi living room.

And I am not a white guy with a civilized job and real problems when I hike an Anasazi hike, I am just some individ who listens, looks and soaks up. I am a guy in love with a landscape, with Anasazi terrain, rock art, and sandstone. I hike Cedar Mesa because I am here and I can.

I do not know if I really "go in beauty," sometimes I doubt it. I do not really think about it. I do know that I try to shape my life so hiking-exploring Cedar Mesa is pinnacle of my week, of my life, and writing about it soothes me when I am not hiking. Most of remainder of 'it' does not concern me, nor draws much attention. I try to bring a book to read at work, when I have to wait, and prefer one about Anasazi, even if some dry archaeological article. It helps give me a

Maria Mitchell' perspective of what is really important in this world [to me anyway.]

My life has shaped me into who I am, what I have become, a guy who only wants to hike and preferably on Cedar Mesa, thru each fall-winter-spring season. Call it an obsession, a mono-mania, call me lucky, it does not matter, as long as there are ruins and rock art I will want to see, for first time or again.

People ask me what I will do when "I have seen it all," meaning all of Cedar Mesa. But, that will never happen, because I have not seen years to come, nor changes, nor people I might meet along my trail, even along my path. I have not seen what it was like when Anasazi lived here, I can only imagine. I think sometimes when I have seen it all, perhaps I will understand. This might seem strange, because there is much more to Anasazi homeland than this corner of SE Utah, in and around Cedar Mesa.

But, I know there is a place inside me where some understanding resides, and is only waiting for fulfillment, knowledge of a complex terrain once home to Anasazi, knowledge of a lifeway and a joy. Perhaps I will someday find this place, I hope to keep looking tomorrow.

I think a big part of this is hiking in solitude, in quiet. For I have experimented by hiking with other hikers, usually just one for a few hikes concurrently. There is too much guidemanship, tho, to these experiences, and not enough quiet for listening. My best hiking companions have always been my dogs, ever eager, ever curious, immured to my spontaneous focus changes, my desire to go "see what is over there," and my shortcuts which perhaps only make sense to a select few. For they do not wonder why, they only want to hike with me, it is all good for them, as it is with me.

Some days, when I drive out to Cedar Mesa, hike alone with dogs, and drive back and see no other cars nor people until near Blanding, it is as if I am in a strange Twilite Zone of Anasazi reality, but Rod Serling has not shown up this sequel to explain. Outside world has had minimal intrusive effect on me, and I have been able to tune out overhead contrails of happy travelers bound for Joshua Tree or beaches in California.

My day has been more about a focus on hiking and exploring than any other reality. An Anasazi reality, although they have long moved away. So, all I have left to see are clues, pieces of a puzzle, with no box cover showing me its design.

My path leads me all over Cedar Mesa, along trails of my making, along routes rarely ever used. There is nobody to consult with, no books to give me ideas about where to go, what to see, it is a solitarily decisive movement thru a cultural space-time. I do my hikes, I see what I am able to see, feel what I can, and think about what it means. In many ways my best friend is a place, Cedar Mesa; my companion in life is a landscape with Anasazi leftovers, where many others have gone before me besides Anasazi, but they came for their reasons, I came for mine. I contain a specific Cedar Mesa within, shaped by hours of hiking and exploring, and perhaps Cedar Mesa has a specific idea of me, and has specific paths just for me, not with any signs, nor cairns.

Perhaps nobody else can see what I see, can know what I seek to know, can have same experiences as I, but this is ok, for I do not want to know someone else's ideas of Cedar Mesa, to know their landscape, nor their map. I follow my own path, and lead my dogs.

CHAPTER 10
TRAILS I FOLLOW

Commonest sort of trail I follow does not exist except in my mental map. Or it exists, but only after I have left, marked solely by my footprints.

This is so because I often have no idea where I am going until I am going, or I know where I want to go, but finite details do not matter, and I always wander over a landscape as vagaries of mood take me.

It might be an interesting hoodoo, cliff face, shadow, or patch of slickrock that draws me; sometimes it is just varieties of terrain that push/pull me. If a cliff band blocks my way I will have to find a way thru. If a canyon blocks my way, I will have to describe a detour. Or if cryptobiotic soils are in my way, sometimes if I am fresh I will make a wide detour, if not I will probably pick out least destructive path; sometimes there is no avoiding cryptogramic soils, nor any animal trails to follow.

I do follow a lot of cattle and deer trails, preferably latter. On a lot of my Grand Gulch hikes, I will follow meandering deer trails across alluvial soils rather than hikers' trail. In last few dry years [late 90's to early 00's], most hikers follow streambed, as a result most alluvial trails have overgrown with brush.

Time is such a relative abstract, tho, and I would rather know that I have seen what there is to see rather than passed by what I could not see. It all depends on what flavor of hike I plan, making-miles, or foot-by-foot.

One of my favorite types of trails is not even visible to me, and only signatured by little dried up piles of scat: coyote trails. Dusty can find these trails, unerringly; perhaps there is some remaining affinity she feels for wild dog's travels and searches for food. Perhaps it is just that she smells their trail markings and scent. Either way, often when I try one of my in/outs to a Cedar Mesa canyon, it is sight of coyote scat which tells me that we are ok--in a sense that our route will go even if I cannot yet see final conclusion.

Often my in/out routes hide parts of themselves and I do not see a key until I turn extra corners, having faith [I suppose] in sandstonicity. Only rarely do my in/out routes have footprints, or human trails.

One, near a popular ruin, I scouted thru binocs but could not pick out a key, or could not quite see if any key 'went'. When I started up, knowing I had time to retreat and return to my entrance route, I found an obvious human trail. It helped me, but soon it faded and mostly disappeared. My guess is that it provided a vue point for photographing. On one ledge I had to contour along several hundred mostly easy yards before I could turn a corner into a key slickrock gully. Any cliff band could stop me if I could not get my dogs up it.

Key gully went, and quite easily, and I was up and out in no time, with only a few 'moves' on a steep stretch of slickrock, mostly trusting my shoes for gription. Once on top, I took a break to admire vue, and out of exultation at a new route scouted, tried and achieved, to be marked on my map and later repeated.

Some of these routes I use frequently, returning again and again to favorite parts of favorite canyons. By this use, I form a trail, but one with no signs pointing a way, and no cairns [which I never erect--often destroy].

Sometimes I come across a single set of footprints, even my own, and may follow them for a short distance mostly to avoid damaging cryptobiotic soils. But, always, another hiker's trail cannot be my own, as where he went rarely is where I am going. Or what he was thinking is never what I am thinking. If I choose to follow another hiker's trail, then I could figure out his thots in general terms, but only rarely am I interested in some other hiker's thots/findings/ goals. This equally applies to my own older tracks, but I look at them as an artifact of who I was then, or what I was thinking, where I was going. I almost visualize my earlier self as a wholly other person, only distally related to me. As if we were in alternate universes.

I prefer to follow deer trails, as they always seem to go interesting places. And, when I need an in/out route, if there is an easy one near, deer will have found it. In one canyon I followed a bighorn trail to get out, tho of course deer also use it. I even privately named one side canyon 'Bighorn Canyon' as route seems like one that they would enjoy most; tho I could have named it 'Anasazi Canyon'.

CHAPTER 11
WHY THIS LAND SPEAKS TO ME

I do not know how it came to be that I am as I am, or that I hike where I hike, that I am called by a land as I am. These may be questions for someone wiser than I.

I have hiked quite a few miles on Cedar Mesa, I have seen almost all that I can see, not nearly all I want to see. I am no longer same person who years ago started a hobby of exploration.

Somehow it has come to be that I must write about Anasazi land, houses, and rock art I love so much, and my way of writing is not as another writer's would be. For I have seen a different Cedar Mesa than anyone else, not more intimate, nor complete; and with an understanding I inherited not from any parent, but from a lifeway of wondering.

And this place, these people have somehow chosen me to paint a word picture of their life, of their land, and of their joys. I may not do it as well as another, yet I am not in competition.

And my path is not over, my exploration has not reached a conclusion, a neat ending in some other author's biography of me. Think of this book as but a resting place for me, as I continue on; I am able to stop awhile and chat with you, saying perhaps, "I found this place one time..."

Long ago I evinced a talent for writing, tho I suppose I never had a subject which truly engaged me enough. Perhaps I was picked as a useful tool, one who could be molded towards some level of understanding. Who picked me is not easily answered. Some personages deeply involved with Cedar Mesa's protection wish to warn newcomers by spouting about "Anasazi Ghosts." Ghosts, tho, whether Anglo, Black, Hispanic, Asian, etc, or Anasazi are only effective if you really believe in them. I do not happen to subscribe to that particular belief system, nor to any religion.

My part of bargain is to do my homework, i.e. to hike as often as I can, even to repeat certain hikes, to think without thinking of what I find, and to publicize a very small part of Cedar Mesa thru Internet. In return I am given a call to find certain features, or elements of overall character of Anasazi habitation. And I include them in my psyche, later they pop back out in my writings shaped differently, disguised even.

Why me? I cannot really say, as I have no clue. I do know that I am drawn to Cedar Mesa, I am drawn to certain places, certain features, and I often contemplate Anasazi Way as it relates to Cedar Mesa and nearby areas.

CHAPTER 12
LOST HIKER MAP

One day, years ago, on a hike to a certain place I found a folded up topo map. I opened it up but could not find any name or address on it, decided it was now mine.

It covered an area I had wanted to explore, had heard about, barely been to before. It was labeled, "Lost Hiker." It was a 1:24000 scale map, thus did not cover a very big area; of course on foot it could seem like a big area. All depends on your mode of transportation, I suppose, or even your mode of thinking.

So, next weekend I drove out to one of a few roads marked on my new (used) map, thinking person who had owned it before had no time to add any notes to it.

It had wonderful place names such as "Enigmatic Route" or "Disappearing Stream," "No Way Mesa" and "Hidden Cave." Large parts of it were without place names, tho canyons and mesas were shown.

I decided to be cautious and get a gps fix on my vehicle location before starting out. I was not taking too seriously map name, but neither was I taking foolish chances.

As I entrenched myself in this landscape, which I had mostly only seen from a distance before, I thot it an intriguing area. There were many canyons leading into a main canyon, which itself dropped down into a main river drainage which eventually drained into Pacific Ocean, or used to before being diverted for California irrigation.

Orienteering seemed difficult, I found, as many canyons were spread out like fingers on a hand, and it became a matter of finding correct ubiquitous mesa area which would lead to my chosen ridge, which would lead out to a vuepoint.

Sometimes I would try to use my gps, set up a route in advance, and this often helped somewhat. Sometimes I would use a compass heading to get me started. Sometimes I just started and let happen what sandstonicity dictated.

I found much more than I expected, more than I knew might be out there where this map designated, and less than I hoped. But perhaps this is way of sandstonicity, that I cannot predict, nor control, that rather I have to yield to another style of reality. One not so much unreal, as just slightly shaded strangely; as if sunlight were filtered thru a cloud with off-color properties, much like alpenglow late in a day after thunderstorms.

I one day noticed that I returned again and again to this particular place, this artificial boundary as marked on this paper quad. There was something about it which drew me, something which came to me just before falling asleep. Perhaps it was miles of slickrock promontories with hoodoos and rock islands, perhaps lack of people, perhaps clear and quiet air.

I never really got lost; it is more that I might not know where I was at any given moment, and this is how I found much, but overall I knew where I wanted to go, where my hike would have to end, and where my next might start. So, in a sense, I was lost to outside world; I could not actually describe to an armchair explorer where I had been nor what I had seen. He might not comprehend joy, delight, and ambiance I received, might not understand my vuepoints where I watched canyons as our sun rolled over to increase or decrease shadows.

How could I describe why I had to return to "Lost Hiker" area, confined by no actual boundaries, nor landscapes, in terms someone who was not a fellow-hiker could understand? If it was color of distant canyons winding around each other in some squirrel fashion, or complexity of an intricate system of drainage, or small and private sites I came across, or small and long-forgotten rock art panels I could perhaps explain. But it is more a totality, a combining of separate aspects; or perhaps separativity is only my civilized brain working overtime.

Perhaps if I could come about to an Anasazi way of thinking, of seeing this land, this particular area, feel as they did, know their struggle of living, and delights in beauty, there would be no need to explain. Then merely doing a hike would be its own reward, to know I was moving and resting in a home. And not a home of walls, or with a roof, but one of openness and landscape.

Perhaps this was meaning of "Lost Hiker"--that a modern hiker who explored this area, and later reported it, found himself lost, and happily so. That he, too, found what he was looking for while not looking, or while lost. And this labeling of a quad map was a recommendation to other hikers not to try too hard, nor to worry overmuch. That if each of us is meant to find what is there, we will. Sandstonicity will help us. But, he could not call this map "Sandstonicity Way" as that would confuse; nor could he call it "Serendipitously Hiking" as that would be a bit obvious. I like this label as it stands, I like hiking this area, do not mind my own lostness.

It seems a bit of a creative process, or trick even, to deliberately allow myself to hike half-lost and unworried. As if I were some Tibetan guru fully in touch with his helper spirits or guides. I think a problem arises, tho, when I try to return to a certain ruin or rock art panel; trying to direct another to any feature would be hopeless. If I found a place while lost, how can I hope to ever return? Or should I return soon so I will not forget?

I find pithouses not marked on this "Lost Hiker" quad, when not even looking, when just walking along to or from an area. At times I cannot avoid them, they seem as ubiquitous as jp's. Some are preceramic, or thoroughly cleaned by archaeologists, some are postceramic, meaning a rough dividing line between styles of culture. Long before I came along pithouses were cleaned of useful timber or non burial-associated tools by a returning band of Anasazi, come home to Cedar Mesa after a long hiatus and change of culture-technology.

I wonder, sometimes, how returnees who came to Cedar Mesa after sometimes hundreds-year-long hiatuses knew where to find housesites of their ancestors. There could be a mental map passed down thru time and generations. More likely, they are busy exploring every inch of their new home, of their ancestor's fabled homeland, and find ruins as a matter of course.

New inhabitants are determined to erect homes in entirely new kinds of landscape, under rock shelters, e.g. overhangs. It is as if they are a new breed, with new ideas. They may not have been a new breed, but their ideas are new; archaeologists call these cultural phases or traditions, and label new people as if they were genetically different--as perhaps they sometimes were.

But, former inhabitants lost their way, whether thru climate change or over-use of farmlands, and had to leave. Hundreds of years later, sometimes less, new people came to make homes on Cedar Mesa. Perhaps they had more and better crops than earlier inhabitants, perhaps beans and new, tougher corn with bigger ears/cobs. Perhaps they made pottery, rarely used baskets. Perhaps they used a bow and arrow rather than an atlatl and dart.

So it was a new way, and life was good for perhaps another few hundred years, joy and beauty was found, but lost again and people left, few or none remained. Perhaps it was rain and snow that was lost.

They are all gone now, and only a few hikers come here

today. Unless they as individs can unthink their civilized selves, hike as Anasazi did, they too are lost. So, perhaps a label such as "Lost Hiker" is a warning, a kind of invocation of a way I as hiker must follow to enjoy this particular area.

Perhaps this is why this map is my favorite, why I return again and again, hoping while lost to find Anasazi Way, to understand.

CHAPTER 13
SLICKROCK DOGS

My first dog, Cookie, did not get to hike much slickrock with me. She went flying with me once, in a small plane. She went on many San Juan and Dolores river trips. She and I hiked and biked around Durango for years. She was part Samoyan and part Blue Heeler, small and very smart.

Then, Goofy came along, and I began to hike more and more on slickrock. But Goofy, tho a good trail leader dog, is deaf and more or less went her own way. I could only control her if she was in sight of me, and noticing. Eventually she got hit by a car at nite, now is crippled too much to hike--tho she loves her new guard dog duties around our house and imagines every vehicle she notices coming by is a potential threat to be barked away.

Dusty, whose mother lived next to my last house near Durango, either chose me or I chose her [cannot remember] to supplement Goofy as hiking-companion. Goofy and I took little Dusty on her first mountain hike in La Platas, one of many to come. Goofy, part Red Heeler, and many other mixes, loved to chase butterflies on mountain-tops. She always loved to chase anything flying, whether planes, birds, bees, luckily she never caught any of these. Goofy also loved to dig up molehills wherever she found them.

Dusty's mom was a purebred Queensland Heeler, very smart but with a full range of neurosis such as fear of thunderstorms and nervousness while traveling in a car. Many times I took her along with Dusty and Goofy for short dayhikes near Durango. Dusty's father did not introduce himself to me, but was probably part pitbull or some similar breed-mix. She is relatively small, but dense and almost looks fat.

When Goofy got injured too much for hiking, Dusty took over as 'Trail-Boss' dog. Her son, Browny, was runt of her one and only litter before I got her fixed. He is just a bit smaller than Dusty, and Goofy is only a bit taller than Dusty.

Dusty's first real hike was up Gibbs Mtn in La Platas, near Durango, Colorado. Goofy and I were to show her how, and Dusty was pretty small. Since Goofy is deaf, I had to lead her on hikes using her eyesight and smell; she would get distracted and find me again by smelling my tracks. Goofy, as we were descending Gibbs, was scouting all over while Dusty tried to keep up. For awhile they were out of my sight, and I started calling Dusty.

Soon I heard boisterous barking, even plaintive perhaps. Little Dusty came bounding downhill above me, perhaps not knowing who I was, or mad at being abandoned by Goofy. Goofy soon joined us, unawares she was supposed to be puppysitting Dusty. All were together again.

Since then, Dusty had a litter before I got her fixed and I kept Browny, who was runt male. Dusty and Browny are both small dogs, heeler size and part-breed. They have hiked countless times with me, mountains in summer, Cedar Mesa in fall-winter-spring. I would guess there are very few humans who have hiked Cedar Mesa more than they, or at least in last few years.

They evolved thru time to be fine slickrock dogs, and by that I mean wise to ways of my hiking style in canyon country, and ins and outs of our routes. Usually I pick routes that are 'dog-friendly' over more sporting routes I might take if alone. Dusty tries to always lead us, finding a route before Browny and I have even begun, usually waiting above us and looking down at us, thinking "well, come on, what is your holdup?"

Dusty took over lead when Goofy stopped hiking, but as she ages sometimes she lets Browny take over for brief spells. Usually Browny, proverbially-speaking, dogs my heels, with brief forays to hunt with his mom when he is fresh.

When it is time to get a boost up a steep slope, they often act timorous, reluctant to be assisted. Browny is lighter and easier to get up, usually willing to go first, and this helps Dusty with her motivation qualms. She does not like to be helped, likes to be in control I think. Browny will try to help when I lift him, and immediately scrambles on his own once I push him. Dusty tends to squat down in protest or trepidation and does not help. Since she is heavier, boosting her becomes a chore. And when I release her, unless she can easily see a way, she will sometimes freeze until I can get up a bit and give her a last butt-boost upwards. Sometimes he will follow me where she will not, across skinny ledges. Then, of course, when I have them boosted up I have to prove my chosen route by getting myself up.

As soon as I 'top out' Dusty and Browny are there to greet me, she wagging, he faking it [he lost his tail when shot years ago] as if to say, "Gee, dad, we did not need any help, we could'a done it on our own."

Whenever I take a minor shortcut which is ok for me, not so for them. I may tell them, "find your trail" or to Browny, "follow your mommy" as Dusty will always seek out a nearby doggy route. Browny will try to follow me, but sometimes defers to his mom's route. He got shot just in front of where his tail was connected to his butt and a Vet had to cut off his tail and replumb his digestive system somewhat. Since then, he has hiked intensively for almost six years, tho, and does not seem to miss his tail. He often likes to get atop some small boulder along our path, perhaps it makes him feel bigger and more able to look around.

Dusty is more timid than Browny along skinny ledges, or

along sloping slabs of slickrock. Often she will try to find an alternative route and usually succeeds. Browny will more often follow me than Dusty, but sometimes I tell him to "follow your mommy," which he understands. When I ask him, "Where's your mommy?" he understands who I am talking about and will wag his butt and look around for her.

I try to encourage Dusty by telling her "Find our trail." Which usually works. This just means for her to go ahead and pick out a route thru some cliff band and that I will follow with Browny.

Rarely, but it does happen, that I must leave them momentarily to crawl along a ledge to photo a site, where I do not want them to go. I will drop my pack and hat near some shade and admonish them to "stay." Usually this works, sometimes Browny gets antsy if left too long, and will try to follow. Thus, I may decide to return to a place I want to go without them rather than chance that they will obey. Anyway, this only works well if I am still within their hearing and can continually tell them "stay," or if they can also see me on a higher ledge.

Coming down a slickrock slope is almost as much fun. I tell them to "stay!" until I have gotten down halfway, or to a stable stance. Sometimes I lower my daypack on a short rope to free myself up for chore at hand. Again, Browny is usually more willing to come down to me, I catch him and lower him on down to either where he can continue safely or I have to step down to boost him safely down again. Then it is Dusty's turn. Once she has seen Browny get down ok, she will eventually come down to me. Sometimes, tho, it is just "not a go" and no matter how much I encourage they will not come down. Then, of course, it is time to retreat and try to find another way. I have hiked into Fish Canyon when there was some snow and lowered both dogs down that little cliff route, then later gotten them up and out, by myself. Of course, there is a little flat spot about a third of way up that helps.

Sometimes Dusty gets impatient when we are trepidatiously scouting a cliff break, and in one side canyon of ggulch, she jumped down a small cliff rather than wait. Soon I found a rock pile and helped Browny down thru it. I think Dusty must have jumped down a 4-5 foot cliff onto relatively soft fill, as she was not hurt only stiff later that nite. I have to verbally restrain her sometimes, and watch her closely when we contour along above cliff bands. Going up is totally different, as usually she will have found a route before Browny and I. Usually she is upslope from us, scouting around and stops to look back at us as she rests in some tree shade.

Normally, tho, things are not quite so dramatic. When just hiking slickrock our usual mode is that Dusty finds a cliff-band break, whether scented by coyotes, deer, or man, and Browny and I follow along. She prefers to be ahead of us scouting and hunting. Browny tires soon into our hikes and tends to follow me.

Only wildlife we ever see are chipmunks, and they are never very successful at chasing them. Once they "chased away" a cougar, which is really a case of lion retreating and Browny and Dusty thinking they were tough. Sometimes we see rabbits, but jackrabbits are very fast and my dogs not that fast. They do better at home, out-waiting rabbits in our culvert pipe. Once I saw a coyote up close, but neither it nor my dogs approached each other.

On a practical level, hiking with two dependent dogs keeps me from taking too many chances, restricts my choice of route, perhaps keeps me out of trouble. I do not mind at all, for benefits of sharing hikes with dogs out-weigh any routes I skip. Quite regularly, Dusty will find a hidden route out of top-cliffs by sniffing coyote scents, before I may have spotted tell-tale scat.

They help me see routes from an animal's perspective, which is different from a human's choice of routes. And I think Anasazi found many of their trails by following deer trails, perhaps even coyote trails. I have never read that they had dogs in Cedar Mesa phases of occupation, perhaps elsewhere or later on.

Dusty does much better when there are plenty of pools for her to drink at, or bathe in since she is dark colored. Browny seems to get by with less water, happily. They usually seek out shade whenever I stop for a break or just to look around, even in winter.

Hiking-day is always their favorite day of every week, whether it comes only once or more. They know when it is Saturday, and try to wake me up at 6am to get me started. It takes me an hour to get to mouth of Arch Canyon, sometimes about 2 hours to get further out on Cedar Mesa, depending on road conditions. That is all nap time for them, coming and going.

While I am getting my 'act' together at trail head, they are out scouting around, rather I should say they are sniffing around to see who was there recently. I lead us by my eyes, they lead by their noses, it seems we make a fair team.

There is another positive benefit of hiking with dogs, for them and secondarily for me, it tends to keep them out of trouble later in our week, as I am off working and they are at home alone. It gives them something to look forward to, our out-there time; it also makes them too tired for a few days to even think of how to stir up trouble. Doggie-trouble in this case is them roaming around outside our yard, crossing a county road where drivers do not care about dogs, themselves, or each other.

Our hikes together give us more intense time-together than even when I am home, as I am usually busy with chores or reading, even relaxing and not always paying much attention. On our hikes, we are involved with a low level of survival and with particular in's and out's of our day.

I have gotten so used to hiking with my slickrock dogs, I would rather be with them than without. There is a kind of joy we share, of outdoors and our hikes and places we go to see. My enjoyment is slanted otherly than theirs, of course. They are there to hunt, to smell, to return to some atavistic level of being I have long forgotten. Their hike is in many ways harder than mine, as they run around more and their legs are shorter. But their 'four-leg-drive' flexibility helps them in many ways, specially when going uphill. I am much better at long range strategy, at planning our route and seeing our vehicle on our return; they are much better at details, at finding coyote routes, at smelling out who has preceded us. We work well together as a team, I would not have it any other way--than hiking on slickrock with Dusty and Browny.

CHAPTER 14
TREPIDATION BLUES

When I look back on who I was as a hiker just a few years ago, I sometimes laugh. I return now to do hikes in places that I thot very difficult and find them only moderately so. It is not so much that I am more skilled, or a better rock scrambler, but my knowledge of slickrock and its vagaries has enlarged, my inner confidence has enlarged and I know my physical and mental boundaries.

I stop often to soak up new vistas, some seem daunting in their complexity, their maze-like qualities. Two in particular, one on each side of lower ggulch, are approached from a height as if specially designed for an explorer. There are multiple small canyons leading in a zigzag fashion seemingly nowhere fast. In between and above are jp flats with hundreds of interesting hoodoos, and it all seems dry, vast beyond belief and too complex to know.

But, only solution is to just dig in my heels and start. I pick a likely looking lane thru hoodoos and small gullies, ignore my map and entrench myself in landscapes. As I get myself 'lost' inside, it all becomes more familiar; if, as often happens, I come back out another way later on, I can stop on heights and look back to recognize some hoodoos I passed, some canyons I skirted, and places I scouted thru binocs.

When I return later, one more section of Cedar Mesa is now familiar. And it is a gradual process of repeating these short hikes, stitching them together and making notes on my paper maps, entries in my journal, and memories reborn when I return that open these complexities up. Trepidation lessens with familiarity.

Sometimes trepidation is a good thing, it may save me from a too-risky move thru some cliff-band, or convince me not to try and boost my dogs up, to go around and find another way. This is all part of Sandstone Way, keeping trepidation under control and using it as a tool for exploring. Trepidation will not lessen unless I test a new corner of Cedar Mesa, entrench myself in its confusions, and give myself up to a certain trust in my own abilities.

Sandstone Way is not part of any Navajo chants as far as I know, nor can it be found in any but a Slickrock Dictionary. It is a path of learning, of knowing how to shape myself to a humble skill at wending myself thru Cedar Mesa. Trepidation is merely a portion of learning this path, sometimes to be ignored, sometimes to be heeded. Sandstone Way is a balance between pure knowledge of where I am at all times, and a realization I have never been here before, will not know until I turn every corner, with trust, what is here.

Sandstone Way is with me every step, every pause I take to look around, it rises in heat waves which are absent in winter. It is colored buff, and red, same color as mud on my boots, same color as mud plaster on rock walls built by Anasazi. It is an ambiance of knowledge, gained hour after hour, it is a calm certainty I am home, that sandstonicity will provide a path. I feel it as I walk along second or third ledge, a canyon on my right, a cliff on my left, nobody around except two dogs leading. We skirt boulder falls, avoid cryptogramic soils, dodge entrenching gullies, admire lithic flakes; it is cool but not cold, a sweater is enough, sometimes second ledge is so clean it seems someone swept it yesterday--of course rare but strong rains suffice for this chore. I see no footprints, no sign anyone has been this way for perhaps a thousand years, but I know this is my favorite path.

Juniper and piñon form shade patches, which Dusty and Browny make use of whenever I stop, even in winter. Underneath are little gardens of debris, collections of animal nests, small holes where perhaps someone once lived. I often break off a dead twig of piñon and swing it like a wand as I walk on past, perhaps mouthing incantations to make my day last longer, delay my return to civilization.

Shadows of mystery beckon from my left, underneath shallow overhanging rock ledges, little caves of possibilities. Although none today have artifacts waiting my discovery, all look interesting. Browny likes to explore them, maybe he thinks he will find a bear cub to play with, more likely a bone to dig up. I follow a deer path thru small boulder gardens, rather than dodge around near cliff on my right. Sometimes I look down over edge, looking for any hikers, ruins, or rock art panels.

Sometimes I must stop to scour opposite cliffs with binocs, looking I suppose for some sign this place was important to Anasazi. It may be that I find an art panel on my left, a place to stop awhile. It is all up to Sandstone Way, what I will find, or who depicted on a rock face I might meet today, what he will tell me.

Sometimes I find a small, seemingly insignificant ruin, just a granary and small house, wide open to weather, tho sheltered from most. An oval sandstone slab door is still in place, and I cannot resist gently moving it aside and poking my head in. Mostly what I find are a few cobs, spider webs, and much packrat dung. Coyote, I see, has visited recently to dig around hoping to catch packrat, to make a good meal for her pups. She may have succeeded in her grocery shopping. I replace sandstone door, move off again. Perhaps I pause to photo-op this place, hoping thus to preserve some memory.

Memory, tho, is a tricky thing. I may very well forget this place, not remember it again unless I revisit years later.

Again, it may be that I cannot forget this place, and I could not say why this is.

We continue along our ledge, sometimes we can stay on one level for miles, usually we must move up briefly, or even down to third ledge. It all depends on erosion, a history of rainfall, and how tough sandstone is, how weak it is.

None of soils I pass are very deep, I have to go high on mesa top for that. Juniper and piñon, tho, seem to do ok--finding enough soil for their shallow roots. Some have been toppled by unchecked wind blasts, blown up from a blast furnace south of here, what we call 'desert.' Sometimes I admire dried and bare tree limbs, branches and twigs of a dead tree, now laying over on one side with pieces broken off during its fall. It reminds me of a skeleton I once saw near here, tree and human body look complete as if merely resting before a slow return to soil or mineral.

In winter, there is a void of sound made by birds and small creatures but I know that under my footsteps some are merely sleeping until spring, some have flown south and will return along with hikers. I rarely meet other hikers, or see any far off; it is not so much that I am first one here, but that few hike in winter, few hike exactly where I hike. This is ok.

Sometimes when I stop to rest, I excuse myself by using my time for admiring a vue, with or without binocs. There is not exactly any goal I have in mind, I can return or continue as I choose, time has not begun to run out on me yet. I have not explicitly managed to switch time off and turn on eternity, but it may seem so sometimes.

When I stop and sit down I become very difficult to see, as if I shrunk somehow, or become diminished. When hiking along I stand out, am obvious. It is not as if it was highly important, merely a thing my father taught me about hunting long ago. Now I am not hunting, yet this thot impinges anyway; I realize Anasazi knew all this and many more tricks, if a time came when enemies threatened. This kind of trepidation shows in certain ruins, in loopholes, in some choices of where to build, in defensive walls.

Archaeologists write that these defensive sites came towards end of Anasazi culture, and of their habitation in much of Four Corners. Perhaps they abandoned much of Cedar Mesa before leaving Four Corners. Who their enemies were is still open to argument, some say each other when agriculture failed, some say invading newcomers such as Athabaskans or Paiutes. Granaries attest to some trepidation, some need to hide food supplies. Yet, evidence of actual violence is scarce and widely scattered. Perhaps trepidation backed up by true stories from further north, or west, were enough.

Abandonment, retrenchment to a safer environment or a better watered one, did not come about merely because there was a threat, there had to be some real tangible danger, or perhaps some sure certainty that this could no longer be a good home. Perhaps Sandstone Way had shut down, failed to protect a happy lifeway of a people used to hard work and hard times, mixed in with certain landscapeal goodness--with horticultural goodness, richness and with occasional joy and happiness. Life was not easy here, but it may have been rewarding[1].

Where Anasazi original homeland was, where and how their culture started, why it became so pervasive and persuasive is open to conjecture. I do not have any good answers, I forgot to bring that book today. If it was merely that ancestors of modern Puebloans knew something others did not, fine. What if, however, it was not all that simple. What if they knew Beauty Way and later taught it to Athabaskans [whether directly or thru example]? What if their knowledge of Sandstone Way shaped them to be a certain kind of spiritual people such that visitors to their landscapes were just a bit in awe, wanted to emulate them?

Wanted to borrow some of their culture as if they could absorb and understand it?

What if later on when some force took Beauty Way away from Anasazi, whether climate, hunger, indifference to beauty, aggressor-aggrandizement from some visitors, some internal error or mistake in their path, or even some freak of nature scared them, convinced their shamans that an era had about ended, they knew it was time to leave, almost simultaneously. When beauty leaves, what is leftover? Who would wish to remain?

If it was a cataclysmic or freakish event, it may have not taken much but a few well spoken tales, and a wave of abandonment began with a few families then increased rapidly. A wave of terror may have swept Anasazi from this land as certainly as wind sweeps my path.

For I am on a path, of discovery, whether I call it a dayhike or my lifeway. It is all Sandstone Way, I am given abilities and desires, shown places and rock art in some Heuristic Way. I have filled my journal with more questions, but not sort I can pose to any archaeologists, for they have their own concerns and questions. I have no fever to receive answers immediately, am content to let some few answers come to me sporadically. And they do, tho I cannot yet read that kind of writing shown out there. If a ruin or rock art panel takes a certain 'stance' perhaps much is said thusly. There is a kind of literature of meaning Anasazi left behind; while there is sublime beauty here, there is also subtlety.

Sometimes I have to clamber down a crack between two large boulders to descend to first ledge, and imagine this was Anasazi Way, this path was theirs first, it must lead somewhere. I find a rock art panel, several actually adjacent. There is a surrounding void of rock art or ruins in both directions near this place, thus I know where I am meant something to Anasazi. What does it mean to me? I cannot say, perhaps it is too early. For my path to get here was not Anasazi Way, it was White Man's Way. I must come back, park away from here and hike up this slope to get here, perhaps then I will see.

I do see what is meant at some panels, tho I am not given an exact key to understanding each element. I sense a general intent, a kind of meta-message, made as clear today as long ago. It is no great struggle to understand, but I am able to because I came to these places with effort.

As I continue my hike, sun moves around relentlessly giving me indications of Anasazi time, of a day trying to end eventually, putting boundaries on my hike. I did not start my day with limitations, parameters certainly, but felt open to anything. I have seen some of what I thot to, more sometimes, and call my self satisfied. After all, it was a Sandstone Way hike and for me those are always best. Some of Sandstone Way has soaked into me, I am not same person as start of day, nor will I be next time I return. This is all good.

I have overcome some trepidation, I have enlarged my internal map, some resting spot will recognize me when I come back and I will know some kind of Anasazi door opened up for me, I have a few keys now and there is now more of Cedar Mesa I can call home. Sandstone Way continues without me, as I return to civilization; coyote hunts packrat and rabbit, badger sleeps her winter days away, plants slumber until spring, a cool breeze comes along, lizard scampers under a warm rock as dusk approaches and moon is eager to lamp another Cedar Mesa nite.

Sandstone Way is my path and I am but another creature following it. Where it leads is around another corner along second ledge or perhaps finally to a home I have forgotten, but will know when I find it.

CHAPTER 15
SANDSTONE WAY

Once upon a time a prince lived in a far off land. His life was charmed, as everything "seemed to go his way." Lacking another way to explain this phenomenon, his friends called it 'serendipity,' because country where he lived was called Serendip.

I once thot that if coincidences seem to go my way while hiking in Anasazi homeland, I should call such a trend "Anasazity" but this seems not appropriate somehow. I prefer 'sandstonicity,' as it is while hiking, resting, or viewing sandstone that "things" happen.

What does happen is that after time I have figured out that ruins, rock art panels, and artifacts find me, but only if my being is in a proper state of receptivity.

I have noticed that there are alignments of certain features on Cedar Mesa, whose meaning escapes me at this moment. I wonder, tho, if these alignments, these in-sight fixes were meant to protect Anasazi in some way I cannot fathom, for my experience is too civilized, too fast-tempo, and too unaligned.

I am a disparate character, a personality intent on exploring and learning; can you really program your own education, tho, or is it a life-long process of evolution? If a species can evolve, could I?

When I hike a new corner of Cedar Mesa, I often know where I want to go but not how to get there. Sandstonicity provides clues as I hike, or as I rest, sometimes early in morning when I awake for no certain reason. It may be a path thru some boulders, it may be a sandstone bridge around an entrenching slickrock gully, it may be a perfectly placed boulder fall, with in-built soils providing a roothold for jp's, it is all out there and only waiting for me to come along.

I rarely run into other hikers; sandstonicity provides me with an appropriate solitude that I can learn at my own pace. My education, my understanding is enlarged in steps, cliff bands.

When I hike in winter, I seek out sunny spots for warmth, often resting out of wind with sandstone as backrest, a vue ahead, and know that tho no other person rested there, many Anasazi did. This does not mean I am an Anasazi-wannabe, merely that I unconventionalize my walks, I see creative lostness as an art, and I know sandstonicity will show me a way.

One time on a hike I came to a ledge-end. I could not go on, nor up or down; I sought to return way I had come but found I had forgotten who I was. I realized I was changed somehow, no longer who I desired to be. Leaving my desire to be, I sat and thot. It turns out I never left, I had to die there.

One day I imagined myself reincarnated as an early explorer. But how could this be, to turn back tic-toc-tic of normality? As I hiked it turns out I had no self left afloat, no desire to find treasure, no certainty I knew it all, and no idea where I was. I was not lost, however, for I knew where I had been, or who I had been.

I think as a new land opened before me, it shaped me in new shades of color, some pinks and buffs of slickrocky persuasion. As if I had been dropped into a dream with new rules of thinking and perceiving. But it was not a dream, it was all real.

There was a cliff and gravity to remind me of mortality, there was weather to remind me of home, and there is hunger to remind me I am not Anasazi, that a nearby granary is not full, and that on next ledge my wife is not waiting to cook me a meal.

I am a modern explorer, but I seldom use new tools or technology. I prefer to find myself as I am hiking, this has something to do with an "a-hah!" epiphany when I recognize a sandstone ramp leading me on my way, as if only just placed there for my benefit. Or rather it has always been there, and only Anasazi and I know why. Maybe it has to do with dinosaur dreams of a creature who will follow, and needs a good path thru life; dinosaurs swished their tails that we might climb here.

Why Anasazi left this area is not nearly as important as why they came here. It is so much easier to abandon, than to imagine and create, rather to see one's reflection in a land and know it is home. I sometimes ask wind: did Anasazi follow a different path towards beauty when they moved off mesas to live in sandstone? Were open lands too spacious, unbounded? Did Anasazi need to shelter in sandstone overhangs because they needed to know sandstone?

Their life was composed of sand, clay, and water; those three bound them, provided for them, and made their bed. People of Mud, I heard when I was not paying attention.

But, I did ask, "Why were overhang caves, alcoves, made with water nearby, and access to mesa?" perhaps meaning to ask instead "Why was a home made here for Anasazi? and by whom?" Well, these are too many questions. Now we ask "why is existence?", or "why is there something, rather than nothing?" but these are not questions Anasazi needed. Theirs was a world of beauty--in a far-off mountain covered with snow, in a nearby canyon with a spring, in soil fit for growing corn, beans, squash, and what we like to call 'weeds' because we have no use for some plants.

Anasazi saw some of their land, some of fellow inhabitants with love, it is clearly expressed in their drawings; it could be that some of their world brought them only fear.

But, I am not an Anasazi, I have come too late for that! I find their drawings and houses, where they farmed and played, maybe where some were buried. I find these aspects without looking anymore, they stumble upon me as if I was a butterfly traveling thru.

I find their routes, with hidden steps carved in sandstone. I find their paths, winding across slickrock. I find their early homes, clearings in open sky-land. Why me? Because I am there, because I wander their land without any particular desire or need. Coyote and raven try to sign me a way thru, showing me what they are most interested in. Raven is interested in food, so is coyote. One flies, other trots. I can imagine spatial identity of both, combine their vue into mine. I can pretend to think as they do.

I can pretend to think as Anasazi did, but have accepted too much acculturation. I can open myself to Sandstone Way, this I have done. For it is out there, thru cliff-bands, down slopes, across ledges, under overhangs, below skies. It is there where I perch above a canyon, watching hikers down below. I think they cannot see me, because they are not open to Sandstone Way. They cannot know I am watching, because they are protected by their culture of laws and technology.

But, I could erase all that with a well-placed boulder, and I choose not to. It is not so much that I fear getting caught, rather they are meaningless, not worthy of enemyhood.

These, of course, are Anasazi fears; concerns of who is friend or foe, and are not aspects of Beauty Way.

When I meet hikers plodding along, I ask them what they have seen. Usually not very much. This is not because they are necessarily stupid, or blind, but they cannot see what they are not ready to see. If I rolled a boulder down near them, I would educate them to a newer level of seeing, but I think "should I?" Is it my work to educate, or would I rather illuminate?

A boulder makes a certain statement when it crashes near your head. It is loud and exuberant. Rock art is hidden, subtle, and quiet. It is for you to notice and understand. Some house ruins are well-hidden, more so for granaries. Hidden from whom? Whoever wanted to take what was not theirs. Some rock art intends to warn, to inform these strangers that "you are not welcome here," some intends to protect in other, more sublime ways. Some rock art says "I am here, I passed thru, stayed awhile."

Those hikers I watch have their books and maps, they talk to rangers, browse an Internet, they know where they are going, what to see. They do not know how to look, to see what they do not know is there, nor what to make of something when it finds them. It is all a test, it is a way to taste those who come thru.

My boulder crashing nearby is only a scare, real fear is seeing unknown, knowing there is something ineffable out there that civilization cannot prepare you for--Cedar Mesa is one small corner of this 'out there'. We can pontificate endlessly, read correct books, take classes, but who can answer questions such as "what did Anasazi believe and see?" or even "why did they come to Cedar Mesa?" Did they come for reasons due to population increases, a hiatus of bad weather, inability to get along with older relatives, old traditions souring? Or did some come for beauty, to absorb it as a lizard soaks sunshine?

I hike Sandstone Way, I hike paths too obscure for modern man, I absorb an ambiance too sublime to describe in modern text, there is an elusive suggestion I listen to which shows me routes too prehistoric for most. I have not found any answers, may someday run out of questions. I no longer know what forces mold me, when I am out there hiking. I suppose it has something to do with Sandstone

Way, Anasazi, and who I am.

Perhaps it has to do with sandstonicity, and a quality of guidance I have only to open myself up to.

I walk on sandstone, sandstone walks on me
I walk on beauty, beauty walks on me
A lizard dreams of me
and I thank her for knowing
we are both alike

* * *

Deja Vu, I have heard, is a feeling you have been here before, experienced this line of time, known this person before, and are about to repeat a happenstance of life. What if, however, as in my case I have spent so much time hiking a particular kind of landscape that it almost all seems overly familiar. It is as if 'ahah' experiences have happened so many times that each becomes commonplace, rather than special.

Ubiquitousity is more than a word, it is reality, when thinking of slickrock. I find same kinds of breaks in sandstone cliff bands, I find same kinds of boulder debris and blockages when hiking various ledges of slickrock canyons. It is there in same kinds of light and shadow, how far off mountains look at certain times of day.

I prefer winter sun, there but not overbearing, and providing a kind of warm ambiance of help--not hurt. Of course I am not an agriculturist to desire heat of summer sun for my crops, I bring food with me from a grocery store.

I love those moments sitting out of wind on slickrock, back against a cliff foot, dogs nearby, nobody for miles, and a twisting canyon below me. But it is moments when I enter a new canyon, or an old friend at a new place, even specially a small insignificant sub-canyon on Comb Ridge, I know I can find my way; I know I will find breaks and difficulties in a manner dictated by rules of Sandstone Way. I have learned to heed these unwritten rules of a lifeway on slickrock, and whenever I see specific features I know I have seen them before, as a type.

For it as a typology that Sandstone Way proves itself true to form. I have become molded to a creature of this other reality, I know paths and ways few can see, could believe if shown. It is all there in front of me. When I stop along a canyon side, look across its depths, and see a new-to-me granary tucked away out of sight under a shallow overhang, I know that I would find it there; besides a call to this land, or from this land, I know each granary is placed where it needs to be to serve Anasazi. There is a level of truth, a following of Sandstone Way here, and I have followed its path for some time now; for so long I may never be able to leave.

When I meet other hikers, which happens rarely, I may indeed be invisible in many aspects of my character. I am no longer within any sphere of their reality as hikers, whatever goals they intend are alien to me. I have not yet a perfect knowledge of Sandstone Way, nor of this place and people, yet I know what I seek and where to find it. I can no longer follow a canyon bottom as if it were in sole possession of truth, as if it alone were a key to experience or certainty.

This is so because canyon bottoms are too dangerous, or were, for Anasazi. A place to be, yes, but not to linger unless certain nobody will harm them. This was not always so; but canyon bottoms were not really home for Anasazi. Home was elevation and vues, openness and sunshine. Even later on, their homes in cliffs faced winter sun.

Some inhabitants preferred shade and coolness for their houses. Some wonder at this, thinking early Basketmaker wo/man a bit crazy perhaps. There is another logic, however, at work here and modern man may have a hard time comprehending truths beyond his education. Basketmaker made small structures, not much more than camps. When I see their walls, placed as they are, a certain knowledge of purpose osmoses its way inside me. Anasazi logic was very real to many people over a long period of habitation, much longer than modern man has proven capable of so far in this country.

Perhaps 'logic' is not correct, too formal and too constricting. Perhaps 'Way' is better, and its use started long ago with a translator of Navajo chants/ceremonies. Lifeway makes more sense than cultural evolution or other modern terms.

For it is as I find my way on Cedar Mesa, and often repeat my way around and thru that I feel most of it is homely, that it was important at different times to Anasazi. Some places give me no feeling of home, no welcome or unwelcome. There are places that feel quite friendly, where some kind of happiness was absorbed in some manner I cannot quite get to with logic.

I see places with no apparent use for moderns that indicate to me importance for Anasazi, whether scientists call them limited activity sites or skip over them in ignorance. It was Anasazi lifeways that decided what was needed and what not, in conformity with Sandstone Way.

For Sandstone Way was their reality, Anasazi Way their dream.

Where good soil will be for crops, where warmth will linger late in a summer, where water will course its way and can be paused for irrigation, where springs will forth out at certain places, where shelter can be molded out of soil or rock, and where a path along a steep slope can be hammered, or where rock art is best placed all seemed obvious to Anasazi.

Now, I hike thru with my home 70 miles away, with a vehicle waiting to whisk me home later in this day, with food and drink on my back, dogs at my side and front, a certain freedom from concerned family/friends. My solitude is a shield when in civilization, now it is merely a tool in some entrenchment process.

When I wind my way thru Cedar Mesa, wherever my day takes me, I am looking for signs of earlier habitation or resting spots, even for lithic debitage or shards, but I am doing more than that. I am thinking how my route is good, not just for me but earlier for Anasazi. I am thinking of how to grow crops here, where to corral water when it rains or snow melts; I got an early education in irrigated farming in desert country, I know some of those problems. I am thinking of where I will build my home, in my mind anyway; I doubt BLM would agree to my living here in this life. I am thinking of where there is a spring, how to get to it. I am thinking of where I would play, hide, or work, dream and even be buried. Where my children and wife would live while I am out hunting or trading, tending crops perhaps, scouting sometimes. Of which places speak to me, which landscapes need adorning with my art, what it would thus tell friends and enemies.

I know that when I first saw Bear scratches on aspen, high in a mountain meadow, it spoke to me of power and intent, of a territory marked but also more than that. This is a sign that "This is my home, I alone decide who else comes here," and I knew I could do likewise for my own home. So, I might have left my drawings on rock to show that this is my home, instead I left pieces of myself. I have followed Sandstone Way and here is my map, here is what I thot or dreamt, here is where I came to know who I was and what my life held for me.

Moderns like to say "vision quest" but have no real idea what they are speaking of. For this process of seeking self-awareness is neither a Buddhist sort of search nor a quantum I can teach you, nor you I. It is, rather, a process of each Anasazi quieting other people's noise and listening to Sandstone Way, which taught him how he fit into his family's or band's lifeway, how he as individ could best contribute to survival, not merely of himself but of those he loved, hated, or must deal with. For even his enemies were part of his responsibility, his to deal with as he may. Each Anasazi individ knew his own balance and harmony were his to shape, and accept, and he only needed a time of clarity to see his lifepath. So, I have found some of these places he went to know himself, but it was not for me to learn myself in this manner.

I came about to know myself on other paths than you will find on these landscapes of slickrock or aspen meadows, of canyon depths or rims, across sage or jp complexities. My way was thru civilization and people I met, battles I fought against tradition or "way it is". I chose to come here to make a home after seeing some of our world. My lifeway is now traced on but a few paper maps, not found in most stores. Mine is a way of hiking and knowing that what once drew Anasazi now draws me. My lifeway is Sandstone Way, and my home is Cedar Mesa; when I come back each time I know I am welcome.

There may not be any more to know about Sandstone Way.

CHAPTER 16
ENEMY WAY

There is a certain responsibility inherent in having an enemy, for it may be that such a person feels a close tie to you, and you to him. I suppose it depends on what quality of Enemy Way you desire.

Or perhaps you do not really want such an individ to think of you as enemy, that his animosity comes for no clear flexic[1]. You may feel nothing but bother or sadness that your enemy sees fit to hate you and constantly attempts to interfere with your lifeway. You may actually be indifferent to his hatred, and just prefer to stay away from him, interact never at all.

There are many reasons for hating another person, your enemy could very well choose any one or several and never tell you why. Thus you may merely be baffled at his intensity.

It may be that you hate this person, for hating you or for peculiarities of his being-personality. And you may engage in activities of Enemy Way against this person. There may be a shared respect from mutual knowledge of each other's powers and strengths.

This all indicates that Enemy Way is a complex path, for Anasazi as well as modern man. Scientists today can fathom some of this thru examination of house ruins and skeletons or mummies. Some is mere conjecture. Modern psychologists have written much about pathology of hatred and Enemy Way. In this period of time life can be very complex, with many interpersonal interactions in a day; for Anasazi life was perhaps simpler with less people around to love, like, or shades of dislike or indifference.

However, his opportunities for individ escape were perhaps limited by lifeway circumstances. Emigration could have been one such escape, perhaps his society had other formalized releases available. Some of this remains unknowable.

There are two main classification of enemies apropos to Anasazi: personal enemies and unknowable enemies. Within these types are individ enemies who are understandable and those who are incomprehensible, or crazy, pathological in our terms.

With a personal, face-to-face enemy each and every primitive man had limited but often very clear courses of action available. These could range from personal combat and defeat for one individ to some organized societal game where personal tensions could momentarily be eased. Perhaps ball games at Hohokam villages served a like purpose. Perhaps neither course served, and a lifelong animosity rankled, spreading out to family members.

In this path, Anasazi could know his enemy, could learn his ways and maybe even circumvent his future actions, or he could emigrate out of his enemies' sphere of influence. Moving to a new home would work best if he had relatives, or his wife did, to ease his transition.

With a stranger as enemy, even as another tribe or breed/language group as enemy, less could personally be done, but again perhaps less face-to-face contact gave some measure of tranquillity most times. This kind of animosity is our "us-them" category, and usually it is expressed as intertribal [or interband] war. So, few individs know their enemy as individs, more as a type, and their knowledge is shared, gossiped and cycles whenever any new skirmish brings forth new material

Another side of this Enemy Way is healing ceremonies by individ's society/religion or sodalities as anthropologists believe. These ceremonies serve to leach out negativity, strengthen his ties to his own people and their lifeway/belief system, bring him back to a sane self, and away from immersion in depths of his shared animosity. For, his people know that any over-prolonged focus of hatred can rot his spirit, sap his path towards harmony.

Perhaps this is all only Navajo lifeway and had nothing to do with Anasazi, perhaps Pueblo do not have these ceremonies. Maybe, tho, Navajo learned some of their chant/ ceremonies from similar processes thru early Pueblo interactions. No doubt for ethnologists to learn.

When I see certain features of Anasazi houses such as defensively aimed 'loopholes' and inaccessibility as an architectural style in their late period of habitation on Cedar Mesa, but archaeologists report little and scattered signs of mass violence indicative of an invasion, I think more in terms of a perceived threat than a real one. In other words, there was a real enemy out there, but perhaps Anasazi's real enemy was fear/terror of what could happen, of what they knew would happen, sooner or later. Perhaps stories came their way of northern incursions and violence, or from some other cardinal direction.

Perhaps an underlying current of fear was worse than an actual face-to-face enemy, one that could be studied, stymied, or even combated directly. That tool works today as well as ever, as we have learned.

There may have never been any deliberate campaign of terror, it might rather have just been an effect of some other people's famine, hard times, or over-population pressures, a need for new territory. Perhaps Anasazi's enemy had encountered them in an outlier area and learned to envy, hate, fear, and desire to kill them. Who can say for certain?

There had to have been some congruence of factors which caused a wide-area and time-wise condensed abandonment of most of Four Corners area. Usually suspected as culprits are climate degradation, arroyo cutting, and others as 'push' factors and reports of better places as 'pull' factors. Rarely do archaeologists write of any real threat of invading enemies, rather they tend to speculate that degradation of agricultural conditions and other factors lead to famine within greater Anasazi culture, thus bands turned on other bands for food supplies; have's versus have-not's.

It is appropriate to mention that "Anasazi" had an earlier meaning than we give it today. To some "Enemy Ancestors" or "Old Ones" indicates less than enthusiastic regard for Anasazi, perhaps some respect tho. Today most of us think of Anasazi as a wonderful civilization living in peace, harmony, and plenty in a beautiful part of this continent. Actually, realistically, Anasazi are known for their brilliance at adapting to life in many eco-zones of basically a dry part of our world, some more deserty than other sections where they lived and farmed. For adaptive farmers is what they evolved to.

And their cousin(?)/neighbor bands of Hohokam were even better at irrigation and surviving in a true desert. Anasazi, like Mogollon, survived in usually higher elevations than Hohokam wherein different techniques, architecture, and farming were required. Anasazi had a different cultural level than Mogollon, Hohokam, or other neighbors. While it was not necessarily better, it seemed to be more respected, or more desirous of imitation. Whether it was their particular lifestyles, their manufactured products, or their 'religion' is open to question. There was some kind of powerful influence or sway that Anasazi held for their neighbors, in time and space.

Perhaps this was a cause of envy or hatred also, and it is possible that Anasazi gained an enemy they neither wanted nor could quite handle. Perhaps their enemy, tho, was of a special category of incomprehensibility or craziness and nothing sufficed but to leave and reconsolidate elsewhere.

Some historic pueblo locations are clearly defensive in nature, perhaps one element of their 'push' away from Four Corners was an enemy.

Some archaeologists wonder that abandonment seemed almost perfectly total, even tho there had to have been ecological certainty of survival for a smaller population. Probably, tho, another kind of structure had abandoned Four Corners, and individ families could not choose to remain without it. Such as, for instance, a structure of mutual support, trade, and society, since there seemed to be no empire or state as there was in Central and South America.

Perhaps Anasazi chose that facet of Enemy Way, to give up and abandon a whole vast area rather than give in to particular demands of hating their enemy. Perhaps they chose not to 'own' their enemy in modern terms; perhaps in Anasazi terms they chose not to 'be' their enemy [i.e. accept, think as, or behave like]. We may never know, because architecture, artifacts, and burials do not always tell a complete story, and modern Puebloans are either not talking, or have forgotten.

In my hikes on Cedar Mesa I do not need to dwell on Enemy Way, or on my perception of it, because I seldom get a feel for hate/dread/fear/violence. Rather I see loopholes, and guard towers/lookouts, defensive architecture etc and I think it sad that some effect of human nature caused this. But I also sense an earlier harmony and even comfort out there, and I think on balance Anasazi found more beauty for more years than Enemy Way.

There are a few Anasazi house sites on Cedar Mesa, while placed in defensive positions, that show an extra effort to attain comfort, safety, or beauty, or that demonstrate a pride in workmanship and appearance. People only expend extra energy for aesthetics if there is no immediate threat of warfare or danger. Perhaps this path towards beauty was an effort to ward off enemies--those who hate.

CHAPTER 17
SEARCHING FOR BEAUTY

When I hike Cedar Mesa, I am not carrying along a dictionary meaning of word 'beauty' nor giving such a concept any philosophical thot. I surely recognize much beauty out there, some sublime, some subtle, some in landscape, some in house ruins, some in rock art.

It is all same to me, just shades of beauty as manifested. Whether it is truly all in eye of each beholder also matters not at all to me.

I do think that Anasazi recognized landscapeal beauty and in certain instances chose to reflect it in their house sites and rock art. They did this by picking places to build that when seen from a distance mirror as much beauty as I am capable of withstanding or absorbing. Their house sites also, when sat in front of, reflect a vast beauty of vue which I am sure Anasazi selected for.

Overall, on Cedar Mesa, landscapeal beauty comes in forms of vistas, of changing lite patterns as day and season progress, in many shades of same few basic colors: green, red, buff, white, blue, black and shapes of sandstone, whether canyons, cliffs, mesas, slickrock flats, ledges, arches, hoodoos or mesa tops.

In rock art, beauty is similar to that of any man-made art form, derived from skill, form, color, subject etc. Beauty may even result from some enigmatic qualities of rock art, such as what is depicted and why. Questions for classrooms, I am sure.

Hiking across Cedar Mesa on my way to some canyon, I am winding around thru jp's and shallow gullies, with small rock outcroppings to explore, possibly ancient house sites with resultant shards. Sun is warm--but it is winter and will not get hot--sky is clear and dogs are happy to be out hiking.

Bear's Ears are north of me, always, as some kind of guardian spirit--a reminder that this was once Bear's home. Then came Anasazi, now I come. I saw a mountain lion once, up close, on Cedar Mesa and another time a deer carcass she had stashed for a later meal. Bear may not have actually roamed all of Cedar Mesa; he certainly overlooked it from Elk Ridge/Dark Canyon Plateau.

I am following a faint deer trail, once used and now abandoned due to some vagaries of deer flexic. It shows me easy ways to skip thru cliff bands and goes generally where I want, towards another canyon. Mostly 4' tall sage surrounds me, soil is not quite right for jp's here, so my vues are 360 degree. I can see where White Canyon and tributaries hide, I can see Salvation Knoll standing guard, I can see south into Monument Valley, west to Clay Hills, and east Comb Ridge is out of sight, but waiting for me to notice.

There are few birds this time of year, and it is quiet if I ignore overhead jets. There are no other hikers within miles of Dusty, Browny and I, perhaps some may be in ggulch. Some woodcutters may be relatively close, gathering juniper cuttings for their long winter nites; or Navajos collecting for their ceremonies.

I feel a kind of peacefulness to this stillness and isolation, perhaps an easier openness to beauty. I am not deliberately looking for beauty, it comes to me anyway. It seems I have evolved into a creature sensitive enough to recognize many levels of beauty in this landscape.

Even if jp covered mesa top areas of Cedar Mesa are infinitely ubiquitous, each little gully and outcropping or shallow ridge system has character, each once-dammed intermittent stream course does also. These kinds of features are, to some, merely a prelude to their real intent in hiking canyons. A kind of bland purgatory of terrain to get thru before their real hiking begins. For me, tho, Cedar Mesa's jp flats and hillocks/gullies are important. I know they were very important to Anasazi, I see it everywhere.

Even so, once at a canyon edge my vue changes dramatically. There is a broad statement made by a Southwestern canyon cutting thru a landscape, and depending on each beholder may seem forbidding or merely interesting. I have evolved from daunted to a kind of calm acceptance of coming difficulty. For me, crossing a Cedar Mesa canyon is not a trial or tribulation, it has become a variety of metier I am well adapted to. Few entrench themselves so thoroughly that there is no shortcut across or down into them.

So as I stop to look around, part of me is involved with finding my route, part of me is looking for sites, part of me is just soaking up whatever ambiance presents itself. I look up and down canyon, across to opposite side, and below me for whatever trails runs along streambed. Once these chores are done, I can admire a vue as nothing more than that.

There is a place inside me which hungers always for beauty, whether landscapeal, in an act of loving between my dogs such as when Dusty tongue-washes Browny's ears for him, in an isolated shard, or in a vue. Even when I am hiking along some canyon bottom, turning corners, new vues constantly present themselves. They appear, then fade as I progress, seeming to fill my mind one minute and recede into memory later.

One aspect of beauty which I have wondered much about--I think beauty found while hiking is more mean-ingful than any I may see while driving. It is not so much that one comes with effort, but that lack of speed gives me time to absorb. I noticed this when I used to mountain bike, speed/progress can become its own reward, possibly to detriment of actually seeing something.

There is, then, a kind of catching of breath pause which blends quite well with absorbing a new vue; as if my bodily needs rhythm out an acceptance of beauty only adapted to physical exertion. Why this should be is unclear, perhaps some momentary shortage of oxygen in my brain helps me recognize what otherwise I might be too busy to notice. Time, then, might be a shade of beauty only ticked off by a pulsing of my blood. Perhaps it is only that increased intimacy comes with a mild desperation.

For beauty is there in front of me, and I see it as much as it sees me. We can for a moment become one. Later when I return home, a certain smile shows that I have seen beauty, when it may be that I did not expect to.

Some kind of intimate distance in each and every Cedar Mesa vue only comes with many hikes out there. That is a kind of beauty in itself, to know that what seems vast is also a friend, sometimes a home. There is a similar beauty in final stages of each hike, when specially doing a loop, that I have circled a section of Cedar Mesa in an Anasazi way, not having to repeat my route in.

There is a warm beauty in sitting with my back against a sandstone wall, sandstone under my butt, a jp in front of me, with dogs resting in shade, not far in front of my feet a canyon depth, across a certain distance an opposite cliff face full of promises, and a rustling breeze not quite reaching me.

There is a warm beauty in knowing I got myself hereand will get myself home today, that I visited another corner of Cedar Mesa, whether new or not. There is much beauty in every approach I make to a house site, whether along an easy ledge or a tricky one.

I know a house site on Cedar Mesa which accepts much responsibility for beauty by hiding, in an accessible way as if to say "to find me you must search long and hard, you must learn to care." Not many people, it seems, have known this beauty nor have visited this site, perhaps one person in every 6 years, as if '6' were some kind of special number.

I know a rock art site near Cedar Mesa which many people go to see, some have tried to destroy its beauty, as if ashamed they could not have conceived such beauty. Fear of beauty, tho, is a limit I choose not to accept. I am searching for beauty, whether this is foremost in my mind or not.

I recognize beauty when I am ready, sometimes I pass it by until later when I have properly evolved. This process is a kind of entrenchment of spirit, as if I were a flat landscape such as Cedar Mesa, just waiting for a canyon to cut thru me. Waiting for a day when hikers would travel thru me, marveling at my subtleties.

I am not a mesa named 'Cedar' tho, I am a hiker who recognizes beauty. Every hike is thru beauty, it is for me to notice. And I see beauty in other aspects of life, but I prefer that I find on Cedar Mesa.

I also notice certain patterns of beauty, between similar rock art panels or similar house sites, as if some ancient conference of Anasazi decided to copy each other. Emulation of beauty can be a form of love, tho, a borrowing of uniqueness for oneself. I see patterns of beauty in rock art, that sometimes a story is told, sometimes a message is conveyed, sometimes love is expressed
for a favorite animal or artifact--sometimes rock art may be drawn for its own sake, as if beauty were enough.

Many times beauty is expressed in simple locational proximities, to shade, to water, to farmland, or to each other's houses. Archaeologists can study these patterns of culture, others seem too vague.

So I suppose I cannot really define beauty as I find it on Cedar Mesa; I can recognize it and absorb it, share some of it, hope for more understanding, and keep looking. I do know that what beauty I find on Cedar Mesa means more to me than almost any other species or variety. Why this should be, I cannot imagine.

When I hike, I have to look down often to make sure I do not stumble. I find much beauty under me drawn in certain ways on cryptogramic soils, with little gullies coursing around obstacles, small dams of flotsam or jetsam, and bushes thankfully absorbing any lingering moisture from melting snow. I find beauty as I look up to check where I am going, or where I would like to go, where I may be looking into shadows, as if under cover hides an answer to most of my questions.

Every jp I pass, brushing closely by, perhaps even picking off a cluster of leaves to crush in my fingers and smell, speaks to me of beauty; yes even in sameness I can find beauty, for each jp is similar, but unique. Each accepts its environmental adaptation in its own way, as if to say, "here I make my home, that you may find shade here, that you little animals may find a home under my branches, that you birds may linger here a moment, thinking your birdthots."

When I stop atop a canyon, standing still on its slickrock skirts, and plan out my next route, there is a waitingness quality of beauty in front and below me--not so much waiting for me to discover, more that it is content to be beautiful unobserved, as if hubris is ok if your name is Cedar Mesa and you wear sandstone as a cloak. A kind of smugness I find appealing, a certitude of worth. A sandstony quiet, not quite secretive, but different. Mesa top is a world of wind, vues, and civilization busy flying overhead, a land where vastness is well-represented. Below my feet another variety of intricacy and infinity of shape hides from vue until I make an effort to visit. Waiting, quiet, alive, and vital in a wholly other way. Knowing that altho I see her clearly from above, yet unless I get down in there I won't know her.

When I am below looking up, all seems distant, too high and unreachable. Then, as I ascend my perspective changes, I see paths unknown from below--when about half way up I share part of an upper world and part of a deep world, both related but different. When I am again on top looking down I see depths otherwise than remote, secret, because I know I have just left. I find I continually must take these steep and efficient routes into canyon depths to refresh my spatial identity, or even more generically my Sandstone Way identity--my relatedness to Cedar Mesa. I cannot hug her close unless I have experienced her differing aspects, as if a place was a person with facets of meaning explicitly hidden in her depths.

Then, as I walk along a canyon rim I imagine I feel a bit like a raven flying overhead, looking down always. I cannot as quickly get down into this canyon's depths and hidden ways as he, but I know that I have been down there sometime before, and I put these two flavors of experience together as a whole. This forms a kind of gestalt, an inner map not at all as two-dimensional as when on paper.

If you visit a Grand Canyon rim an overwhelming sense of possibilities may push you back to your car and safety in boundedness. That place seems so vast, it cannot be fully absorbed. Some people, after years of exploration can see such vastness and look deep inside, say "ah, one year we camped there. Then another time we climbed up there to look around," and their feeling is one of familiarity, of knowledge of secret ways of where to hike thru, down and around.

With Cedar Mesa canyons, there is a wholly different flavor to canyon depths. They are not as well entrenched, they are not as wide. Neither are they stepped, in slopes interspersed with cliffs in quite same way. Many Cedar Mesa canyons drop sheer to their streambeds. There are ledges, but all supremely narrow by Grand Canyon standards. Along these ledges, hidden, are little isolated Anasazi house sites, and granaries.

It is as I find a new-to-me building site, resting half in shade, half in a warm winter sun, with its small area of rubble and shards, and few if any footprints, that I may hear a certain whisper of beauty that no other area may know. For I have found much beauty standing atop a Colorado mountain, knowing for one moment it is mine to hold and love, and share. And another sort of beauty, a flavor in some shop which sells many flavors, waits here. This is no Mesa Verde large site with many rooms and tourists scrambling thru with their "oohs" and "aahhs." This is a private, quiet, solitary little building. It has calmly waited for perhaps years for someone to visit, thinking its granary thots.

I had no idea, after reading my map, that I would find this granary--a purposeful little building now empty--but when I came to it I somehow knew I would. I had not seen it from around any corners, nor across canyon. There was no sign on this ledge holding out promises of discovery, even beauty. Beauty Way works thusly, tho, it is for me to find and recognize. This granary sees me, knows me, and for a while we share a kind of resting remembrance of what once was.

For this granary has seen much, provided safe storage for many years, for many Anasazi. It was appreciated, looked after, rebuilt, checked often, needed. It was hidden from animals, unfriendly people, and now--by time. I stop to sit down and rest near its presence, thinking granary thots myself.

For granary is no longer used, nor needed much; when I come upon granary and stop to think awhile, tho, I do need it. It fills in one more corner of my map, of a question too broad for any book to answer. This granary knows a beauty that once was, it shows its own beauty of purpose whether that purpose is current or not.

It hides on its own ledge, tucked into a corner of a disappearing ledge act, overlooking one section of one Cedar Mesa canyon. Perhaps in some archaeological file there is a mark for it. I wonder, tho, if whoever first surveyed it and made an 'x' for it on some governmental map, bothered to sit down and think about it. Such as why it was here, who lived nearby, how those Anasazi brought grain to it, how often they retrieved it, how this granary kept rodents out, and moisture at bay. There may be a kind of beauty to scientific knowledge, of certainty to knowing how this granary fit into an overall habitation pattern of culture, here on Cedar Mesa. But there is a real, present, more vital kind of beauty here, and I stop to soak it up.

I see how its doorway is shaped to fit a certain sandstone slab, one picked out in advance. I see how its lintel is up about 12 inches from sandstone floor of this alcove. Its depth is sufficient to hold much grain, yet still be reached by a people smaller than I. Perhaps Anasazi children were given task of crawling inside whenever more food was needed. Now, 1000 years after its construction and use, plaster still covers its stone walls. In places this plaster is weakened by moisture and time. I wonder, tho, how my house would fare given an opportunity to try for 1000 years?

Its color blends in very well with background sandstone, as if Anasazi had ground up nearby slickrock to form a color tint for their plaster; a kind of primitive camouflage. In overall shape it suggests a kind of beehive, with smooth sides, and without bees or honey. It rests against sandstone walls of this alcove, at end of narrow ledge, and its walls rest against ceiling of alcove, a kind of borrowing of architecture; each granary and house is unique in their specific adaptations to each locale. What works in one canyon, on one ledge, may not in another.

This granary is only one of many, spread over greater

Four Corners area. As such it has no great significance, nor importance. Yet, since I am here I study it, for other than a vue of canyon in front of me, there is no other scene. There is no other object quite as beautiful, it seems to me, as a purposeful little Anasazi structure tucked safely away waiting to be needed again. For I do admire all kinds and shapes of slickrock complexities, but Anasazi buildings make a kind of sentient statement--as if to say someone once needed this land, someone once loved this land. Sandstone Way without Anasazi structures is vital in one way, I prefer its vitality where once Anasazi lived.

This is so because I have always admired man's efforts to live off a land, or to extract minerals from his environment. Every different culture shapes and molds its landscape in unique ways. I cannot help admire how Anasazi adapted themselves, and their landscape for survival--for their deserty eco-system is not as friendly to all those people who have tried to live in it since Anasazi retreated south.

A simple utilitarian structure that we call 'granary' shows me a species of architectural understanding and skill that no bank or post office ever has. But it was a bank, an Anasazi bank for food, for a security of survival. Anasazi planned and labored to shelter their food for coming winter, and worse for coming spring--before plants could again provide a harvest and animals resume their fattening-up process.

Even more than a granary, when I see a house site I marvel at how Anasazi planned, organized, shared, and dreamt up their house to match its surroundings. For I have never seen any Anasazi house that seemed awkward, seemed not to fit, or not to belong to its landscape. This kind of perfection of architecture, or more primally of a gestalt of place has to come from individs with what we might think of as a magical gift of perception or understanding. Or with a genius for seeing what could/should be. Who these individs were, how they fit into their culture/society is unclear. Perhaps they were merely unique Anasazi individs, just as we now have our creative masters.

All these kinds and shapes of beauty, whether landscapeal, building situation, style, are all reflected more so in pottery decorations or rock art. What I find, tho, are not full pots, rather shards with pieces of each puzzle; I find shards with decorations which hint at what its pot looked like. But I think finding these pieces is better for my imagination than finding whole pots--they give me something to wonder about.

When I find rock art panels something different happens to me, some other shade of beauty appeals to me.

There is a purpose here, otherwise some Anasazi individ would not have put so much effort into these depictions. But his or her purpose and meaning may not be clear to most people, nor to me. First, I look at each panel as a kind of billboard, and wonder what it is advertising. Not trying to sell, tho sometimes that seems possible--selling a warning loud and clear.

I look at which direction each panel is facing, and this suggests much to me. For each panel is placed in specific locations for specific reasons, not white man's-way reasons nor bowing to our forms of logic, but in a pre-puebloan kind of flexic that current puebloans may or may not comprehend. I have seen many alcoves that did not have a house site in them and I have seen many wonderfully patinated rock faces with no rock art on them. Yet I find rock art on cliff faces in remote locations, on ledges difficult to access, facing directions with no discernible meaning.

Until, that is, early in 2002 I began to notice some other kind of structure to rock art panels, or rather organization. It came about thru a temporal juxtaposition of two random-seeming happenings. One was a book I was reading, another was me resting in front of an old and unique panel in a Cedar Mesa canyon. There was a connection between these two unrelated actualities, and that was me. I noticed that where a certain rock art panel was facing, in rough terms, there was another panel upcanyon. Downcanyon, almost in sight was another rock art panel. As my memory went over other panels further up and downcanyon, I pulled out my maps and pored over them. There seemed to be a linear connection, for possibly several miles, of a line of sight between rock art panels.

This theory I began to test by projecting into unconnected areas of this canyon. In some cases I was able to find rock art panels judging by my guesses, always only approximately in line-of-sight proximity to each other. What this all means is still in a speculative stage.

Herein, however, lies some kind of beauty of intent, of purposefulness, of a certain knowledge of landscape and possibly of what we call religion or spirituality. I do not believe that exact line-of-sight was ever specifically intended. Perhaps, rather, a symbolic connection, an approximate line-of-sight, that those 'spirits' designated in rock art panels would be able to see thru intervening trees and even around physical rock corners somewhat. These 'spirits' were guardians, perhaps, and their connectedness was reflected in a desire for protection by Anasazi; maybe Anasazi were put at ease knowing that these linear alignments symbolically pulled their disparate residences and personalities together, to form a kind of extended civilization instead of merely isolated families living their own lives unconcerned with neighbors.

And in some circumstances these placements of rock art panels matched small zigzag patterns drawn as parts of rock art panels, a kind of map of intent was drawn to scale to show each other how all were connected. Much as a teacher draws on his chalkboard to show patterns of cultural change, or Lewis and Clark's explorations.

When I discerned this possible pattern of connectedness,

of alignment of intent, and continued to look for it elsewhere on Cedar Mesa, a warm kind of beauty soaked me. It arose from an increase in understanding Anasazi, but one I self-generated rather than one I read in some ubiquitous archaeological book. For archaeological literature is full of theories about rock art panels and elements, their meaning and artist's intent. I cannot hope to ever understand an artist's intent, tho, if I cannot get 'inside his head.' This is very difficult [or impossible] to do across time and cultural boundaries.

I can walk up to an understanding of these line-of-sight placements, but may not be able to prove anything scientifically. That is how Beauty Way walks, tho, as she intends. It is up to us to follow and notice. It helps to be open to her ways.

Part of being open to beauty comes from a carefully imposed solitude, a certain quietude to surroundings, and a willingness to accept concepts and realities not of one's own making. For I am not Anasazi, I merely wish to understand their inner being. I can best follow this way by hiking Cedar Mesa, and knowing that all paths lead to and thru beauty, if I can only follow them.

CHAPTER 18
MIRROR

And sometimes people go to a place or another person looking for a mirror. They may not even know that they are doing so, but it is so. Maybe there was a need for reaffirming, or reassurance. Maybe you were just looking for yourself, reflected in a landscape, in a slickrock pool.

You may have walked far thru many hardships, or you may have gone to your neighbor. It does not matter.

And you may have found what you were looking for, or maybe not.

But you should know that often people walk out upon this land seeking a home, and they never find it. Sometimes they become lost and do not know that they are. Sometimes they find something which they think is a mirror and are thus made happy.

So you need to remember a particular idea. It is this: there is no mirror where you may find it, there is no home waiting for you, there may be no mirror wherever you may look, and yet you will find yourself if you walk this land.

For here is a place which waits for you could you but know it. It is written upon rock walls in certain places, once where people stopped to rest or to wait for a cooling of late afternoon. Here is what you seek. And it is to be found in a shade of a dwelling carved of sandstone, hi above your head with no way in.

When you first gaze up at a cliff dwelling and flexic that it may have been waiting empty forever and needed only that you wander by, you may find a mirror. You may see in each small window some part of what you seek, some part of yourself. You may rest long in shade of a cliff dwelling that you have never seen before and feel you are finally at home.

You may feel sad that no one waits for your arrival to shout with joy to see you.

You may stop a climb up sandstone to look down into a deep canyon, thinking only to pause for breath, and see a small cliff dwelling hiding and waiting. You may feel a deep silence, and a gracious calmness as you breathe and look down on a place of living so long ago abandoned that you may not remember if you once lived here.

You may have climbed up a sandstone ridge thinking only to get a vue of eternity, wondering if maybe you could see into a place you once heard about, but had never seen where you no longer need to search. And once on top of a sandstone ridge you worked to get to, you stop to gaze into one face of beauty which is always turned to greet you.

As you are about to give up and return to what you call home, your final parting glance finds a small dwelling perched under an overhang, surrounded by sandstone, built of sandstone blocks very near top of sandstone ridge. You may ask yourself some 'why' questions, you may wonder, then you may decide to walk over.

And you may not know this, but every step you take across sandstone to see this dwelling up close is your mirror. For this is where you are, it is where you have always wanted to be, and you came here already knowing this.

You may have once stopped beside a small pool of water carved out of sandstone, perched hi above a land of canyons cutting thru a plain of sandstone, and leaned against a lone juniper or maybe even a pine. You may have come to look out upon a vue, but find yourself gazing at ripples on a pool caused by wind, bugs, life, or yourself. You may be thinking that just beyond your pool perhaps is a small side canyon which will lead you down to a sandy bottom which you can follow and discover a way home.

You may spend a day walking on sandstone seeking, you may spend a lifetime, you may spend no time, or time may even be a concept you are unfamiliar with. For you may come to walk on sandstone unconcerned with passing of time, have no thot towards leaving at a certain time to go elsewhere.

You may wander about, seeking without seeking. You may have come here just to be some place different from where you were. You may just be walking thru to get to that mountain just beyond, or not.

You will find what you are not seeking, wherever you walk, because this land is yourself. It may be only when wind threatens to blow limbs off trees, or when a gentle snow falls and covers all sharp edges, it may be at all times and all places in this land of sandstone.

Maybe this land is only a place to travel thru as you seek out cliff dwellings, looking for signs of man's life on sandstone. You may not care about sandstone unless it leads to another dwelling or artifact. And with each dwelling found, you decide this is one more place of sandstone you need not come to again.

You may think if I had lived here, I would build in this overhang, not that one. But not every overhang with room to build a dwelling is a good place to live. That was how another people found their mirror, by knowing where and when to build. Yours may only reside in finding where others chose to live.

Your mirror may have nothing to do with sandstone. It may be that deep in a canyon bottom on a warm bed of sand beside a small stream of water, surrounded by trees, sung to by birds you can be happy, you can find your home.

You may find yourself only while asleep with a gentle breeze stirring your hair, with a dog beside you and a partial moon above dreaming of a place you may never find but know is your home.

You may think your mirror is just around a corner, and keep turning them. You may find your mirror on a hot day with no shade nearby, plodding across a sandy plain with tuff shrubs impeding your progress, with tall sandstone cliffs far off on both sides of you and in front a slowly narrowing canyon, and below you dung from various animals who have come before you.

You may become convinced that you will never find your mirror, but go upon sandstone to look anyway. You may find joy in a search, tho hope is just a word you cannot feel. You may think if only you can cover every gully, every canyon, every sandstone mound some time you will find your mirror.

You may stop to watch a deer graze, unaware that you are near, and know that her comfort is kin to your certainty that each cliff dwelling you encounter only awaits your discovery. She may be thinking deer thots you can never comprehend because you cannot learn to unthink yourself as does she. And when she looks up finally to see you, you flexic that she has never seen you before yet she knows you very well. For she knows that you are her mirror, and you promise more than she may want to accept.

You may look out upon a vast stretch of broken sandstone and try to decide which way to go, where today you wish to walk and where today you think to stop, what you wish to see. But sandstone knows, even if you do not, it does not matter which way you go. For when you walk where you need to be to find your mirror, you will find it, and there is no path there for nobody has ever been there before. There is no sign to show you a way, and there is no drawing on a rock wall to show you.

It may be that you listen to every eagle's cry, hoping to learn of what she sees, thinking she will tell you where to go. It may be that you learn that eagle or hawk is busy even when he is floating hi above and seems asleep. He has many concerns which have nothing to do with your journey, but it may be that you can find your mirror when you see eagle or hawk flying overhead, for as much as anyone can be a mirror, they are.

Coyote may stop as she runs away from you, turning to look at you for a flexic you may not understand. Here is everyone's mirror, but few know this. For coyote's gaze is a signal from a world man is but a small part of, and man knows little about. She will always stop to look at you, because she knows who you are, as does deer. Coyote recognizes you, and knows she has always known you. And you have always known her, but you have chosen to forget this.

For there are some mirrors out upon sandstone too vast or too intimate for you to accept. And tho you actively seek to find one, you shy away from coyote's gaze. Looking into her eyes is too utterly primal, and throws you back to a time you would rather forget. But coyote can read more than a being's genes. Coyote gazes back at you that you would know who you are, and who you will be.

Most people choose to temper their mirror, to mold it to fit their own vue of themselves. But certain facets of beauty, and coyote is one, cannot civilize any mirror held up to you. You must accept it as given or not.

And few people ever learn that when they seek a mirror, whether they find it or not, what they really want is a capacity to gaze upon every facet of beauty and not turn away. For most people find each face of beauty all too much but do not know why. People have always looked for beauty, especially upon sandstone, but not known what they find.

For beauty walks sandstone, more than some places, and when beauty builds rock houses perched under a sandstone overhang and puts a veil of time and some mystery there, very few of us can flexically know what we gaze upon.

For it is here, as much as anywhere, that we find beauty displayed in complete openness, in compliant willingness to be found and known. It is in every cliff dwelling we unknowingly stumble upon. And she even shows a way. She has left openings in each rock wall which beckon us to look within. But few can do so, for to look within beauty, some think, is to cease to exist.

Beauty is everywhere upon sandstone, and many other places, and she waits patiently for us to come by, stop awhile, and share with her.

She gives us a cottonwood for shade, water to rest near, and a vue far off to west. She gives us each small cliff dwelling long silent, and crumbling from lack of use.

Beauty gives us a small deer path to follow when we are lost. She gives us a mountain to look down on a vastness of sandstone, and a cool breeze in an evening canyon to cool our imaginations.

She puts a river deep in a sandstone canyon, lined with trees, home to birds and many small animals. She gives eagle and hawk warm rising air to soar in.

Beauty puts herself in every place we may look, everywhere we seek she is already there. And when we sit above a vast land with rock towers as remote as any star, and wait for sunsetting lite to reveal angles of terrain we could only imagine, she is there.

Beauty puts her hand to shape white sandstone mounds lining tops of some sandstone canyons, forming a land of no visible use to anyone, yet necessary to complete a landscape.

Did beauty form this land, and all others, that man may one day come by and find a home, did she know that if she puts water here man will come? Man and woman may forever ask themselves questions such as these and never find an answer. And may gaze in all faces of beauty and shy away, trying to explain in terms only he or she can comprehend.

But I wonder, do coyote and deer, bighorn, eagle, hawk, and rattlesnake know beauty as we never can? Does beauty flow thru every move they may make? Are they each so far beyond any need to comprehend beauty resident in each and every facet of our world? Are they so complete as extant that beauty finds a home therein?

Man, or I, can ask these questions and not get answers. And each man or woman may walk upon sandstone looking for a mirror. Each may stop when he or she encounters some aspect and think this is beauty, and not flexic that beauty has no limits, has no borders, nor allies herself to any individ's understanding. Beauty is what she is, she is where she is, and it is up to us as humans with our particular gifts to find her.

And we may forever seek her, and indeed find her, yet until beauty can find a home within us just as any individ seeks to find a home within another or himself, or with a horse and a dog, we are lost. We may think to find ourselves in a shadow of any cliff dwelling, may look for ourselves on a map, we may stay upon a hi overlook forever gazing about and not find ourselves, nor find our mirror.

And if we can venture upon a land with no sandstone, where we think there cannot be beauty, yet find it and feel a certain surprise we may find a way. If we can look upon a face of another individ where we think we mite not find beauty, and find some internally flexiced beauty perhaps resident in such an individ and know surprise we may find a way.

For our way is to beauty, therein is our mirror, and she awaits us. This I have learned, and this I know. I walk upon sandstone, and she walks upon me. I walk upon beauty, and she walks upon me. I am of beauty, and she is of me. And we are one, while we are two. Beauty comes this way, and may stay awhile. And beauty may find a home with you and she may stay awhile with you. For it is her way.

And you might ask yourself, 'can I stand up and look beauty in her face, whatever face she presents to me, and not turn away?'

And can you know that here is your home, one that you have always been searching for? That once you can gaze upon any face of beauty and grin with joy, you are home. That even tho soon you may choose to walk away to another place, you have come home.

And you may carry her with you always, once she has found a home within you, and even look upon a strange land and recognize her face.

And it might be that others may see in your face that beauty has found a home with you and say of you, 'he walks in beauty, beauty walks in him and he walks in sandstone, sandstone walks in him.' For they will have seen, even if you cannot, that you are now a creature of beauty. Just as coyote, deer, eagle, bighorn and rattlesnake are her beings.

And none will have to say to you, 'go in beauty,' as a benediction of parting for they will flexic that soon enuf you will be back, even if they are not still here to greet you. For as they might wish to walk in beauty, and do not, or might seek a mirror and know it not, yet they can recognize one face of beauty. And for them there is hope.

And then, in parting, I say to you, "seek your mirror, that it might show you beauty". And even if you cannot comprehend that which you see, make a home for it, and beauty will make a home for you. And others then will say of you, "she walks in beauty, and she knows."

Nor will any map show you a way.

CHAPTER 19
SOLITUDE

There is a kind of freedom granted a man when he learns his own dance of life. I have always walked alone, in my mind and on my path, but perhaps I could not really think I would always walk alone. Acceptance has finally appeared as I turned a corner in some nameless canyon.

I think there are many shades of solitude, some joyful, some not so. I really could not say what particular color my solitude is, perhaps I hug it too closely to see it well. I do know sometimes I carry it along as a shield, sometimes as a weapon. It seems to serve.

When on a hike I need silence of surroundings and thots to help me find my path. This is not really physical silence, so much, rather a kind of openness to hear what is being said. Solitude often settles in around me, similar to a shell of possibilities and certainties. Such a state of being helps me see what is before my eyes, and believe that what I see is real.

And I find it easy to know solitude even tho most often I am accompanied by two dogs, two slickrock dogs well adapted to my pace of exploration. For their silence is only broken by chases after small elusive animals. They hike to a different rhythm than I, yet we manage to complement each other.

That solitude I am thinking of is more ephemeral, even elusive. Many people when in backcountry alone may be thinking of elsewhere, elsewhen, or someone else. I have no one else to think of, have no desire to be elsewhere until later, and find reminiscing not very rewarding.

This does not suggest I am in some kind of perfect zen world of my own. I think rather that my kind of solitude comes from knowing I have talents as an explorer, I am able to listen to silent suggestions, and I often find what is seldom known. There is nobody I have met who can really show me where to go, or what to see, and therein lies another shape of my solitude, that nobody can completely help me, tho many try to nudge me in some other direction.

My dogs and I have formed an understanding bond of skills, sometimes it is my turn to lead, sometimes they make suggestions. I have rarely found them to be wrong, they have learned Sandstone Way in a style unique to their abilities and senses. We share our hikes in many ways, yet in some ways I am thinking thots unrelated to their doggie concerns. I watch them for clues into their psyches, but also am focusing on my surroundings, on finding rock art panels and even house sites.

And I have hiked alone, leaving my dog-companions at home; that is another kind of solitude I do not like as well as sharing my hikes with them. It does have benefits, but we have formed such a fine team that without them I feel a bit too much solitude.

For there is a map I have of solitude, and on one extreme there lies a shade of madness, and near to another edge lies sanity or even genius. I have heard of and met people who have stepped off one edge or other, and cannot seem to get back. Solitude is no better than many other states of being, it holds no surety of benevolence. Some can handle it in large doses, some cannot. I prefer mine tempered by otherly-sentient beings who are concerned with their own explorations. Their thots are much closer to ground than mine. Perhaps, tho, this likens them to Anasazi in many ways.

My map, then, has paths of exploration marked on it and it seems they do not include other people. This kind of solitude, of non-sharing, means that what I find or do not find I am responsive to, and for, in my own style. Nobody is arguing, nor helping. There is nobody showing me a way.

I have tried hiking with other people but too often it seems their questions clutter space between us, their concerns are too uneducated for me. By uneducated I mean that they have not done their homework, have not read about Anasazi, nor on a more basic level can they seem to pay real attention to our surroundings.

There are no books, nor any libraries full of archaeological books which can fully educate anyone to Anasazi reality. There are many archaeological sites, however, which can provide a tempering of what one does read. For I think it is by a gradual absorption of actual Anasazi landscapes, lifeways, and their building or rock art sites, thru a physical visiting of them that one attains a true Anasazi education. Books are full of opinions and misconceptions, stages in archaeologists' own education, or certain competitions to prove one theory or another, but Anasazi sites speak quite well for themselves, if only one is open to listen and see.

Perhaps this is what I really mean by solitude, then, an individ approach to learning Anasazi Way, accepting that I have found no adequate teachers nor guides except myself, at my own pace. I am launched on a pattern of self education; there are no diplomas waiting for me when 'done.'

But solitude is also a physical ambiance, more than a lack of other people near me. It is, as I hike Cedar Mesa, a clear knowledge of self-reliance, self-responsibility, and freedom to listen and see. There is no weight on my back heavier than my daypack, none on my mind heavier than temporal concerns of waning daylite and a return safely home. For as I hike I am focused yet seemingly defocused on my surroundings.

Sometimes I deliberately avoid meeting other hikers when

I see them nearby, mostly not wanting to dilute my intensity of experience with their concerns. In many ways, a physical and mental solitude enhances my experience, and I tend to seek that state of mind more often, hiking places few would consider going, even tho they may be nearby unaware I am there. There are a few times when I will stop to chat with other hikers, but usually our level of conversation is not at a high level of archaeology, rather it deals with directions, locations, water, or accesses.

Long ago I have realized that, in a very real way, I am not you, nor you I and while I may have a talent for a perception of some individs' real character/qualities, and do feel empathy in some cases, yet I sometimes close myself off from other people deliberately. I have found that this kind of focus is a necessary step for discovery. There is, thus, another level of solitude most people cannot understand nor practice. I do not recommend it for most individs; sometimes a deliberate limitation of character or personality causes mental degradation, not everyone can handle it.

It is another facet of my map of solitude, that it takes a strong mind to accept such a state of grace, and a strong heart to survive it.

CHAPTER 20
INNER MAP

When I first started hiking Cedar Mesa, I relied on maps heavily. Those landscapes were unfamiliar, and paper maps helped me find my way. My maps did not have many notes on them, nor provide much help.

As time went on, hikes multiplied, and as I became more familiar with Cedar Mesa, my maps got covered with notes. Some of these notes were even erased, mistakes corrected; I rarely use gps and rely on memory to add notes at rest breaks while hiking or later at home.

I have evolved thru several generations of maps, as they are updated by publishers or as original paper quads become more tears than substance. I even use digimaps on my home computer with many markers and routes added.

But I am evolving, and am trying to change to using paper maps less, and working to increase my mental map towards leaving my paper maps at home where they belong.

This is not a plateau of understanding I recommend for beginners. I once met a young woman hiker with her dog in La Sal mountains who had to ask a map-type question as she had left hers at home. She was in no danger of getting lost, rather wished to re-familiarize herself with immediate surroundings and to pick out a peak to summit. At that time I needed my paper maps of La Sals and it was certainly easy to show her mine and be helpful.

Yet what I want is an almost complete understanding of terrain and landscapes as presented on Cedar Mesa and nearby areas; in summer I am working on such an inner map of nearby mountains, ones perhaps Anasazi visited frequently [La Sals, La Platas, Abajos].

As I hike I am always looking around at near and far landscapes, at presentations of features--I am cataloging, absorbing, comprehending how one canyon blends with another, trying to understand how this area was important to Anasazi and how they not only saw it but how they got around thru it. Routes into or across canyons have become important to me, as I have evolved to an Anasazi Way hiker.

Most hikers do not know that Anasazi did not consider canyon bottoms quite as important as they do. Canyon bottoms were not primary avenues of travel as they are considered today, they were extra resource areas for Anasazi. Places to sometimes grow crops, and always to hunt-gather. But originally, or primarily Anasazi lived on Cedar Mesa, and farmed mesa-level areas as much or more as canyon bottoms. Down inside a canyon could be where water was, but sometimes it was uncontrollable, and always unpredictable, sunlite exposure was always limited.

As Anasazi clustered around canyon heads for water, near springs, in drier times perhaps they had to adapt to a dryland farming technology, which they mastered. Currently Pueblo tribes in Greater Four Corners are excellent dryland farmers.

I had a fair grounding in desert irrigation farming while a high school student, and tend to look for signs of Anasazi fields or irrigation. Mostly all that remains are building sites, yet sometimes a pile of rocks near a shallow gully suggests a former dam.

As I am hiking, every hike, usually partly at mesa levels, I am looking for everything, even an absence of Anasazi sites suggests something. When I find water I know somewhere nearby Anasazi would have made use of it, either for a field or residence. Even when my hikes are bland or I find no sites another corner of Cedar Mesa has become familiar.

And every bit and piece of increased familiarity, every landscape seen from different angles, from perspectives shaded by personal relief, tiredness, or hope as I start a hike all blend into my inner map. When I stop atop a highland and survey a lowered landscape, a terrain I am about to engage in, it looks one way. As I entrench I may forget overall details of a large area, and concentrate on specifics, how to get thru, down, and around. Perhaps later, returning to my vehicle I stop to look back often. These final looks help with 'ahah' moments; as I turn back for another look I see how everywhere I just hiked fits into an earlier survey--but now shaded by a more complete understanding.

As I stop for breaks and when at home I add notes and markers to my paper map, draw routes I have learned or repeated, new sites I have found or minor details to ones I have visited before. I can look at my map months later and remember what I saw, but I think until my paper maps become obsolete, until my mental map is complete, I will not be satisfied.

Sometimes I cycle thru many consecutive hikes in a particular area, or around one canyon system. Some hikes may be rimwalks, some canyon bottom, and others combinations. As I see new facets of an area, I am intrigued for another hike to explore what is across canyon, or half way down its heights. Sometimes I merely repeat an area I have been to before, but take more time to explore every nook and cranny. Sometimes I find new-to-me art panels, sometimes new building sites. Sometimes I explore where I have gotten a tip to go see. There is one confluence of canyons on Cedar Mesa that I have hiked to from all possible different sides; I have taken rim-breaks to admire vue from each angle as if there were some special message only I could decipher--given enough time. Sometimes I 'bounce' around Cedar Mesa with consecutive hikes in completely different areas. It all depends on my inner guide, my interests.

One big difference between a paper topo map and my

inner map--one is lines and letters, other is sceneries, landscapes and vues. One is one-dimensional, other is multidimensional. For time, interest, energy-level, awareness, evolution of character, and understanding all contribute to my inner map. A paper topo is drawn from aerial photos, supplemented by some on-foot explorations and checking. My inner map is drawn from many hikes, and many experiences and discoveries, at ground level, and what may only be a vague topo line on one map may be a fine ledge system with a house site, or rock art panel. I cannot really add enough notes to my paper map to represent all wide ledges, or where house sites hide exactly, or where a fine place to admire some vue is. But my inner map remembers these places, even if only when I return years later.

And I think it is a map in memory which has more space for those individ experiences at each place, those aspects of exploration which add flavor to a landscape. For how I felt, what I saw, where I rested, which ledge I followed and thot full of beauty, where I found a possible field, or dam, or rock art panel, house site, or where I boosted my two slickrock dogs up, how we found a perfect Anasazi-deer path across our canyon, where I found water, where I found unexpected marvels all add flavor to my inner map. I am quite sure I cannot fully share this map, for I may not know official names of house sites, nor numerical designations for them, and any experiences which flavored my map could not match someone else's, nor would I wish it so.

There will always remain a few sites on Cedar Mesa I know of yet am unable to reach, particularly some house sites. It could be that once a tower or series of log ladders granted access to Anasazi, all long gone or fallen down; it could be that Moki Steps are now worn out and no longer provide help. I will have to satisfy myself with a study thru binocs, and thinking about what I see. This is ok, for without a few minor mysteries my knowledge may become commonplace and unfresh. I have no desire to cover every inch, nor to enter every ruin; I want a comprehensive and finely tuned knowledge of Cedar Mesa but I am not Anasazi, merely a modern day explorer thus a few places should keep me at bay.

My map can never match an Anasazi inner map, for I merely come for dayhikes, I rarely camp out anymore, and I have never tried to live on Cedar Mesa nor attempted to survive off its bounties, year after year, season into season. Nor have I migrated into or out of Cedar Mesa, sharing hopes and worries with fellow Anasazi as climate waxed and waned. I am an observer, not a participant. Yet I observe carefully and openly and this suffices for me. My inner map is filled in under my own fashion, thru my own efforts, and shaded by my own thots. Its value, then, is for myself to savor and sometimes share.

CHAPTER 21
MOUNTAIN WAY

In summer, while too hot for Cedar Mesa hiking, I hike/ explore nearby mountains, mostly La Sals and Abajos. La Sals have more 'real' mountains, Abajos have easier and longer hi-country trails. La Sals have more streams and are cooler, Abajos are close and sometimes I do not feel like another drive, after driving all week. There are mountains in Colorado, nearby, and sometimes I hike in La Platas near Mancos.

While mountains and my hiking them may have nothing to do with Cedar Mesa, yet to all western US prehistoric, historic, and present natives mountains are sacred. Desert people, in particular, understand this because mountains are a supremely vital force in nature. Mountains are where a desert-dwellers' water sources originate, and he well knew this. They are also where many herbs and plants grow, and wildlife such as deer and elk migrate to in summer.

I think and feel also that mountains, by their remoteness and prominence always beckoned to Anasazi. I feel while looking at them across a Cedar Mesa top how far away and unreachable they seem, yet I remember quite well my hiking/exploring, even driving thru them, and how seemingly vast distances to them fade as I travel towards their heights.

In some cases Anasazi lived around mountains' shoulders, such as Abajos, La Sals, Mesa Verde, Navajo Mtn, Francisco Peaks, Black Mesa, Mt Taylor, and many others. When hiking Cedar Mesa, unless entrenched in a canyon, I cannot avoid seeing Elk Ridge or Abajos, and far off to west

Navajo Mtn. They form a kind of landscapeal wall, or backdrop to my hikes. It would probably seem odd to me--if I hiked on Cedar Mesa without mountains in background, for then I would be on just another mesa top, with a dropoff on all sides.

And when hi above, resting from some climb, as I look down across Cedar Mesa [best vue is from Bear's Ears] I can piece together a vast landscape thru which I have spent so many hours exploring. It all looks different, yet somehow quite truthfully portrayed--as if in some fashion my paper maps really represented an actual place. For so often a two dimensional map seems to be a little silly, showing what a bird would see but not really what a hiker wants to.

Aside from their potentialities as vuepoints, mountain hiking gives me much joy. I love sitting on top, or even on a shoulder quite close to top, out of wind, and simply looking around, with or without binocs. I love vagaries of terrain, with entrenched and sloping valleys--often called basins or cirques--sometimes full of trees, sometimes open tundra meadows, with little glacial ponds here and there.

I love that seemingly impossible climb ahead, daunting in its heights while I am struggling along some winding trail or primitive route. But as I climb up, I stop to admire vues below and above, and gradually I do get atop each mountain. When I look down, it all looks easier, different, yet later as I am leaving and look back, again it seems too distant, unreachable. This is a particular magic of mountains, tho, that they reveal their secrets slowly.

Often enough their secret ways have already been discovered by elk and deer and I enjoy following primitive deer routes as often as easy hiking trails. Maybe more so, as often what man conceives as a good route is over shadowed by a fine little secretive deer trail. Man comes in with his chain saws and horses to clear a trail, deer accommodate windfalls by detouring or jumping over. One method is labor saving, other is flexic.

Even when I have to or choose to cross talus slopes and flats, where I prefer more stable deposits of rock, there is some stark simplicity beautiful in its complexity. For hiking a cleared trail is one thing, crossing a vast talus field another. One allows looking around, but confines to a narrow track; other provides unlimited choices and requires intense concentration and focus. How fast I move across a talus slope [and I am slower at 50+ than 20 years ago] all depends on what kind of "day I am having," in a physical fitness way. Some days I do not even have to think about it, I just automatically cross. Even tho I am intensely involved, I often stop to look around. And I am able to admire many shapes and fits of those rocks I borrow temporarily, even while I remain alert for unstable appearing individs.

Above and beyond talus I love tundra slopes, with their little mole hills, natural gravel patchworks, scattered alpine flowers [I admire but do not know names/species] and built-in steps for ascending/descending assistance. Only problems I see with hiking across tundra are that when dry it is unyielding and hard on my ankles, and there is rarely any trees for shade or wind-shelter--mostly for my dogs. I can always fall off a lee slope to escape wind or go behind a manmade rock wall [recent hikers] but my dogs often try to hide in my shade, such as it is. Mountaintop time is probably not what they enjoy about hiking mountains most. Dusty prefers mountain streams, with thickets to sniff out small animals from, and water to cool off in or drink often. Browny seems content to follow along usually.

Certain mountain ranges, or parts of mountains where I hike have few other people. In Colorado, accessible mountains are becoming more popular, and for solitude often I have to be creative, get off beaten trails. On one hike in Colorado in 2002 I counted 25 people, 5 dogs, and 4 horses in a mere 4 hours. In SE Utah few hikers go into mountains. There are people driving around and camping or trying to fish in tiny 'lakes' but usually only people I see are on distant peaks. Some hikes I never see anyone. Often I put together creative routes seldom hiked except by hunters. I am more interested in exploring what is there instead of following a normal trail to get to 'point B.'

'Peak-Bagging' has become less and less fulfilling as I age. I do still enjoy vues from atop any peak, and almost every hike is to summit some mountain. But, I will often look for loop routes, or a route with plenty of travel involved, perhaps merely crossing low passes, or circumnavigating a mountain. This, when combined with a scout from a summit, seems to help me fill in disparate pieces of a landscape. In other words, it is often not enough for me to look down on a cirque or a low pass with an interesting basin nearby, I want to get down into it and engage or entrench myself; I want to explore a country below me, not just look down on it from a distance.

My mountain time is more than an interlude while I am waiting to return to Cedar Mesa, it provides me with a balance, even perhaps a more complete Anasazi Way of hiking. Mountain Way and Sandstone Way are on my path; where it leads is towards understanding Anasazi Way.

CHAPTER 22
ANASAZI ODDITIES

There are some strange 'artifacts' in a larger sense than shards that I have found while hiking Cedar Mesa. So far I have only discussed two with a BLM archaeologist.

I have found many, almost ubiquitous, tree lines near where Anasazi lived in pithouse villages and farmed. Whether these tree lines are merely a result of a nearby drainage channel, or are artifacts of hundreds of years of habitation by Anasazi remains to be seen. These 'tree lines' are rows of single trees usually only about 20-30 feet long, mixed pinyon and juniper growing close together and surrounding empty spaces, and rarely very near a pithouse site, but close by. Whether these tree rows were deliberately left standing as windrows such as modern farmers use to slow down winds near their fields, or not is uncertain.

It seems improbable that jp's which are only hundreds of years old, or less, could form rows to copy those that Anasazi encouraged 900 years ago. Perhaps there is some other phenomena of nature at work, perhaps there is some deficiency in soils upon empty spaces next to these rows of trees.

Beginning in 2002-2003 hiking season I also began to see another artifact, one which is writ large on landscape, which is difficult to see, and which is even more difficult to believe [perhaps]. These are trails on slickrock near areas where many Anasazi lived for hundreds of years [off and on]. I do not at all mean trails laid out such as Anasazi 'roads' are laid out, with cleared paths and rock borders.

When I first realized that a route I was following along

one rim of a popular Cedar Mesa canyon, tho where few people ever go, seemed smoother than nearby slickrock I imagined that it could be a trail. It seemed to go on for miles, within 10-20 feet of nearby rim-cliff, across slickrock mostly, and I could pick it out by a certain look and feel to slickrock beneath and in front of me. What I mean by smoother is more worn down, and after awhile I could pick out this path without even trying. This is so because it followed a naturally easier on-my-ankles way than trying to walk over humps adjacent to it.

There was no other discernible geological phenomena to explain this faint, wandering, smoother path on slickrock than human intervention, and I know that livestock, deer and bighorns prefer to walk on dirt. Flexically, also, it made sense as it connected several small Anasazi villages together, and a sidecanyon below it was very hard going, chock full of boulders and narrow.

My next hike I found another short section of an Anasazi trail, but this one seemed harder to believe because it could well have been caused by a dripline of cliff above. I started to think, tho, that it made sense in several ways for Anasazi to want to walk on slickrock than on nearby dirt. There was more chance some enemy could see where they walked, thus lived, if they tracked across dirt patches than if they walked on slickrock. Their footing would have been more secure, with less chance of stepping on a small rock and twisting an ankle. Plus, as original trail showed, they wound around taking advantage of flatter terrain amidst humps of slickrock; when I followed their path I felt this ease of travel also.

In some places their trail crossed short stretches of dirt but were blocked by deadfall or growing trees. Immediately I detoured these areas, tho, I could see where their trail resumed. In places I lost their trail across slickrock, whether thru looking around or not paying attention. But I soon found it again. And I noticed an internal process happening--that it was easier to find and follow their path if I thot about it less and just let my feet and lizard brain be in control.

To prove that this phenomena is factual I intend to, while rimwalking other canyons in future, look for more Anasazi trails. I can look back to places I have walked and think where I would most likely find these trails. One obvious candidate is across Comb Ridge, specially where I have found long series of Moki Steps across slickrock slopes on its east side.

I have already found that once I have stepped over this heuristic block, finding their trails becomes automatic and easy, in some kind of art-rather-than-science manner. I think it is progress along a path leading to understanding Anasazi lifeways, at least as applies to Cedar Mesa.

One other thot I have had about why Anasazi fascinated so many people, for why their culture influenced so many people particularly while they still thrived and why they were copied came to me just now. Prior to their moving into that phase of life and culture characterized by stone and plaster buildings they lived in temporary and crude pithouse structures just as everyone else did. But eventually they began to construct solid buildings aboveground, and later whole 'pueblos'. They were not first to do this, perhaps they saw and copied builders from far to south in Central America or Mexico.

One facet of Anasazi buildings, whether under rock shelters or out in open, is their permanence, their prominence, and their sheer advertisement as massive, impregnable homes. I believe that a certain level of awe was engendered in passer-by when first spotting a pre-puebloan stone and plaster building or village. Just as today when first we see a far off caprock ruin fairly well preserved, seemingly waiting our personal discovery and arrival. I imagine with people living in them, smoke arising from their roofs, and noise emanating from them, a certain impressiveness came naturally.

I doubt few visitors could resist feeling a bit inadequate and perhaps uncouth. Some of this is seen in our time in old Western buildings with false fronts, in modern advertising billboards, and in designs of some buildings.

Along with some permanence of habitation came an increase in exchange of ideas about pottery manufacturing techniques, about art, about 'religious' ideas, and perhaps an increase in farming efficiency. Many other hunter gather tribes would only have been able to keep what could be carried on their backs, and to see richness of life of pre-puebloans must have been a bit of a culture shock much as happens in our time when an aboriginal human leaves his jungle home to travel to Buenos Aires or Los Angeles.

Perhaps some similar awe struck first Spanish explorers when they came within vue of Pueblo villages. They exaggerated to their 'bosses' and served as catalysts to later Spanish entradas.

Another question occurred to me while rim-walking a popular Cedar Mesa canyon in 2002--did Anasazi also farm inside dirt-filled tinajas [slickrock pools]? Larger ones tend to trap loess, and must retain any moisture for quite some time. Most have jp's, grasses, and small shrubs growing in them. In some, soil is fairly deep, most are shallow. I have never read anything one way or another about horticulture in tinajas, but would be surprised if Anasazi did not take advantage of them.

CHAPTER 23
WALKING LIGHTLY

When I start out on a hike, it might almost seem as if I am not really there. I am there, but I am not heavily there, I do not intend to make noise, to change any landscapes, to leave more than a few footprints; I do not think I own this land, or that nobody else has any right to travel thru it. I am just there.

I do not really claim to tread lightly as in some idiomatic mantra of several organizations out to save this or any other 'wild' country. I am a heavy guy, and often I do not really pay attention to where I am stepping, too busy looking around maybe.

What I do is think quietly, I progress quietly, even if I stumble sometimes and move rocks, or break off twigs to fondle them in some prehistorically sensual way--perhaps assuming I too can pretend to be an aborigine. In a sense my hike is conducted like a hunter out after game, he is quiet, cautious and careful to remain behind cover at all times.

But I am not a hunter, although I am out looking for Anasazi signatures, signs they cared and dreamed. I am not a zen hiker either, out to out-japanese myself in some style rarely seen these days.

I am a modest hiker, in that I am out to hike and explore--whether new terrain or a repeat of familiar geography--and I prefer to soak up what is there to see than write my presence on this land. But my presence is there, I have been over this place too many times, thot too much about it, and even had a few dreams I keep to myself mostly. So this land is modified by my passage, by my path of water, as I am modified by it. We are not who we were before we met, and this is good. I have not chained this land for my cattle, ridden across it with my dirtbike, torn up new roads for firewood, nor drilled holes for profit.

But I have insinuated myself in a landscape, not just a physical landscape; this land remembers when I was last here, longs for my return. And I walk quietly thru, every hike. When I see other hikers, most often I stand back behind cover, or watch them from above; I am able to read their intents and progresses, their fears and their hopes in how they shoulder their packs, how they eagerly or tiredly dodge every intruding boulder. For there is a language of body I see in others, it is part to do with how they perceive this country, part in how they look about. Sometimes I see them walking with head down, or studying a map as they walk, as if unable to await their arrival at a convenience store even if in this case it is merely a campsite.

I have stood quietly near my tent as a backpack-burdened hiker walked right by me, barely 10 feet away, seemingly unaware I was there until I spoke. Was he tired, bored, thinking about his city-life or job, or was he just not really there?

When I am not really there, I suggest that I am aware, I am looking around, but I have not brought any preconceived notions, or theories with me. I have read many articles, many books by various archaeologists, some in agreement, some not with each other. I am not an institutionally educated expert, tho, and I do not bring along their variety of knowing-it-all.

I hike alone, with my own thots, as my dogs are busy with other concerns. I am light on this land because I want to see what it has to offer, what it has to teach me, rather than I instructing it in how to behave, how to respond, or how to care. I do not expect it to care, but I know it does. How is this possible? This I cannot explain, you either know it yourself or it does not happen for you. Navajo know it, or some do; Puebloans know it, most of them; and some anglos may know it. I think it has something to do with many dead Anasazi buried here; that a land can assume a *landality*[1] of those who once lived there.

It has to do with a land that was once lived in, cared for, and where some Anasazi are buried. Once this kind of process happens, a landscape changes--it morphs into a lifeway of terrain, in some kind of mode I can perceive but cannot quantify. And as I hike I am open to suggestion, I am amenable to instruction, I am a heuristically ready individ.

I travel light, with a daypack and barely what I need to point A-to-point-B myself. I travel light, with no more expectation than is warranted by weather, energy level, or prior knowledge of where I am going. I travel, tho, with joy, happy to again be out on Cedar Mesa, away from four walls and appliances.

I can feel myself move thru an excess of quiet air, of stillness partly formed of knowing nobody else is around, partly thru knowing I am on my own as nobody knows where I am, but I am not really thinking here of solitude, for that is a different flavor, a different spice to my hikes. Solitude is a kind of ambiance, a kind of temperature of surroundings--as if it were just a bit warmer or cooler, hard to say sometimes. I am thinking, instead, that I am moving thru this Sandstone Way landscape as if invisible. As if I do not exist; and this is true, I have had trouble in life partly caused by not actually existing most times. For I am an individ always on a cusp, always changing, always learning new ways as if life were only true for me as a student, and all other creatures and humans were teachers, as if canyons and slickrock, trees and bushes, even nameless grasses, or mysteries of Anasazi were just part of my classroom chalkboard scribblings. I do not think I have enough answers to spread out to more than my immediate locale, perhaps this is why I travel light. I have not enough strength to carry latest edition of "Book of Answers[2]," as if it were necessary in order to survive away from sight of neon.

And I have poured thru its many pages, many long nights when unable to sleep, even tho I need to. I have seen answers we are not ready for, I have seen answers nobody has asked proper questions for; I think some answers should remain unused for awhile. So as I travel Cedar Mesa, and cannot remember all these answers, I may be open to new ones, forgetting I have already read all I need to for this life-way I call my own.

And it is not just over Cedar Mesa that I travel lightly, for I have no friends that I can count on, I am not attached to any recent ideologies, I do not participate in local affairs, I do not have normal concerns most people may feel, or if these concerns come to confront me I usually shrug them off, say "I am not at home, sorry." I cannot be bothered with normal trivialities, and I sense a new chapter for that "Book of Answers" boiling up somewhere in my mind. It needs but a few more hikes, a few more vistas, and a few more reststops on slickrock.

This travel is what I do, it is what I am, not completely but enough for labeling. I mean travel on Cedar Mesa, by foot, pausing to form new questions, stopping to grin a place welcome, knowing I am home.

You may see me moving about in normal city-life, and ignore me as is your way with most strangers. It does not matter, tho, I was not really there, what you saw was a persona I project until I am back on Cedar Mesa. That is where I live, tho I do not sleep there; that is where I think and dream, but I do not make my meals there.

Let me tell you of a few things I have seen.

I found a skull, stuffed in a shallow alcove and mostly covered by packrat nesting; I assumed its skeleton was there also. This was a sole individ's burial spot, and after looking around carefully, touching nothing, I left. I have only told a few people; I have only told one archaeologist an exact location [it was already known about]. It will remain secret, I do not think it is particularly some sacredness which keeps me silent, rather I think you do not have a need to know. If you did, you would find a skeleton. Luckily most grave robbers are just part of our history.

I found a historic pot, whose meaning does not seem all that important. It is metallic, blue-enamel coated, totally ubiquitous in most hunting camps. I uncovered it and placed it on a nearby ledge.

I was helped to find a prehistoric pot, have returned a few times. I have taken a very few people to see it.

I found some cans in a baggie with a note from Fred Blackburn, I was told where it was [by other people]; he thinks it may have been from late 1800's, from a camp of Wetherills or contemporaries.

I found a heavily pot-hunted pithouse site, and promptly informed BLM [they knew its location, but not any vandalism to it]. ATV tracks led to it. My footsteps in a rainstorm led away from it.

I have found many rock art panels, some rarely if ever visited. Perhaps those who came before wore rags on their boots, perhaps nobody really cares to visit some of these places anymore. I have found small, remote ruins rarely visited. It is not so much that they are hard to find but that few people now are driven to find them.

I have found so many 'wild' shards I lost count before I was born. By wild I suggest a shard away from its place of origin, where it was constructed and used, and laying randomly on Cedar Mesa. These quiet little reminders, I think, are more interesting than shards surrounded by their friends at a house site. For these isolated shards carry a story with them, and it is up to me to fathom it.

I found, in one day, a stone axehead I was given directions

to and another I found "on my own." One I hid, other I left close to where I found it.

I have found a few more artifacts, pre- and historic, but there is not a thick book cataloguing all my 'finds' and this is ok. That is not my particular emphasis, not my metier.

And to return: my traveling light on Cedar Mesa means that whatever I find, or do not find, each and every hike, is a piece in a puzzle. It is a complex puzzle, and perhaps that is why I leave my "Book of Answers" at home, it over-burdens my Heuristic Way hike.

For I am a hiker thru more than just a terrain, a landscape or a lifeway, I am a hiker thru time, thru space, and thru a culture no longer extant, yet not far away. I am hiking towards an understanding of a people's lifeway, and for me answers are 'out there' and not already written in ink.

And I think I will leave a trace, I will leave a sign I have passed, and I will modify a landscape--but you will have to know what to look for, as within months of my walking thru, no tracks will remain. I will not be building any houses on Cedar Mesa, but I will have visited many; I will not be living in any of them, yet they will be living in me. That may very well be enough to show you a way, but it will be your way, not mine. Mine lies along my path of water, and yours along your path of water.

CHAPTER 24
WATER

In early September, 2002, I hiked into ggulch, went downcanyon about 5 miles, then hiked out. As I was returning to my pickup I tried to beat an approaching rainstorm. I was unsuccessful and got thoroughly wet, even with a poncho. Lightening crashed, but none very close. I stopped a few times under a jp, once I peeled my wet tshirt and donned a pile jacket. Mesa soils got so soaked that I sunk in almost every step, and my boots were thoroughly wet since I was not properly prepared for rain as some Washington native might be.

Later I stopped at KGRS and chatted with Scott [resident BLM ranger], and it was obvious we both felt same way about this rain. It had been a very dry season following a dry winter, and a previously not-as-dry summer. Scott and I were quite happy about this rain, even tho I had slogged thru it for an hour or more.

This rain was coming down so heavily it was certain to cause some flashflooding, wipe out sections of dirt roads and trails, perhaps endanger a few other dayhikers still in upper Kane Gulch. It would not be enough to really replenish springs much, or not immediately anyway, nor would it do more than cause a temporary runoff in canyons. But, it was rain, and it was much needed water, even if too late in a summer growing season.

Once, long before this summer, while living north of Tucson my sisters and brothers and I splashed in mudpuddles near our country home after a heavy rain. Our nearby river was flowing higher than we had so far seen it [many years later it twice flooded our house, after most of us had left]. We had certainly seen rain before, living in Montana for several years previously, but I think we already knew some way how desert dwellers revere rain, rare as it may be.

This is a strange phenomena, personally because I do not really like to get wet and I am not now a farmer who relies on rain and snow to grow his crops. I know full well I cannot enjoy my hikes if my surroundings are scorched by water shortage. I hike in mountains in summer and do not like it when I get rained on. I do not like hiking in super lush shrubbery, prefer alpine tundra and sparse forests with deer trails. I enjoy desert hiking, or nowadays a variety of hi-plateau desert such as on Cedar Mesa.

In winter I will not usually hike when it is snowing, nor in deep snow. I no longer go into mountains until late spring as snow is melting or gone. On Cedar Mesa if snow is too deep, I go elsewhere such as lower elevations to hike. But, I also know that snow as it melts provides water for my dogs and of course for resident deer, coyotes and rabbits. Snow depth is rarely much of a hindrance to my hiking/driving Cedar Mesa as winters in SE Utah are usually fairly short and mild anyway.

But, there is also a part of me which sympathizes with a dry landscape, starving for some rain or runoff. I suppose I add my 'prayers for rain' tho not to any now recognized god, rather I pray to same forces Anasazi must have prayed to.

I think I have lived in deserts long enough to know what rain really is: life. Not so much for me directly, but for whatever particular landscape and bioscape I am hiking thru or living in. And I am enough of a desert dweller to recognize a landscape happy and drunk with water-joy, and to share in this.

* * *

Craig Childs writes an interesting book[1], about his years

long obsession with searching out sources and places of water in various deserts. He categorizes water in various ways.

Mostly in last few years on Cedar Mesa there is no, or infrequent, running water. There are three other kinds of sources which Childs writes of. There are springs, slickrock pools, and runoff. I differentiate running water from runoff by thinking of former as a stream, more or less permanent, and runoff as temporary result of snowmelt or rain.

Years ago there was often a stream in upper Grand Gulch, and other Cedar Mesa canyons, and spring was a favorite time for hikers. Usually these streams would last until early summer and be replenished by summer rains. Perhaps in some future, these streams will return.

I hike usually with two slickrock dogs, who allow me an illusion that I am in control, and most water we find is in rimtop slickrock pools. Partly this is because we hike canyon rims more than bottoms. Some slickrock pools are large, known as waterpockets or tinajas. Childs differentiates between these, depending on whether they are in a streamcourse [tinaja] or not [waterpocket]. I prefer 'slickrock pool'. Dusty loves to find slickrock pools [whatever I choose to call them], but often I have to call her attention to them.

When we hike a canyon bottom, most water we find is in form of springs--usually where a change in rock strata occurs. A harder, more impermeable layer sheds water in a few pools. Fish Canyon is a good example, and has relatively permanent water in many pools.

Another location for springs, and one very important to Anasazi all over 4 Corners--prime examples are found in Hovenweep and Mesa Verde--are canyon heads. On Cedar Mesa there are a few places where Anasazi utilized this water but usually they just built nearby. Sand Canyon Pueblo, near Cortez, is an excellent example of this practice, and is under excavation by Crow Canyon Arch. Center. It arcs around and adjacent to cliffs at a formerly well-watered canyon head.

Anasazi utilized runoff on mesa-top streambeds by building small dams. Few remnants of these exist, yet there are a few on Cedar Mesa. Most have long ago been washed out. Arroyo cutting eliminated many of these. From resultant pools, they presumably carried water in baskets and later pots to water their crops. None of these pools would last forever, but could prolong benefits accrued during rainstorms.

Anasazi also deliberately built pools with dams [I've seen no evidence that they hammered out pools from sandstone] right next to rimtop cliffs. This water then percolated down thru 10-20 feet of sandstone and fed springs. Good examples of these pools can be found in Hovenweep or Mesa Verde--I've noticed most on Cedar Mesa are washed out.

There are even a few cases of defensive walls or structures near water sources. This suggests a need to guard water during dry times. Perhaps lack of water led to wide-area abandonments thruout 4 Corners [actually a retrenchment to other areas].

I think Anasazi built up inner maps of their landscapes, and water sources were extremely important--not to be taken for granted. I, on other hand, most often carry enough water for myself, and help my two slickrock dogs look for it. A few hikes I have to carry supplemental water for them, usually when following Mountain Way in summer.

We so often find little shallow slickrock pools where we hike that springs or streams are no longer vital for our happiness. There have been a few Cedar Mesa hikes when Dusty and Browny only found one pool and had to make do. But, I noticed, water came when we most needed it--as if my dogs also follow Sandstone Way.

CHAPTER 25
HIKE IS OVER BLUES

There comes a time in every hike when no matter how reluctant to leave, specially if I am lounging around enjoying some scenery, that I know it is time to go. Where? Home, to a house I built. To a house that is first I ever owned with no mortgage, and perhaps will become a place I spend most years of my life. For my life was one of a wanderer, both jobs and houses, even as a child it was part of my father's job, to move often.

When I tell dogs, peacefully napping under a tree, it is time to go they get up and stretch. They are not into admiring vues and prefer to snooze.

On some of my hikes I have gone a long ways to get to Grand Gulch, hiked a few miles in it, and now must return a few miles to my pickup, tho usually by a different route. And usually I have to return across ubiquitous jp flats, across heart of Cedar Mesa. I rarely follow trails, unless cattle or deer trails, and often they lead where they lead, not exactly where I want to go. Sometimes animal trails work for me.

Sometimes my return is a long, curving, arc described only on a few maps, and if you were watching me from a space station. Sometimes I, like most Indians native to America, follow a straight line, cutting across shallow heads of tributary canyons, not at all deterred by a rise and fall in elevation, or required route finding to manage many cliff bands.

Dusty likes to lead and usually she will find our cliff breaks, following animals' trails I can neither smell or usually pay attention to. When we are going across jp flats, she and Browny, unless very tired, will be scouting to both sides for rabbits, chipmunks, or coyote scent. I am left to my own devices, which do include broad-scope route finding for our small group.

Mentally, I am in plod mode most of time. I often stop to look back and to sides, sometimes using my binocs to see some feature or shadow closer. But if my feet are tired, or if weather is cold, or if I am regretting an end to another fine hike/day, I often get into plod mode.

Plod mode, as I think of it, is mental state of not-thinking, ignoring discomforts and miles to go. It is a different kind of not-thinking than sort I use to find Anasazi sites. That mode is a hunting mode without being necessarily alert or aggressive. Return non-thinking is more of a shutting out of distance I must travel, obstacles I might have to skirt, growing cold, tiredness, and soreness. Both are necessary.

End of hike plod mode helps me get back to my pickup, so I can go home, shower, have dinner and relax either with a book or in front of tv. But, I have to put aside those future comforts a little, and remain in this hike even tho in final stages. I have to stay alert to my route, weather, setting sun, situation as it develops.

I like to park my pickup on a height when possible. This makes it visible from miles away, helped by binocs, and both gives me a positive direction and a mood boost, knowing that my goal is in sight and more or less near. Even so, sometimes I stop for a last break in some nondescript place, with a few jp's around, some slickrock, and of course cryptogramic soils, and maybe a break from wind.

Sometimes my end-of-hike is best part. If I have had a beautiful hike, on a warm winter day, dogs did great and found water, or I found some new in/out route or rock art panel; and although tired I feel fulfilled. So, tho thots of home intrude, I am still with hike and in mode to enjoy

Cedar Mesa.

I think a high percentage of Cedar Mesa hikers mostly enjoy canyons, thinking perhaps that is real core of Anasazi outlier homelands. But more and more I tend to spend a lot of time up in jp's, getting to a canyon and back, or rimwalking. A canyon is a place for me to drop down into, see sites, and get back out of. It is not an avenue, or only avenue for my progress.

I think 3-dimensionally about Cedar Mesa, and find almost as many sites, whether ruins or rock art panels closer to mesa level than along canyon bottoms. There are exceptions, of course. But, I am a type of hiker who likes to be able to see far, to see across canyon, to know I can get in and out of any canyon almost any place I wish. Of course it takes time to know in/outs of any area, as with any person.

So it comes about that I find as much and even more beauty on mesa than in any canyon, and my finest resting places are near a canyon, out of wind, with a fine vue and some sunshine. And as I plod back to my pickup, it is a recent memory of my latest resting place, or vue-spot that I take with me. It makes me grin, and keeps a glow with me as I get across miles to my parking spot.

And often I mull over what I have seen as I hike out, and what I saw that I want to return to someday, somehike. I can plan my next hike if I am into a 'plan' of exploration of a certain area, and use consecutive hikes to fill out my mental map. Some series of hikes, 5 or 6 in a row, are all in same area, and while I do not design a mental flow chart, I know I am intrigued by a collection of sites, vues, or landscapes and will be 'hooked' until I fill in dots. Then I might be off to a different area for months or years.

As I am plodding along, these kinds of thots intrude more than thots of work, or problems, future concerns not related to hiking. It is easy to do, as I have tended to simplify my life, down to basics, and pigeon-hole problems for a later day.

So, in a way, end of hike is not really an end, it is merely a break until next one. An interlude, when I rest, shower, eat, relax, work, deal with 'real world' and think of my next hike, or go write about one just finishing up. A sort of continuity of hiking, and a return to my vehicle is just one part.

CHAPTER 26
HEURISTIC WAY

I don't know when I first realized that my path of discovery and exploration on Cedar Mesa had as much to do with self-education as it did with hiking every gully. I certainly did not at first think of this facet of myself as I hiked Cedar Mesa.

There was an odd attraction I felt towards certain features on Cedar Mesa. I would be drawn to go see a place but usually put it off for later. When I did fulfill this need I was always rewarded by new knowledge.

I would, early on, look at a mesa or canyon side and feel it was "impossible" or extremely difficult to climb, years later I would have to laugh at myself for my trepidation--my ignorance of sandstonicity. But my skills at hiking slickrock had improved, as had my certainty of Sandstone Way.

My sense of responsibility towards this place and towards Anasazi Way grew as I logged hours and miles of hiking, or even as I spent hours just admiring a scenery. I would sometimes do a hike just for potential scenery value.

I eventually got better at finding sites, both rock art and buildings. I got better at noticing certain other aspects of Anasazi Way while hiking canyons.

I learned to recognize landscapeal features as friends, places I had hiked to, nearby, or even perhaps sat under for a break.

I learned to fight my waning alertness, my growing fatigue and indifference to "go that extra 100 yards," to realize that only by putting energy into my exploration was I going to learn anything.

I found that my metier was doing solo dayhikes and I have only backpacked a few times in last 20 years or hiked with others a very few times in last few years.

But beyond all these facets I have learned to see more and more of Anasazi Way, specifically how Anasazi lived on Cedar Mesa and perhaps why. Some of this I discuss in "Anasazi Oddities," some in "Anasazi Way."

Along with my hikes I have read many articles and books [certainly not all] by both archaeologists and historians, which helps give me a basis for my imagination to work on. There came a point, tho, in my research when I realized that many articles by archaeologists are nearly worthless, for me anyway. By this I mean that some archaeologists write site reports, some condense info from many site reports, some argue with each other under a guise of another goal, some make mistakes or errors of judgment, some authors write authoritatively when perhaps they should not, some seem to publish only for recognition--not out of any real ability to contribute, some devolve into lengthy mathematical calculations divorced from reality, and some just plain "don't get it."

I sometimes get to a point I cannot or will not read any more archaeological articles, and prefer to go for a hike and "see for myself." By this I mean that it is while immersing myself in an environment rich with prehistoric culture I feel that I soak up a bit more understanding, empathy, and ambiance.

I do not claim to have finished my evolution, my Heuristic Way path of knowledge of Anasazi, but I can see better where it may lead. I am better able to look at a site and assess its meaning, value to Anasazi, difficulties of lifeway. I am better able to see their terrain and know how they modified it, or utilized it, maybe how they felt about it.

My inner map of Cedar Mesa as Anasazi saw it is enlarging; I have to mentally subtract our modern roads, trails and vegetation [i.e. Tamarisk] to visualize how Anasazi saw it.

I do not carry along in my daypack enough hubris to convince myself that I am an Anasazi Expert, and I have a hard time remembering specific dates when each cultural tradition started or stopped. It does not seem all that important, somehow. I would rather look at differing Anasazi sites as progressive improvements or enlargements of their own Heuristic Way. I think their path of evolution is evident, if I can clear away my encrustations of civilization enough to see.

As I start each hike, I lighten my pack of everyday concerns, reshape myself to fit my environment, and forget roads, airplanes, other hikers, or "later in my day." My outlook is one of joy, gladness to be back hiking Sandstone Way, and Dusty and Browny always share this joy. Often I conduct my hikes as if I was carrying corn or water back home, constantly on lookout for resources, enemies, or other Anasazic realities.

* * *

My Heuristic Way journey is, in some ways, similar to Moki Steps. Hammered out in hard sandstone [my ego and pride], worn out by time [maturity], and often switching mid-course [differing paths of interest], but always leading up to some new facet of Anasazi Way, a building site [enlargement of self]. Without being too cute, I will say that I can see definitive steps along my process of learning and expansion.

Years ago, when I first started hiking here, I was intrigued but not obsessed. I wanted to return, but lived far enough away to make frequent trips slightly difficult. I never backpacked, nor camped on Cedar Mesa, and this may seem strange to fellow hikers. Some of this was due to many years, earlier in my life, when I did camp out and live out of my backpack. I had no real home. When I bought my first house and began remodeling it--I think it gave me a real sense of belonging-to-place.

Gradually, this place became Cedar Mesa, but still I somehow did not really want to camp out. I wanted my comforts of home or I wanted some kind of retreat from over-Cedar-Mesa-ization, I suppose.

Then, my obsession grew. Eventually I managed to move to SE Utah, quite close to Cedar Mesa. As I began hiking more, and reading more archaeological material, understanding grew. There came certain plateaus of comprehension, new facets I 'discovered.'

Not to get too carried away with my analogy, tho, I became very interested in finding Moki Steps, and routes. I started noticing other aspects of Anasazi Way also, some explainable, some not easily explainable.

One odd focus to my path is a reluctance to explore other areas of Anasazi Way not on Cedar Mesa. I do hike around Moab and Needles a little bit, have explored White Canyon, Sand Canyon, Hovenweep, Horseshoe Canyon, Salt Creek, Davis and Lavender Canyons, Abajos' south side, Yellowjacket-Lowry areas and others. But it is always back to Cedar Mesa that I unquestionably return. Why this is so is a bit beyond my vision, just now. Around some corner of second ledge.

I see several other steps on my path, looming now only as potentialities. They serve as 'pull' factors, drawing me forward. I do know that when I am not hiking Cedar Mesa, I am merely resting up for my next hike. In summer I take Mountain Way hiatuses from Cedar Mesa; I am not that fond of 100 degree days. But I know I will be back.

Every path I follow, every site I visit, every place I rest or stop for a vue, every rock art panel I admire or puzzle over becomes a part of me, and vice versa. Heuristic Way is merely one possible path towards knowledge, and it is certainly interesting.

CHAPTER 27
HIKING

For me hiking is a way to attain several pluses. It keeps me fit, it gives me a way to see outdoors and it is how I navigate thru Anasazi Way. For I see Cedar Mesa as one huge Outdoor Museum, with perhaps less artifacts than a 'real' museum, but spatially more intriguing.

I came to hiking rather early in life, but it was a secondary effect of hunting, or fishing; rather it was a benefit of pretending to care about these endeavors. I tried Boy Scouts but did not fit in. Hiking began to be an effective escape from family arguments.

While in high school, my only friend and I would often hike southern Arizona mountains, foothills, go to old mine sites, or just drive in desert country. Sometimes I would just leave my desert home and family, and hike thru heat of day towards nearby foothills/mountains, without driving. It became a means of escaping large family stresses.

When I was hiking in Grand Canyon, which I did off and on thru 70's alone, I lived in my backpack. I had no real job to return to, nor any pressing social engagements. My guides were two books by Harvey Butchart, and a few maps.

One time rather than try to hitchhike to Havasupai trailhead, I hitched to Grand Canyon Village. I hiked for several days along a seldom used 50 mile dirt road which connects GC Village to a road to Havasupai trailhead. I got only two rides, both short ones. Last one was with two Supais who tried to scare me with tales of scalpings, but they were drinking beer and tossing their cans out; I did not take them seriously.

I hiked thru their village but did not stop to pay for that 'privilege.' I stayed in a campsite for a week or so, and only saw one other hiker but basically had it to myself. I only went as far as Beaver Falls. Eventually, spring break with crowds, an approaching snowstorm, and an invitation to leave by a local Ranger [they needed plenty of sites for college students] got me to hitchhike back to Flagstaff.

On another GC hike I hid out in upper Phantom Creek for about a week, exploring around. I saw nobody, and when I came back out first people I met were two women who informed me that Nixon had won--what a welcome back to reality!

I encountered a few Anasazi sites in my years of GC hiking, most between Nankoweap and Unkar Delta, but I did not specifically go looking for them.

I hiked a few other places such as Paria River narrows, Dark Canyon, upstream from Sedona in Oak Creek Canyon but these places did not engage me fully. While living in Flagstaff, Arizona, I began bicycling relatively long distances. For several weeks I camped out and used my bike as means to bring fresh groceries down from town.

While living in Durango I got heavily into mountain biking, locally or a few times near Moab. It became my obsession, and my only hikes were into La Plata Mountains west of town. I continued an obsession [thru 80's] with rafting, which became a means to do great hikes while in Grand Canyon, on San Juan or other rivers.

In 1990, I stopped rafting and mountain biked much less. I began more and more to return to SE Utah for dayhikes, or biking [started going there in mid 80's].

A few watershed events in my life eventually brought me to living in SE Utah, and hiking Cedar Mesa almost exclusively. Whatever serendipity helped me, there was already a desire. And I found myself evolving to hiking as my sole outdoors physical activity.

Work became more and more onerous, and solely a means to an end; or several ends some of which I have accomplished. People I worked with could not understand my wish to have weekends off, for hiking and getting away from my job. These were people who mostly thot work was life itself. I have never been a workaholic, however.

* * *

Hiking is an intimacy, with me. A way to touch sandstone, to move thru its vagaries and cope with its exigencies. It sets rules, and I obey. But, of course I am human--and man always wants to master his environment, to change his surroundings to give him some comfort. So I, too, seek easy paths. Not always.

Sometimes where I hike only Anasazi would have. Most guys or women have goals they wish to own. They want to hike standard hikes. They may want to hike to find ruins, rock art or artifacts with modern names they learned somehow. I often desire these also. Other times I just hike Cedar Mesa for more subtle reasons, or for no discernible reason at all.

Mountain biking is a lot of fun but one thing it cannot do for you is give you intimacy with a landscape, or a culture. You are buzzing thru, only somewhat slower and less comfortable than if you were in a SUV. You are engaging, of course, but at a higher speed than I prefer. Sometimes a mere process of riding becomes its own goal--a physical challenge and mastery. Nor can you bike or raft everywhere you can hike.

Rafting is fun, but it seems again to be another form of driving. I have flown small airplanes, as pilot, to some interesting places. But rafting, flying, or biking are mechanical processes, man coupled to a machine.

Hiking is an Anasazi Way activity. Stating an obvious fact, Anasazi had no other alternative. He had no beasts of burden, nothing but his own legs and sandals. But I think hiking was more than just a means of getting around. Or perhaps an Anasazi did not hike, per se, it was more of just walking. By this I suggest hiking is a more modern activity for "doing something fun." Anasazi may have often felt tired when thinking of a long walk to get water or tend his crops. He often lived remotely from his fields, water, or game--even in some places from firewood. Maybe dayhiking is just my simulation of Anasazi Way.

I have followed a few Anasazi trails, tho, that suggest admiration for a vue. And if I may backtrack a bit, I suggest hiking is walking with a burden which Anasazi certainly did a lot of. They had to carry their corn, beans and squash back to granaries for safe-keeping, or water to their homes. Often their trails skirt cliffs overlooking other housesites, or places they valued.

I have read that pre-puebloans were highly mobile people. Not only did they often migrate, take hiatuses from areas such as Cedar Mesa, but they often walked long distances to visit relatives or friends. Their descendants still do this except usually with vehicles. Navajo people, who of course are not Puebloan, in some communities spend a great deal of every day driving around visiting, or shopping, when not at work.

I have seen some house sites with very scary entrance routes, whether using ladders, towers, or Moki Steps to in/out. I know their children learned to scramble all over cliffs and boulders--having nowhere else to play. Walking would have been much more natural to them than to us.

I inwardly laugh when I read Ferguson's comment about how an Anasazi mother would feel more secure knowing her children were protected by a bannister or wall at a Mesa Verde ruin[1]. While this may be true, it is another example of modern man projecting his feelings towards a lifeway he may not fully understand. Evidence is everywhere that

Anasazi children emulated bighorns to survive, to get around, and I think modern rock climbers can better see this.

There are Anasazi travel routes, more than trails, that show where they stopped--usually near water or shade--and where they 'hurried' thru, also where they often paused long enuf to etch or draw on nearby rock. I wonder how far they usually walked in a day, normally. I have read some estimates, studies based on their sphere of activities around communities or unit pueblos, generally about 'x' number of kilometers.

Of course how far they walked in a normal farming day all depended on many variables, some probably walked further than others. In some periods of their occupations, they deliberately lived on remote mesa tops in defensive sites. Unless Anasazi had waterholes on these mesas, long walks ensued. From what I have read, often they lived in 'field houses' near their crops--probably to protect, water, and generally tend them. Perhaps they all helped harvest and carry their food home--this could be what is depicted in so-called 'procession' panels of rock art.

Another thing I wonder about is motivation for long walks. When I hike, my motivation is different depending on if I have a goal, or am just drawn on by expanding curiosity. Sometimes I just want to make-miles and do not stop often. Most archaeologists' articles that I have read indicate Anasazi lived a purposeful life, with seemingly little time to 'goofaround.' In other words they had to walk for water, food, or firewood, and that is all work, not fun.

Someone, tho, had to walk to originally explore new country. Someone had to re-explore a country long abandoned by their predecessors. Someone had to find best migration routes. Anasazi often, as I've read, had to meet their fellow to exchange info about where conditions were favorable for living, or where there might be rich food resources.

They had to walk to exchange goods also, and I have read that some desert cultures migrated constantly, similar to Australian Bushmen, following water and food, knowing that to linger was to deplete local resources and starve.

If Chaco Canyon was a center for cultural persuasion and/or trading, Anasazi often would walk there. Not all of them, perhaps there were 'pochtecas' [traders] who performed this task. There are even pre-historic 'roads' all over greater Four Corners area, many are near Chaco. I do think that roads are an ostentatious display, perhaps reflecting a desire to emulate 'big city folk,' e.g. Chacoans. Often, as is claimed by archaeologists, these roads would serve functional needs of Anasazi, whether to assist them while carrying logs, for trading, or to point a way to newcomers. Other archaeologists think these roads served a more ceremonial purpose or perhaps an advertisement of magnificence.

There were probably few roads on Cedar Mesa, at least few have been found, but none of these are very obvious today. I imagined that I saw a remnant road recently while admiring a vue from atop Cedar Mesa's eastern escarpment. It pointed diagonally [compass-wise] towards Comb Ridge. Later I learned from a BLM archaeologist that another archaeologist was finding road remnants east of Comb that pointed directly where I had stood, intersected by Moki Steps on Comb's western cliffs. Several ruin sites lined up along this projected road-route.

William Ferguson[2] shows a photo of a road remnant very near Arch Canyon, and diagrams of others nearby.

I have found, besides Anasazi trails, another sort of route that may very well be one Ferguson shows in a map. This is a kind of hanging valley near a main streambed, which stretches for a mile or more. It is very easy to walk thru, relatively flat and only interrupted by [at least] one shallow streambed. It is near several ruin clusters, indeed connects them, and has at least one ruin next to it. Its other end leads to a route which crosses over into another drainage system.

On another hike I was returning to my pickup along a popular sidecanyon of ggulch, when I decided to follow a faint set of footprints up a fork of this canyon. Judging by my map, this fork was insignificant--but what do maps know. I soon came to a small cluster of ruins, some relatively well preserved, some next to a shallow streamcourse, some higher up.

This, and other discoveries all come at a price--which I pay gladly by hiking. And it has become, for me, more than a process or more than a means to an end, it is my metier, altho I do not think of it as work--except sometimes late in a day when returning to my vehicle.

CHAPTER 28
BINOCULARS

My first pair of binocs were Jason 'fixed-focus'. It were okay, but I thot soon after I needed a lighter pair and/or something that I could focus. Then I bought a small collapsing telescope, which I hung around my neck and kept in my t-shirt pocket for ready access. It was also okay, but took some practice getting used to--holding still. Later I realized that its eyepiece was scarring my prescription glasses' lens.

I carried that small telescope for about 5 years of hiking, found it very helpful. I remember reading, I think in "Wind in the Rock" that someone told Zwinger to leave her binoculars at home--that only way to see rock art or ruins was to hike over to them. I did not buy into that theory at all.

In 2001 I did a few hikes with a guy who had a pair of Swarovski binoculars. His were moderate power, 7x35 SL I think, but I was amazed at their optics. Later I did some Internet research but could not find them on discount anywhere. I settled on a 10x42 EL pair, which are expensive, but I quickly came to love looking thru them.

I also bought a binoc sling-harness that suspends my heavy binocs from my shoulders rather than my neck, is elasticized and adjustable. They not only ride comfortably but its elastic keeps tension on binocs while I am looking thru them, and helps me hold them steady.

I no longer think about how heavy my binocs are, and I wear them constantly on all my hikes. I only take them off when climbing a brushy slope, or a minor cliff-band.

Most hikers I meet who carry binocs have small and lightweight ones; I have looked thru them but prefer a larger field of vision.

There is a certain magnificence inherent in looking around at distant cliff faces thru binocs, powerful and with crisp optics. If I spot myself correctly I can look right into ruins in unassailable locations, and there are a few on Cedar Mesa. Of course I cannot look inside their rooms, but very few have any artifacts or murals--in a very real sense once you have seen inside 100 rooms [as an arbitrary quantity], whether kivas or not, you've seen most of any variety that is out there.

I also use them frequently for scouting possible in/out routes, whether from a distance or close up. There is a minor problem, tho, that often I get a distorted vue thru binocs--a foreshortening effect. I have learned to compensate for this, partially by comparing a non-binoc vue, and knowing slickrock. Usually this is only a problem with steep slopes of slickrock, and in some cases it is true that only going close to 'check it out' solves this quandary.

I will spend a great deal of time scouring far-off cliff faces for ruins or rock art, and I love a kind of remote-hiking feeling I get. As if I was really able to climb up, cross this ledge, and jump over to another across some gap. I do find binocs very handy for scouting a route across a skinny ledge to a site, but again sometimes a route looks impossible and only a closer examination helps.

Binocs do save me a lot of needless hiking when I see a promising shadow or overhang--even a well-patinated cliff face. In ggulch I found a small and very old rock art panel which may not be known to BLM [I mentioned it to an archaeologist, it was news to him] but I believe someone has seen it before. It looks extremely difficult to get to, involving a climb up a crack system with or without Moki Steps, and a traverse and climb up a black-crusted slickrock slope--all above a 100 foot cliff. There are only a few elements, notably a long snake. This panel is invisible without binocs, as desert varnish has almost covered it up.

Another facet of my 'prying about' with binocs is that I tend to look at opposite rims, or down below in canyons when I am rimwalking for other people. I love to find them, then watch their social dynamics from afar--as if I were some peeping-tom psychologist student working on a thesis about hiker-ology.

It might almost seem that I am paranoid, constantly looking around for other people. I am always surprised, tho, that on a nice hiking day when I am in a perfect spot that nobody else is around. As if I should feel guilt at having this place to myself. Part of that is a need to share, and I have nobody to share with [directly].

One time I watched three hikers looking thru binocs at a nearby ruin. I stood beside a tree, and was only partly making an effort to hide. They were across canyon on a bare slickrock dome, quite obvious. I have watched other hikers when I was in plain sight and they never noticed me. It has something to do with a quietude I surround myself with, partly with a lack of alertness [paranoia?] in others. One time, I and two fellow-hikers watched a couple hike to a talus slope, descend, then disappear upcanyon. We sat in plain sight, but I doubt those hikers ever noticed us.

Perhaps it has to do with expectations, that I always expect to see someone hike where I love to hike, but other hikers have no idea anyone else could be around [or care]. I am always fascinated by what draws hikers out to Cedar Mesa or Comb Ridge, and often it is obvious--I just have to read their tracks. I even step into someone else's footsteps and walk where they walked, imitating them--as if I could thus read their mind, feel what they felt, see what they saw. Where they stopped, where they detoured, how many there were, where they went is all interesting. Watching other hikers, and I don't usually do it for long--not wanting to invade someone's privacy--shows me what quality of hike they are having.

When they stop suddenly and set their heavy backpacks down, sit down and begin eating a snack I can see a certain quality of their experience. I watch them thru binocs to see if they are sitting on slickrock or dirt under trees. One place provides some kind of vue, other may provide an atavistic sense of shelter from sky-born enemies. Or perhaps, of course, it is merely hot and they seek shade.

This either makes me some kind of hiker-voyeur creep or indicates that I find other hikers and their experiences interesting [latter is more flattering, ego-wise]. Usually within a few minutes I tire of my spying and move off.

Another time, from far off I watched a couple explore a beautiful ruin under a rim thru my little telescope. I was fascinated to see them engaging in an act of discovery, a first-timer's joy in a new place. I watched them leave, which gave me clues for access. I had seen this ruin but not quite figured out how to get to it. There was no way this couple could have seen me.

Spying on others, I think, was a thing Anasazi had to do quite often. Later in their occupation of Cedar Mesa, when they moved down under rockshelters, and built defensive walls with peepholes aimed strategically they must have had concerns about strangers in their land.

Perhaps these were actual enemies , or potential enemies, who can say. Of course in prehistoric time Anasazi had no binocs or telescopes, but were probably more far-sighted than modern man. Plus, they would not have had smog to hinder their vision, only occasional dust storms.

In certain places you still find little tower walls, sometimes on a canyon rim, sometimes on an isolated boulder. Latter may provide a defensive retreat, or not; former may have served other needs, ceremonial perhaps.

These towers usually provide long vues of surrounding country, or nearby canyons. Perhaps little peepholes [loopholes] provided a kind of focus of vue--an Anasazi telescope. Some peepholes, according to archaeologists, may have served as astronomical observation tools.

Mostly my binocs are a tool of exploration, and I value them highly--qualitatively not monetarily. Another area that binocs with large optics excel at is in gathering light. I can look into far off caves, or overhangs and it is very like looking thru a camera viewfinder with telescopic lens and using a spot meter function.

My binocs are best investment for hiking I have made. Hiking boots, a daypack, and water bottles do not count--for I have to have them. I could get along without binocs, but hiking Sandstone Way would not be same.

CHAPTER 29
A PATH OF WATER

My lifeway is a path of water, coursing across a landscape cut by time, canyons, and a people's prehistory. I hike this path of water; I follow streambeds and I sometimes attempt to change direction. In any kind of ending, however, I came back to this path.

Its ways are too strong for me, too close for me to wholly share with others. Its needs have become my own, and my goals are equally matched by this stream I have chosen to think of as my life. Whether I had much choice or not, matters little, for I have become enlarged and entrenched.

When others may have thot I followed paths across slickrock, across canyons, or along ledges in some realistic landscape--instead I was traveling a path not of this time nor of this world.

For those who would follow a path of water soon find themselves lost to an outside world, a world not composed of sandstone, canyons, cactus, once cherished homes, or drawings on rock with seemingly enigmatic intent.

And you may not sit still in an alcove for long, and return home as same person you were. You may not engage in this landscape where once a people lived, dreamed, and farmed and remain wholly yourself. For it is as you expand out of yourself, as you lose yourself in another level of life, that you know where you were going to begin with.

This place may very well be animate, almost sentient if you listen closely enough. It has something to do with so many years of living, loving, struggle, and joy--then abandonment. And it is forever changed by being lived upon, and by harboring its dead.

And I am no different, I am not who I once thot to be. I have followed this path of water, modified my direction as obstructions dictated, as obstacles molded me, as places I visited asked of me.

Perhaps I never should have napped on a ledge in a winter sunshine, close beside a dwelling.

* * *

A path of water is a strange thing, for usually it cannot be seen until afterwards, in some hindsight-is-perfect way. While traveling it, you often have no idea why life gives you these turns and changes, these 'setbacks' and variances. You think to yourself "why is this happening...?" and rarely know any answers. It is not always good for you to see your path, or to try to change it much. I do not really speak here of fate, that is not a concept I buy into.

I see a path of water as more personal, less objective, for it is those little steps you take which add up, each of us sees ahead, behind, to sides, and above or below differently. We are shaped by who we know, choices we make. All these seem impossible to fore-ordain. It is how you react to some block to your supposedly smooth lifeway that forms your path of water. And I cannot actually show you where yours lies. I can follow my own, perhaps describe some of where I have been to you.

When you come to a place, and seek to understand it, you engage in an enlargement of some variety. It is as if who you were cannot continue to suffice. This is life, and you go on. I have seen many places which changed me, so many that some might think me disparate, uncollected. As if my path of water poured out into sands and was absorbed. Little remained to show I was there.

But I am one of those individs who can simultaneously travel my path of water and see it unfold, can speculate that each odd happening has a meaning yet to reveal itself, and I need only be patient. It is this kind of flexic waiting for an answer which yields many gifts. My path is one towards understanding.

Once I sought a very thick "Book of Answers," yet now I ask for a thinner volume. Perhaps it has to do with maturity perhaps it is merely that I have entered a slot canyon about to reveal itself after time and effort. Perhaps not, for my path of water has many twists and turns, I do not always perch on Mountain Way able to see it unfold ahead.

This is ok, I would not want perfect fore-sight.

I have looked back and seen how some steps along my path of water led to other choices, but I do not particularly desire to dwell in my past. I accept and move on. I wish I could use metaphors or analogies such as those found on a river--eddies, currents, and such, but mine is a drier path, where water is scarce. A kind of deserty path of water, perhaps where water submerges under sand, only to later reappear after some rock bed forces a reckoning.

And my path of water has led me to this place, in this time, and with certain talents or desires. I am here now, and have chosen to walk this path as long as I am able. Whether you see me on a Cedar Mesa path and merely think I am hiking, or realize more is going on, is up to your individ abilities. Or how your own path shapes you.

I have chosen this path, as well as it chose me. I walk this path, it walks me. I am water, I am a path, I walk on. Where it leads is up to me. And there is a sign to show me my way; there are many; it is only up to me to find them. And I ask you, "I walk my path of water, where does yours lie?" Perhaps in some small way, at some future time ours may cross. Perhaps not.

SECOND LEDGE

CHAPTER 30
HONAKER TRAIL THOTS[1]

As I leave my pickup, I get a good look at Monument Valley off in distance. First, I check out what part of San Juan river I can see, but see no rafts. It is in middle of December, just after a storm moved out. Tho breezy, clear and cool I do not really expect to see anyone.

Browny and Dusty jump up and chew on my fingers, a 'thing' they picked up from Dusty's mom, a purebred Queensland Heeler. This signals their eagerness to get going, among other things. So, with a last look around, I shift my daypack and descend.

I am pleasantly surprised to see that someone has recently done a bit of trail maintenance. Possibly Boy Scouts, possibly BLM. Naturally, I stop at 'Little Angels Landing' a prominent limestone point about half way down to look around. I can see many deer trails across and up river from where river runners camp. This point has a crack which splits it into two, but I step down into it a bit, then jump across telling Dusty and Browny to 'stay'.

Later, I lie on sand next to river with my daypack as a pillow. Low winter sun just peeks thru a 'v' shaped notch in canyon rim. My left side is warmed by it, while my right side is occasionally cooled by cycling breezes. I am soon lost in thot. I feel no need to leave yet, as sun is warm, river is green, and a lone bird sends out a strange call, which I do not recognize.

I soon realize that my clock is shadows, as sun moves. At

first I am in full daylite, later shadows cover beaches on far shore. This gives me a growing awareness of time passing, where my wrist watch did not. In front of me, left bank of San Juan River rises in a perpendicular series of stepped cliffs. It is banded by geologic strata I neither care to learn names of, nor think much about.

I had noticed where long ago Anasazi could have climbed down one cliff where miners had used dynamite and a lot of back-breaking labor to build a trail. Any other obstacle on this trail would not have slowed them down much. And I knew that they had come here to camp and hang out. In summer, this must have been a welcome respite with a cool river to swim in, plenty of wood for fires, and sand for kids to play in.

But that was then, this is now. I thank all miners and laborers who helped to build a trail that they barely used. I know full well that nowadays nobody could afford to build a trail without first assaying any potential minerals, that is if they could obtain permits from BLM first. And BLM would never come up with funds to build such a trail which serves no practical purpose, goes basically nowhere, and is not used by very many people. I see that a certain motivation of those miners serves a purpose they probably never foresaw.

A moving shadow stirs me to think of where I am, how I will need to get out back to my pickup, get home and rest for work tomorrow. It is not a welcome awareness. It is very quiet here; a small bird flies directly overhead, crosses river, and lands near a rock on opposite beach. Dusty is busy digging a hole under an overhead tamarisk. And that awareness brings me to think of how completely different this must have been before tamarisk came to this country.

Neither miners [probably], nor Anasazi [certainly] would have found tamarisk here. And I think of ggulch, where I had been hiking side canyons extensively for last 3 months, and how much easier it would have been to raise crops and get around without tamarisk. It is, of course, impossible to realistically think of getting rid of them, and I am now using one as a partial wind-block. But, I would like to see this place w/o them.

It is very peaceful, and I am alone with my dogs. I know there is probably nobody closer than Gooseneck Overlook or perhaps downcanyon in either Johns or Slickhorn. I think how pleasant it would be to have a small rock cabin hidden away in some rock cranny next to this river with a secret route out of canyon. Living thus, soon enough, all of my tensions and angers at life in civilization could float on down river. Staring at a river flowing by all day could give me a tranquil, perhaps hypnotic calmness of mind and allow my disordered musings to geal. Or perhaps not. I had spent a lot of time in grcanyon rafting, and some of it lounging on beach. But, there I was never alone for long.

And solitude, as I now experienced it, comes in these moments. I think it is solitude outdoors that gives me an ambiance of universality, which I try to carry along with me in my mental lunchbox as I work a very mundane job. I can arise above an everyday sort of existence and see a broader world, that of nature, sandstone, and my efforts to explore. It helps give me a sense of balance which I try to use whenever normal workday vexations spring up; perhaps helping me to step back and remind myself, I am more than I seem, I care about more than this in front of me, and I have thots much bigger than this

Here I am surrounded by cliffs, sand, trees and a river. I cannot see more than a few hundred yards unless I move. I am confined by nature. But it is ok, there are none of nature's 'punks' [ravens/magpies] around to pester me.

It is easy to attain clarity, when surrounded by simple scenery, and it helps me to focus.

And soon a lengthening shadow signals, as do Dusty and Browny, that it is a good time to leave. I have a nice, easy climb up and am surprised at how fast I go and how well I feel. There is nobody on trail, no tracks, and at top no cars. Cedar Mesa's cliffs stand back a ways, and eastwards are some marvelously rippled hills next to San Juan river, upcanyon from Mexican Hat. It has been a very short hike, timewise and mileswise, but it feels like a mini-vacation squeezed out at no particular expense, and I am refreshed in a way not much else I do can.

CHAPTER 31
FISH AND OWL CANYONS

I think Fish and Owl Canyons, in these last few dry years, might become a better alternative place to hike than Grand Gulch. They are certainly quite popular. I am referring to fact that Grand Gulch is drying up, there has been no significant stream flow in at least two years [prior to 2002].

Owl does not have as much water as Fish, but it is more consistent than in GG. Fish Canyon is easily best watered canyon on Cedar Mesa. This has to do with where Fish starts, and its shortness. GG also starts in highlands of Elk Ridge-Abajos, but due to its length and perhaps underlying geology, water goes underground more. I think also that further east of GG headwaters, where Fish starts, there is more snowfall on Elk Ridge.

Fish and Owl always will remain popular places to hike due not only to their wetness, but simply because they make a very nice loop hike. They are also scenic canyons in their own right. I have met people who try to do a Fish-Owl loop as a dayhike--I am sure they succeed--and I wonder how much they enjoyed their hike or how much they saw. Perhaps if hikers are bored with what else they have seen on Cedar Mesa, or feel in need of a hard making-miles kind of hike, this dayhike is attractive.

I have mostly given up making-miles types of hikes, though, and I hike Fish and Owl differently than most hikers. I try to hike all of Cedar Mesa as an Anasazi would have--by knowing where I want to go, hiking mesa tops to get there, then dropping down into a canyon. In other words I work to know all of a canyon's in/out routes and use these.

As of this writing there are parts of Owl and Fish I have yet to hike, but it is just a matter of putting together pieces of a puzzle--mostly how to access these stretches in a dayhike. I have rimwalked most of both canyons, though, and in some ways this is better than hiking along streambeds.

Lower Fish is wholly different than its upper reaches. It is wider, flatter, sides are less vertical, and of course it is somewhat drier. Getting in/out is easier than further upcanyon, and usually there are only one or two cliff-bands which cause you to search for a route. Its south side is fairly easy to get up or down, but there are no roads nearby.

There are a few ruins in lower Fish, but they are small and hard to see--some are quite hard to get to. At one place there is an obvious trail uphill to a ledge for several small ruins. Down near Comb Wash are a few ruins with a little rock art, but years of easy access guarantee that they have been thoroughly pot-hunted. At least one is still quite photogenic, and I have a photo in my website.

There used to be a 4wd road into lower Fish but it has mostly washed away, and I noticed recently that only a few ATVs have utilized parts of it. Later in this book I discuss some in/out routes for Fish, and there is a fairly easy one in lower Fish, upcanyon from Comb Wash.

In upper Fish, just as in GG, where there is water there may be more ruins. One facet of Anasazi Way that is scarce in Fish and Owl canyons is rock art panels. There are some small panels scattered around, if you can find them, but there is not an intense concentration such as in GG. I have only found one section of Fish with several very nice panels, and only small panels in Owl [so far].

I have found Anasazi Trails along Fish, Owl, and other places on Cedar Mesa; I have also found many short sections of so-called Moki Steps--'Moki' used to be a popular name for Anasazi--generally I prefer term 'Anasazi

Steps' [I capitalize as they are labels for a distinctive type of archaeological feature]. Very few people will hike along these trails, or notice them if they did; Anasazi Trails are usually faint, unmarked [I discuss them in a previous chapter, 'Anasazi Oddities'] but distinct once you learn to see them. As a matter of exploration, I have found them thru every canyon. Generally they tie together distant building sites along Anasazi-logical routes. Of course, Anasazi-logic is mostly unknown to modern hikers--many archaeologists understand and prove it in their writings.

Fish and Owl Canyons are equally as fascinating as is GG, in their own way, and no small part of this is their pure scenic value. Fish, due to its bold entrenchment, has very steep sides, is mostly slickrock, and when you sit somewhere along its rim, looking up or down canyon, can draw you into forgetting about a constant 'tic-toc-tic' of time [re: Joseph Campbell].

My first few hikes into Fish and Owl were fairly standard dayhikes--in at top and down as far as I could, then back out. Then as I progressed, I [as elsewhere on CM] began exploring in/out routes and figuring out how to see other parts of Fish and Owl I had missed before. There are a few places in Fish and Owl I will never manage to access, such as a few building sites, but I am ok with this. I am, though, very close to an Anasazi Way understanding of these canyons.

CHAPTER 32
GRAND GULCH

Grand Gulch is a complex and long canyon system, and I discuss most of its major in/out routes later. My knowledge of its secrets has followed Heuristic Way. I began, as with other parts of Cedar Mesa, by doing standard hikes. But starting in late 90's, after deciding to write about this area, I began scouring maps, driving many roads, and exploring possible in/out routes--mostly so that I could hike all of GG, if possible, as dayhikes.

I have accomplished this goal, and more. What else I have learned will have to remain unpublished for various reasons. Some of these reasons concern a sense of responsibility; awareness that there are 'hunters' out there; and that as with many other goals in life a realization that my expansion of knowledge was hard-earned and followed Heuristic Way in my own way--and you need to follow your own H-Way path.

My understanding of responsibility is also complex. When I first started hiking CM, I copied others in thinking to pocket any and all interesting shards I found. This is a natural, if deplorable facet of humanity; I applaud those who never give into this--whether trained as archaeology students, or just innately more responsible. My period of collection came to a stop when I started hiking here more often, and exclusively here. Recently I returned a baggie of shards to CM, admittedly placing them with confusing proveniences but also where it is unlikely they will be found and simultaneously in places where their provenience is easily explainable [if they are ever found].

Often when I find collections of shards at building sites, I re-scatter them close by, often when I find 'wild shards' [i.e. away from sites] I move them under a nearby bush, but not always. Many people think to preserve shards or make them more noticeable by placing them on nearby rocks and this practice is frowned on by all Cultural Resources Managers [i.e. BLM, USFS, NPS]. My scattering of shards or hiding them is probably not encouraged either, but in certain circumstances I feel a responsibility to Anasazi Way unhampered by concerns of what anyone "might think."

That is--I am in close and frequent contact with a BLM archaeologist and never hesitate to tell him of any illegal activities I may encounter, I try to adhere to guiding principles of behavior while hiking Cedar Mesa and visiting sites, I would discuss any significant artifact I found that seems unknown, and I keep to myself many features, sites, routes, or other knowledge I have garnered. However, I follow Heuristic Way as an individ and perhaps this also means I have to make up my own mind whether I am ultimately responsible to CRMs or my own integrity. Since I hike alone, I usually lean towards latter.

By 'hunters' I mean that I have gotten emails from people who admire facets of my website, such as photos of ruins and/or rock art panels, and who ask me for locational info. I have noticed a few individs who assiduously and alertly take notice of what I write in my 'NEWS' page online--i.e. where I hike or what I saw--and hope to use these hints to go find Anasazi features. I often obfuscate on purpose.

Fred Blackburn told me once that he led some people onto CM to see certain sites and was "followed" by someone who later returned to remove artifacts. Without discussing complications I see inherent in an act of guiding relative strangers to see a site or artifact, I will state that Fred disgustingly told me he "won't even come here much anymore."

I see a similar wariness in archaeologists in discussing certain sites, but this is largely due to training and rules of ethical conduct.

David Roberts, "In Search of the Old Ones", showed a photo of a prehistoric pot and a photo of a distinctive geologic feature in that canyon then went on to discuss how he "found it". I and others believe he was guided to look where he did thru general or specific hints [possibly exact locational info]. Later on, in a magazine article, he admitted that he made a mild blunder. As a result of his candor, many people have figured out where this pot is and gone to see it. I have had people email me with directions, and have been several times to see it. BLM, of course, is frequently monitoring it and looking for signs of increased visitation at which time they would decide whether to accession it into a museum, presumably Edge of Cedars in Blanding.

It takes time to learn how hungry these 'hunters' are, and how to best avoid them. Some of this is due to laziness, or lack of time to explore heuristically as I have, some is just due to innate hunter-gatherer predisposition.

To return to GG, there is a great deal more than I write about that I know of, but I have learned it as with whom I share that reflects my personal integrity. A case in point was a Utah resident from near SLC who emailed me about some site. He was heavily involved with a kind of techy trend of using gps units to share adventures. This Internet group would leave small ammo boxes at certain places then pique each other with gps locations. Their goal was to go find these caches, thus fighting boredom, seeing more of Utah, and presumably 'having fun with a toy'.

Eventually I invited him along for a few hikes. I showed him some relatively advanced places in Grand Gulch.. I took a gamble that I could convince him not to put everywhere he found out there in a gps hunt website. I think my method worked, and I hope this individ has come around to sharing responsibility for protection of remaining cultural resources. So far I have only hiked with three other parties [total of eight people] to "special" places on Cedar Mesa. Most of these trips have been into GG. In most of these cases, people do not have easy access to Cedar Mesa and consequently there is little likelihood they will return often.

I have seen how publicity, whether word of mouth or written, can increase visitation to certain corners of Cedar Mesa but, as I have stated elsewhere, visitation to some places I have publicized has not increased.

Grand Gulch is certainly an archaeologically rich area, not so much with artifacts but with building and rock art sites. Part of this is due to more water in wetter years, a wider canyon, a north-south orientation thus providing more sunlight penetration, many in/out routes, and many rock shelters.

There are several notable ruins and rock art sites that are easy to see and access, some that are well-maintained. A few are marked on maps and discussed in books or miscellaneous websites. Perfect Kiva, in Bullet Canyon, is very popular and with easy access. It is also better maintained than most GG ruins.

Of hundreds of rock art sites, only a handful are regularly visited. Part of this is due to obscurity, part due to difficult access. There is a phenomena which has occurred recently that has helped CRMs protect these panels, and BLM's local archaeologist has become aware of this. He figured it out after hiking part of GG and I remember mentioning it earlier to him--but often this is how Heuristic Way works. Personally I have visited a high percentage of GG's panels; some I am aware of are extremely difficult or impossible to access due to erosion. I would not yet claim to know of all rock art panels on Cedar Mesa.

Grand Gulch and Fish Canyon remain my two favorite

places to hike-explore on Cedar Mesa, whether for sheer scenic beauty or for interesting features and cultural resources.

CHAPTER 33
DARK CANYON

I first heard of Dark Canyon in mid 70's while standing in line to obtain a Backcountry Permit at south rim of Grand Canyon. A ranger was telling some visitor-hiker that Dark Canyon, which he had hiked recently, was his "favorite place of all" even tho he worked and hiked in Grand Canyon. I listened in and even asked a few questions of my own.

Soon I bought a few maps, borrowed a friend's car, and took off. Instead of starting at one of several intermediate in/outs, I began where road crosses around head of Dark Canyon. That ranger had suggested I might be able to hitch a ride on a boat on Lake Powell.

I hiked all of Dark Canyon but do not remember all that much. I did not explore any side canyons, just sort of plodded thru. It was really my first full-length canyon hike; I had been hiking Grand Canyon but only in pieces.

As I neared Lake Powell, vast areas of bleached driftwood clued me in. Soon, I saw a few wet footprints of two bare feet. I hurried, and saw around a corner a couple arm in arm, giggling and nude, walking towards Lake Powell. They never heard me so I followed them, allowing them to get ahead a bit. When a minute or two had passed, I approached their houseboat and apprised them of my following them. We all had a good laugh, then I asked them for a ride downlake to nearest marina.

It seemed I was in luck, it was last day of a four day holiday weekend, I do not remember which, and they [4 people from Phoenix] were probably last visitors into Dark

Canyon for several days or a week. I would have had to return to my car, and an incipient cold discouraged me from this plan. They did give me a ride, and fed me breakfast of fresh trout and eggs.

Back at Hite Marina, they had no room in their car, so I walked up to highway and sat for about half a day. Finally a couple, possibly honeymooning, picked me up. They were traveling around camping and intended to visit NBNM next. I told them of my hike, where my car was, and was able to convince them to take me to my car. In trade, I shared a camp with them in NBNM, we drove around to see bridges, then went up to my car. Later we both drove to Blanding or Monticello [I do not remember which town exactly] and I bought them breakfast and some gas.

After that, it was years before I got back to hiking/exploring SE Utah, and I was never tempted much to return to Dark Canyon. Instead I was busy hiking Grand Canyon, later I moved into Wyoming oil field towns and took a hiatus from hiking.

Recently, I have hiked down into Woodenshoe Canyon, driven down into Peavine as far as Dark Canyon and down to Big Canyon, then hiked downcanyon. I have also hiked once down Sundance Trail then a few miles towards Lake Powell. I have also explored a little on mesa tops near Woodenshoe Canyon.

Even tho Dark Canyon was my introduction to this area, it has not turned into my favorite place. It is a bit remote for dayhikes, and access is limited. It is also not as archaeologically rich as CM, tho there are some sites.

CHAPTER 34
ARCH CANYON

Arch Canyon is a strange place, nowadays, in that it is not quite part of Cedar Mesa and is not protected by any particular boundaries. There is a 4wd route up it for about 10 miles, and another 4wd route just north of it up past Hotel Rock and onto Milk Ranch Point. Just south of it is a county road which turns 4wd at one hill, closely parallels Arch Canyon, and has two short spur roads to overlooks--one of which has a staircase onto a promontory. So at certain times it is crowded with ATVs or 4wdriving tourists/locals.

Most of these visitors stop at a few ruins near mouth of Arch Canyon, may spot a few other sites upcanyon, but mostly come to see two main arches or just to do a drive. For a hiker best time of year to visit may be when snow stops vehicles. Due to Arch Canyon's exposure to sun, first mile or so is snow packed most winters, but after it turns north-south not much snow remains all winter. Despite this, not many people visit Arch Canyon [or any other part of CM] in winter.

I have noticed that most of these visitors do not even see better attractions in Arch Canyon, which is certainly best for their protection/preservation. For a hiker, with time to explore and pay attention, it is a fascinating canyon. This is so because there are rock art panels and ruins not always visible from a moving vehicle; one needs to take time to look.

I have explored Arch Canyon rims, hiked parts of its bottom, tried some of its sidecanyons, tried some of its extra in/outs, scoured opposite cliffs for ruins, found some of its rock art panels, hiked way up to a third arch most people do not see, mostly in winter. There is some weather phenomena that often keeps storms out of its lower end, while shadows preserve any snow in last mile all winter. Probably due to proximity to highlands and uprising currents of air, I suppose.

Often I detour to hike Arch Canyon when weather elsewhere is marginal, because it is a closer drive and usually Comb Wash/Butler Wash is drier in winter than any highland canyons such as Owl/Fish. In some ways it is one of my favorite canyons, partly for its landscapeal layout, how it looks. There are other nearby areas equally as interesting, short little canyons with a few sites which I return to often.

There is a particular ambiance of entrenchment that I like about Arch Canyon, perhaps easy access has something to do with this. Easier than with Mule and Fish canyons, when I enter its lower end I do not have to hike miles to get entrenched--to get into a 'real' canyon. Of course Comb Ridge canyons share this feature, but they are shorter and wholly different. I step out of my pickup, shoulder my pack, and voilá I am in a canyon.

Sharing a canyon bottom with a vehicle route does not bother me, partly since I hike it in winter, and partly because I can defocus that aspect and look at Anasazi sites prehistorically. I mean by this that I am able to ignore signs of vehicle traffic and look around, imagine what it was like for Anasazi and use my skills to see more of their sites, whether obvious, 'limited activity'[1], or AWUF[2]. For me a road is often just a tool, a way to get in to a place I want to hike, and has no real significance as a "sign of exploitation, or overuse." That is why, as I stated elsewhere, I do not mind using mining or drill hole roads, and am glad most of them are still open to use.

I realize there are some people or organizations who wish to see Arch Canyon closed to vehicular traffic, also lower Mule Canyon, and this may happen someday. I am fine with this, but meantime I hike them anyway and do my best to conceptualize these canyons as they were for Anasazi, not dwell on how currently they are driven thru. After all, I have driven up Arch Canyon myself a few times, and will do so again in future.

THIRD LEDGE

CHAPTER 35
HIKING CEDAR MESA[1]

Starting about 2000, or earlier, there is very little or no runoff thru Grand Gulch, or any other Cedar Mesa Canyons. This trend has continued thru 2002, and is likely for any foreseeable future. There is still water, but it is scarce, isolated, and usually murky. Hikers are strongly encouraged to remember that resident animals need this water also. It is best not to camp near any water source, try to be quiet and discreet around any springs to avoid scaring off wildlife. Hopefully, this dry condition will change soon. I try to give up-to-date info about water conditions on Cedar Mesa in my website.

A very good overall source of map-info is Trails Illustrated waterproof map. It can help you find necessary roads and routes. There are very few maintained trails on Cedar Mesa, usually only sections thru Grand Gulch. Many of these trails are not even marked on maps, so any hikers need certain orienteering skills.

All Cedar Mesa canyons are rugged, some extremely rough. Boulder gardens, pouroffs, rockfalls, trails which constantly criss-cross streambeds--or follow rocky streambeds can add difficulties. There is only one Ranger Station which is not manned year-round. Thus, hikers are cautioned to be careful, to not take senseless chances, and be aware that rescue could take a long time.

Summer temperatures can exceed 100°, and winter temperatures can drop below 0° [specially at night]. In summer more water is needed, in winter more clothing is needed. Best times of year to hike are from mid-March thru May, and September thru early December. I hike from September thru May, then head for mountains to hike. I also hike alone, with 2 dogs, but this is not for everyone either [I have hiked alone since 1973, in Grand Canyon and elsewhere].

Two highways provide access to a central core of Cedar Mesa, Hwy 95 which goes from just south of Blanding up to Hanksville and beyond, and Hwy 261 which goes from Hwy 95 south to Hwy 163 near Mexican Hat. I list many other roads which are mostly built of native clay, and treacherous or impassable if very wet.

Snow is usually not much deeper than about 6 inches across Cedar Mesa, with deeper deposits inside canyons. Usually a few warm days consolidate and melt snow up above, and lately there has not been much snow anyway. Hiking slickrock when wet or snow-covered can be dangerous. There can be periods as long as a week during winter with warm, clear days. Once, years ago, friends and I rafted San Juan river for two days starting March 1.

Most of hikes, or in/out routes I write about are not for beginners. I do not rate routes, and assume any reader has enough common sense to decide his/her own abilities to do a route or not. I do give qualifications for novice hikers in most cases. Thus, you as hiker assume all responsibility for where and when you hike, and consider my suggestions as merely that. Ultimately, you must decide for yourself. Enter at your own risk, and enjoy.

Currently, due to dry conditions, no campfires are allowed in canyons. Cell phones will work in some spots; there are towers on Navajo Mountain and Abajos.

BLM has certain guidelines for hiker-behavior while visiting sites, and I list many in my website. Basically, though, you are encouraged to admire sites from a distance;

stay off walls, stay out of rooms; don't touch rock art, try to hi-light it for photography, or vandalize it; never camp in alcoves with any Anasazi cultural presence, or build campfires in them, or "go to bathroom" in alcoves; respect all cultural deposits, do not remove shards or other artifacts; keep your pets under control and out of Slickhorn Canyons or Grand Gulch below Collins, or leave them at home due to dry conditions lately; remove your pack before peering inside a room, do not use walls for support; remember that certain modern-day Puebloan tribes vue Anasazi cultural remains [of any kind] as their heritage, including all of Cedar Mesa as a former homeland of their ancestors, put succinctly--you are a guest in someone else's "house" and you should behave accordingly.

BLM administers all of Cedar Mesa and nearby areas such as Comb Ridge, Arch Canyon, etc. Pack animals are allowed in Grand Gulch, upcanyon from Collins; they are not allowed in Slickhorn Canyons.

Permits, reservations, and fees are required for overnite camping in canyons. There are restrictions on sizes of groups, and number of days spent backpacking. None are required for mesa-level camping. Dayhike permits and fees are required for hiking most canyons, and an annual permit is available for $20.. These can be obtained at BLM, Monticello [near Conoco station] or at KGRS, 4 miles south of Hwy 95 on Hwy 261. Phone number of BLM in Monticello is 435 587 1500.

ABBREVIATIONS USED

cl: canyon or creek left [facing downstream no matter which way you are going].

cr: canyon or creek right [facing downstream].

mm: mile marker

MAPS

CEDAR MESA
TRAILS ILLUSTRATED #706

1. Bluff NW
2. Bluff SW
3. Cedar Mesa N
4. Cedar Mesa S
5. Cigarette Spg. Cave
6. Hotel Rock
7. Kane Gulch
8. Moss Back Butte
9. Polly's Pasture
10. Red House Spring
11. Slickhorn C. East
12. Slickhorn C. West
13. Snow Flat Spg. Cave
14. S Long Point
15. The Goosenecks
16. Whirlwind Draw

NEARBY AREAS
TRAILS ILLUSTRATED#703

1. Black Mesa Butte
2. Bluff
3. Burnt Hills
4. Chocolate Drop
5. Clay Hills
6. Cream Pots
7. Fry Spring
8. Goulding NE
9. Goulding NW
10. Jacob's Chair
11. Kigalia Point
12. Mancos Jim Butte
13. Mexican Hat
14. Mike's Mesa
15. No-Man's Island
16. Oljeto
17. San Juan Hill
18. The Cheesebox
19. Woodenshoe Buttes

GRAND GULCH

This is certainly most popular canyon on Cedar Mesa. It is on western half of CM, if east-west dividing line is accepted as Hwy 261. Generally this half gets less effective moisture than northeastern part. Grand Gulch is about 52 miles long, according to Trails Illustrated [TI] map, however there is more upcanyon from Kane/Grand confluence, not easily hikable, about 8 miles. Mostly Grand Gulch runs north-south.

Upcanyon several miles from this confluence, both Kane and Grand Gulch get shallow at cliff bands; Kane has a constructed horse trail thru this barrier, Grand is virtually impassable at its major dropoffs.

Grand Gulch is never very wide, except in some wide swinging bays, generally only a hundred yards wide. From Junction Ruin for many miles canyon walls interweave impassable cliffs with broken talus/juniper slopes, allowing prehistoric inhabitants many access routes. Upper part of Grand Gulch also has more springs, denser vegetation both along stream and on slopes, and more sites [both rock art and ruins].

Downcanyon, near Collins Canyon, Grand Gulch entrenches in more vertical cliff bands, one stacked atop another, interspersed with weaker layers of rock. Verticality, however, yields few in/outs. Most sidecanyons provide no access routes at all below Collins, and for miles there is no 'escape.' There are also very few sites in lower Grand Gulch, and fewer people hike it. Bannister Ruin is last notable and well-preserved ruin going towards San Juan River.

Downcanyon from Junction Ruin, hiking is only

moderately rugged, with very few real obstacles such as pouroffs or boulder gardens. In last few years most hikers follow dry streambed trail. Check with BLM for water availability or weather before hiking [bulletin board at KGRS].

Winter moisture is severely limited all across southwest quadrant of CM, thus sidecanyons are not fully developed, nor could Anasazi effectively farm there in most years.

Grand Gulch sidecanyons and in/outs are listed in order starting from Kane Gulch and going downcanyon. Not all in/outs are included, just some obvious ones.

* * *

KANE GULCH

Is standard upper entrance to ggulch [actually an eastside, *cl* tributary to ggulch]. Kane Gulch Ranger Station, only BLM outpost on Cedar Mesa, is located at trailhead. Prior reservations may be needed for overnite camping, thru Monticello BLM office. Most hikers do a Kane to Bullet multi-day loop, either hitching back to KGRS, or using two cars.

MAPS: Kane Gulch 7.5 covers all of it. Use TI #706 also.

GETTING THERE: about 28.8mm Hwy 261; it is 4 miles south of Hwy 95. Park at KGRS, trailhead is across hwy. You could also hike upper Kane Gulch, tho it is shallow and in cattle country, and it runs between Hwy 261 and Hwy 95.

HIKING KANE GULCH: as easy as it gets. Starts across sageflats, then into a gully which gradually deepens, then down a constructed horse trail. Some hikers miss a *cr* detour and go thru a long boulder garden after canyon is entrenched. In one place you hike right thru slickrock gully, where ice could be a problem in winter. I have made it down to Junction Ruin in less than 1:30, and even down past Stimper Arch and back in a dayhike.

WATER: there is an usually reliable spring at Kane/Ggulch confluence. In summer of 2002 this spring dried up. There has been insignificant spring runoff for several years before 2002, someday this may change. Most reliable springs are marked on TI map.

ATTRACTIONS: many, as it is a kool canyon to hike and so many people do it trail is obvious and you do not have to think your way along. Upper Junction Ruin is scenic, tho impossible to get into w/o special gear [do not even try, it is illegal].

Fee for dayhiking and camping.

* * *

SIDE CANYONS OF GGULCH, PLUS MAJOR IN/OUT ROUTES

1) FORTRESS CANYON: a *cr* [north] side canyon of ggulch @5.6 mile, and first major one downcanyon from Ggulch/Kane confluence. There is a better route just downcanyon. Extremely primitive, steep and bouldery, rarely used, not for novice hikers.

MAPS: Kane Gulch 7.5 covers it all. Use TI #706 also.

GETTING THERE: @ 88.6mm Hwy 95 turn south onto SJ231a, same road as for 9 and 12 mile in/out. .8 mile from hwy turn east onto a small sagebrushy woodcutters road which ends 1 mile later in Indian Park, ok for hi-clearance 2wd.

HIKING FORTRESS CANYON: follow shallow drainage nearby. Fortress forms a wide cliffy valley after about 10 minutes. Within another 10 minutes Fortress forms an inner gorge, and you can get into it either 100 feet *cl*, or contour around *cr* for several hundred yards and find several routes down, one has some rocks piled up 4 feet below you. There is a spring at this dropoff, tho I do not know how good it is in summer. Almost immediately you encounter a steep although short drop thru a nasty boulder fall. I elected not to do it with dogs, as it is a bit ugly.

A route that might be better, tho still not easy, is in next *cr* ggulch drainage, which is less than 1/4 mile downcanyon. I have not hiked it, only scouted from above. Perhaps easiest is to start out on a promontory upcanyon from it, find an easy break then walk way around *cr* on a wide ledge and work down a talus slope.

WATER: only in Fortress, below major upper dropoff; this may disappear in dry years.

ATTRACTIONS: I enjoyed vues from above and rimwalked around more than anything else. There are a few sites in Fortress. Two local pothunters were caught near here by BLM about 20 years ago. See "*Cowboys and Cave Dwellers*" by Fred Blackburn for part of this story.

* * *

2) TODIE CANYON: is a *cl* [east] side canyon of ggulch @7.2 mile and only about 1.75 miles long. It is rough, bouldery, brushy, but has a trail and is used more than Fortress. Other nearby routes are easier; it can be used as part of a loop hike. Not recommended for novice hikers.

MAPS: Cedar Mesa N 7.5 covers it all. Use TI #706 also.

GETTING THERE: 25.1mm, 261 Hwy, drive west 1.3 miles on SJ2361 [new style sign] to deadend at a parking lot. Road ok if dry, but is mostly clay and very slimy if wet. SJ County maintains road periodically.

HIKING TODIE: trail starts off *cl* from parking lot, and stays out of gully for about .6 mile to avoid a dropoff. It descends a cliff break thru a gully into inner gorge. Look for cairns, as route zigzags to avoid numerous boulder gardens and other problems. Generally, you can make it to ggulch in 1:30 hours.

NORTH FORK: you can access it either from Long Flat [road is barely visible] or from Todie C parking lot. I hiked over from latter, and rimwalked upcanyon until it got shallow and easy to enter. It, in many ways, is easier to hike than S Fork Todie tho more remote. Only near confluence is some boulder skirting needed. I saw no tracks, virtually no trail, although there is little alluvium so I was forced to hike in streambed.

WATER: a spring at head of Todie, another just up from ggulch, but it is a short canyon and few people camp in it.

ATTRACTIONS: there are a few sites, perhaps its greatest charm is as access to this part of ggulch. Split Level Ruin [see TI map] is about 3 miles down ggulch.

* * *

3) 9 MILE CANYON: is a *cr* [north] side canyon [almost more of a gully-slope] of ggulch, @9 miles. It is steep and rugged, not for novice hikers. This is my unofficial name, I have not seen it labeled on any maps.

MAPS: Cedar Mesa N 7.5 covers it all. Use TI #706 also.

GETTING THERE: @ 88.6mm [or 88.3], Hwy 95, SJ231a heads south and deadends after 4.2 miles at a capped drill hole site. Immediately after gate next to hwy, go left at 'y', then stay on main road to end. This road can be impassable if very wet.1997 version of TI #706 map has this road marked incorrectly, it skirts closely Wilderness Area Boundary, and goes directly to drill hole site which is next to '6408' elev.

GETTING STARTED: from this drill hole site you can also access Pine and Green House Canyon. To orientate, climb atop a low mesa nearby from which you can see for miles. This will also be your landmark for returning; a GPS shot is helpful.

HIKING 9 MILE CANYON: from drill site hike ESE about .5 mile and follow main drainage to edge of ggulch. When you get to dropoff into ggulch look around and upcanyon of two nearby drainages has a scarce but doable ledge thru fall which I have boosted my dogs up and down. *Cl* is a talus slope with somewhat of a trail down into ggulch; you can work down ledges *cr* also, tho perhaps this is easier coming up. Pouroff spring marked on TI map as "*10: Pour Off Pool--8.8 miles*" is just upcanyon.

WATER: probably none, but in ggulch is a usually

reliable spring just upcanyon.

ATTRACTIONS: interesting in/out to ggulch, scenic from rims. Can be used as part of a loop hike. Split Level Ruin is nearby, see TI Map.

* * *

4) 12 MILE CANYON: is a *cr* [west] side canyon to ggulch @12 miles [approx.]. It is short, steep, and rough but it goes. This is my unofficial name, I have not seen it labeled on any maps. Not for novice hikers.

MAPS: Pollys Pasture 7.5 covers it all. Use TI #706 also.

GETTING THERE: same as for 9 mile canyon.

HIKING 12 MILE CANYON: hike along a ridge line just east of drill hole site in a SW direction. Alternatively, rimwalk ggulch until you reach it in about 1.5 miles. Upcanyon from it is another side canyon which probably does not go w/o rope. 12 mile canyon is distinctively at a sharp angle to ggulch, very steep and contained by sheer cliffs most of its way. Hiking it is actually easier than it looks. You may have to walk thru sage flats just above ggulch if streambed is difficult.

COMMENTS: 12 mile canyon is a very striking in/out, perhaps most efficient I have ever used. One could almost say it makes a 'bold statement'. I saw no signs anyone had ever used it until I neared top. To digress: 24 Mar, '01 I hiked down 9 mile canyon and saw no signs of recent human travel. After photo-oping in ggulch both upcanyon and down, I elected to try 12 mile as an exit. I had scouted it from below earlier and had marked its bottom as doable. I could not see enough to know if it went. I started up it at 4pm and knew if it did not go I would be hard pressed to return to 9 mile, climb out and return to my car before dark, not to mention very tired.

My dogs did not seem too reluctant; many times they can smell that a coyote has used a route. I saw no coyote scat until hi up, and felt some hopeful relief. Soon, I could see biggest problem 'went'. Above at a stepup, someone had stacked rocks almost 3 feet hi; about 60 feet away were two logs as ladder. I did not care to try and boost my dogs up this and decided to look for another way. I followed a wide ledge *cr* around perhaps 100 yards or less, and found several very easy ways for my dogs and I. I have to shake my head at idiocy of people thinking an obvious route is only way. I have seen this before in several other canyons. Perhaps an ability to council yourself to look around before trying hardest route comes with experience, perhaps it separates slickrock hikers from rest.

WATER: I do not remember seeing any.

ATTRACTIONS: very scenic and short canyon, makes one part of a very nice loop combined with 9 Mile Canyon.

* * *

5) COYOTE CANYON: is a *cl* [east] side medium length tributary of ggulch @12.8 miles, just upcanyon from Shieks. Most people come into its lower end in search of water at its probably permanent spring. It goes via a southside talus/jp slope, its bottom is mostly easy hiking. With care, ok for a novice hiker adept at routefinding, with other hikers; coming out Coyote [as one part of a loop hike] is easier.

MAPS: Cedar Mesa N 7.5 covers its eastern upperend; Pollys Pasture covers it at ggulch. It is labeled on TI map but not topo. Use TI #706 also.

GETTING THERE: drive to Shieks C parking lot; just north of 24mm Hwy 261 turn west onto SJ251 Shieks Flat road. In about 2 miles road goes south, about 1 mile later turn right at a fork and drive to end. Sign, register and a cute campsite nearby. Look for a faint closed road going north and follow it for about a mile. Actually, when it seemed to turn west I followed a cow trail north. You could also park where main road makes its turn south, but I saw few signs others do this.

HIKING COYOTE C: is quite easy once you get down. There is a very dramatic impassable dropoff similar to that in Slickhorn #1. Look for a possible faint trail and/or cairns, tho I saw neither. I took a *cl* talus/jp slope closest to dropoff [southside], and there may be another further around downcanyon. Coyote is similar to Shangri La as it is flat and open. There is more of a trail in lower section as hikers come in for water.

WATER: a usually reliable spring about .4 mile upcanyon from ggulch.

ATTRACTIONS: Coyote is scenic, sort of easier than Shieks C, and makes a nice half of a loop, with perhaps up or downcanyon explorations in ggulch, and Shieks as other half. The Thumb is between Coyote and Shieks Canyons.

* * *

6) SHIEKS CANYON: is a *cl* [east] side canyon at 14.2 miles in ggulch. It is not as popular as Bullet C. as an in/out to ggulch, and is as rough as Todie C for a short distance only. Ok for novices accompanied by more experienced hikers.

MAPS: Pollys Pasture 7.5 covers most of it; Cedar Mesa N covers eastern third. Use TI #706 also.

GETTING THERE: Turn west at 24.2mm Hwy 261 onto Coyote Flat road, SJ251. Can get impassable when very wet. It goes west almost two miles then curves south. After about a mile take right fork [west]. Left fork goes over to Bullet parking lot [about 1.5 mile]. Mostly an easy 2wd road, maintained by SJ county, until it goes thru some slickrock humps which you can now detour easily. Road ends shortly after in a picnic/camping area with BLM sign and register box, and cute campsite in trees.

HIKING SHIEKS C: Basically, follow nearby gully and it gradually begins to take form as a canyon. It deepens rapidly and abruptly into a full-blown canyon. There are 4 or 5 dropoffs to detour. First 2 try *cl*, next *cr* and last you drop down a very steep and flaky conglomerate slope, *cr*. As you near [soon after it deepens] ggulch, there is a shallow saddle *cr* which leads into ggulch, but you must use a log ladder to get down an 8 foot cliff. Soon after this saddle hiking in Shieks gets easier anyway, and within minutes you are in ggulch.

I have combined Shieks with Bullet for a dayhike loop and/or Coyote C. A nasty detour at last dropoff is easier going down than up, tho I have been both ways thru it.

WATER: a very reliable spring [even in dry years] about .2 mile upcanyon from ggulch.

ATTRACTIONS: there are a few isolated upper sites. More popular, and why there is more of a trail in lower end, is Green Mask site. This is next to a spring and is in most hiking guide books about Cedar Mesa. A small ruin, which is best left alone, as a note in an ammo box clarifies, is crumbling away nearby. Actual Green Mask is hi overhead on a rock face above some boulders, and is only about 8" high. Other interesting rock art is adjacent. Makes a great loop hike with Bullet or Coyote Canyon.

COMMENTS: Two Durango ranchers, Charles McLoyd and C.C. Graham in 1890-91 systematically looted many area ruins, leaving their names written here [they were contemporaries of Wetherills]. Their actions [not then criminal] probably prompted 1906 Antiquities Act protecting art, artifacts, and ruins. There are several books which discuss these early explorations, most notably "Cowboys and Cave Dwellers" by Fred Blackburn.

* * *

7) BULLET CANYON: is a *cl* [east] side tributary of ggulch, perhaps single most popular one, at 15.6 miles. Many hikers come in ggulch at Kane and exit at Bullet several days later. Upper part of Bullet gets rugged, and rough, but so many people go thru there is an obvious trail.

It is a good introductory hike for novice canyon-country hikers, preferably not solo. As a dayhike it is unbeatable; Perfect Kiva and Jailhouse Ruin are within reach of a strong hiker.

MAPS: Cedar Mesa N 7.5 covers its head; Pollys Pasture 7.5 covers it at ggulch. Use TI #706 also.

GETTING THERE: @ 21.75mm, Hwy 261, turn west onto SJ250, trailhead about 1 mile off hwy. There are signs on hwy for 'Bullet C'.

HIKING BULLET C: Trail follows rim, *cr*, for about ..2 mile, then drops in. Bullet starts bland and shallow, but gets interesting rapidly. At first small falls, you make minor detours and walk right down slickrock gully. At end of this stretch, you drop off a small step and stay *cr*. There is one long detour, hi on *cr* which some hikers miss or seem to prefer climbing thru a rock garden. Later, Bullet gets flat and open, and hiking is easier.

WATER: a very reliable spring [even in dry years] 2.2 miles upcanyon from ggulch, known as Jailhouse Spring on TI map. There are other smaller ones upcanyon in wetter years, in streambed.

ATTRACTIONS: most popular sites perhaps in all of ggulch are Perfect Kiva and Jailhouse Ruin, both marked on TI map; former is up a short side canyon on northside and a cairned trail climbs slickrock south of it, then crosses into an alcove. Jailhouse Ruin is in plain sight. Bullet is a very scenic and classic Cedar Mesa canyon; overall it is moderately easy to hike and has some water.

* * *

8) GREEN HOUSE CANYON: is a *cr* [north] side canyon of ggulch at 17.6 miles approx. It does not go thru to ggulch. Upper end is shallow and cow country until it entrenches close to ggulch. Lower end is popular and relatively easy walking.

MAPS: Pollys Pasture 7.5 covers it all. Use TI #706 also.

GETTING THERE: @ 88.6mm [or 88.3], Hwy 95, SJ231a heads south and deadends after 4.2 miles at a capped drill hole site. Immediately after gate next to hwy, go left at 'y'. This road can be impassable if very wet.1997 version of TI #706 map has this road marked incorrectly, it skirts closely Wilderness Area Boundary, and goes directly to drill hole site which is next to '6408' elev.

HIKING GREEN HOUSE C: from drill hole site walk SE staying slope-right on a long ridge, then pick a spot and enter it. Green House is fairly easy hiking until you get to an impassable dropoff not far upcanyon from ggulch.

WATER: a usually reliable spring [may disappear in dry years] .2 mile upcanyon from ggulch.

ATTRACTIONS: it is scenic, easy hiking and most people probably come in from ggulch for water.

* * *

9) STEP AND PINE CANYONS: are really two forks of same *cr* [north] side canyon of ggulch. They begin just south of Hwy 95, south of NBNM, @19.5. Some few hikers come in from ggulch, maybe to see lower attractions. Both 'go' although Pine is not as wide nor easy as Step. Neither are viable in/out routes to ggulch due to remote access. They are rough in places, and detours are often required, not for solo novice hikers.

MAPS: Pollys Pasture 7.5 covers core of these canyons. Kane Gulch 7.5, and Mossback Butte 7.5 cover remainder. Use TI #706 also.

GETTING THERE: not easy. Hiking upcanyon is moderately difficult. Access from above is difficult. From east: 87.3mm on Hwy 95, turn south. There is a long strip of pavement alongside highway here. Road is 2wd for 2.6 miles, maintained occasionally. Then road degrades to severe 4wd where route finding is problematical; very few people drive this 4wd track. This is part of old Mormon Trail and joins Hwy 276 at 85.7. Its last westernmost 1 mile is ok for hi-clearance 2wd if dry. For Pine, park about 1.7 mile from eastern end and hike southeast.

Alternative: for upper Pine, use Drill Hole road off Hwy 95, at 88.6mm. [SJ231a] Hike west from drill hole site which is 4 miles from pavement [just south of pavement, turn left at 'y', pass another rd to east, go on south.] For Step, either hike along Mormon Trail from either end, or drive to its head. This is closer from west, tho after first mile off Hwy 276, is worst part of Mormon Trail. Requires hi-clearance 4wd with sturdy tires, non-novice driver, patience, and even walking to find route; recent heavy rains may necessitate use of a shovel to fill in erosion gullies.

HIKING STEP: after Step C entrenches [coming from head] there are several dropoffs to negotiate. One, you can slither thru, and coming back up it is a bit of a grunt [getting traction]. Lower and bigger dropoff you climb up *cl*, around a ways and look for a skinny log 'ladder' at a 5 foot drop. I have lowered my dogs here easily. In upper canyon there is a nice historic horse camp with grain box, plenty of trash, etc.

HIKING PINE: upper Pine cliffs out where it deepens and is probably impassable. But, just east of S16, and near a small gully is an old trail *cr*. Above, as a landmark, look for a small distinctive white sandstone cone shaped hill. In this area, on *cl*, is a talus slope that looked doable [if coming from drill hole]. Down where Pine joins Step it is thrashy and slow going, with not much of a trail. This does not last long.

WATER: in Step C, .8 mile upcanyon from ggulch is Necklace Spg. There are other smaller springs upcanyon from Pine/Step C in both canyons probably reliable only in wet years.

ATTRACTIONS: it is wild and quiet with few hikers visiting here. I saw my first and so far only mountain lion in upper Step. There are some Anasazi sites here, most notably fine rock art at its mouth. It is possible to do both canyons as a long dayhike, or combined with Dripping, tho perhaps camping makes more sense.

* * *

10) 20.5 MILE CANYON: is a *cl* [south] side canyon of ggulch @20.5 miles approx. This canyon could easily be called 'Short Canyon' or, better yet 'Thrash You Canyon'. It does go, reluctantly. It is bouldery, brushy, has one major dropoff, not for solo novice hikers. Route-finding skills necessary.

MAPS: Pollys Pasture 7.5 covers it. Also use TI #706.

GETTING THERE: moderately easy. Use Slickhorn Rd., as if going to Govt. Trail. At 19.1mm Hwy 261, go west on SJ245 [Slickhorn Rd]. Immediately, you come to a cattle guard where BLM register is. One mile from pavement main road goes left. 2.5 miles from hwy turn right @ sign for Govt. Trail [stay on SJ245]; 4.7 miles from hwy turn right again onto a faint road. This road is ok for hi-clearance 2wd vehicles if dry and is blocked off by BLM after 1.8 miles by some signs and a log. It continues on to a stock pond and ends after 1.5 miles [total of 8 miles from highway].

HIKING 20.5 MILE CANYON: From where road ends, follow a relatively obvious cow trail across a nearby drainage, then NNW. It crosses a shallow divide, then enters a long, wide and shallow dry valley which slopes off towards ggulch. Stay on a *cl* cow trail thru this valley until you begin to reach head of 20.5 mile canyon.

Stay in this drainage. Very soon you step off small dropoffs, and a bland gully becomes a canyon. At only dropoff you cannot step thru, look for a small trail *cl*. It winds about 75 yards along a wide ledge, and goes under a shallow overhang. Just as you leave this overhang, near cliff is a small boulder. Look down and there is a very easy sloping ramp down to a ledge just below you. Follow it less than 100 feet upc and descend down thru some junipers [logs placed for handholds]. Do not get into a hurry, tho, to reach canyon bottom and try to contour downc staying high as long as you can. Then, enjoy boulder gardens/small dropoffs and brush.

ATTRACTIONS: perhaps this canyon's greatest attraction is as access to ggulch. It generally takes about 1:30 hours to get to head of 20.5 mile canyon and another 1/2 hour down to ggulch. From there you can hike upcanyon to Step C. in about an hour, or downcanyon to Dripping C. There is one site in 20.5 mile canyon quite visible when you detour biggest dropoff. *Do not try to climb up into upper section!* Anyone struggling to do this may inadvertently grab already shaky walls and cause more damage. Vue and photo it from a distance, please.

* * *

11) DRIPPING CANYON: is a *cr* [north] side canyon ggulch @ 22.3 miles. It goes thru to ggulch, is moderately rugged, has one major dropoff, is scenic, and not for solo novice hikers.

MAPS: Pollys Pasture 7.5 covers most of it; Moss Back Butte 7.5 covers remainder. Use TI #706 also.

GETTING THERE: it can be accessed from Mormon Trail. @ 85.7mm Hwy 276 turn east on a barely visible road, look for a small BLM sign. Park after 1 mile approx. at edge of Cow Tank C. Hike across from edge of Cow Tank C, or with sturdy 4wd and experienced driver continue on to Dripping C, which is next major drainage. This road is VERY ROUGH. Some people may hike in from this road's east end. @ 87.3mm on Hwy 95 turn south onto a maintained dirt road. After about 2.5 miles west it degrades into severe 4wd.

HIKING DRIPPING CANYON: is harder to get to than it is to hike. It is pleasantly easy, and scenic, with one significant dropoff and several smaller ones. I usually park my vehicle next to Cow Tank C. and sagewhack across to Dripping C and enter where 'canyon' printed on TI map ends [there is a distinctive 'rock island' next to streambed]. Starting here there are 3 dropoffs close together, but if you follow a small trail *cr* and stay out of inner gorge, you miss all and then descend thru a slickrock slide. Downcanyon there is a seemingly impassable dropoff: skirt it *cr* along a narrow ledge to a talus/juniper slope, which my dogs have done with my help. NOT FOR BEGINNERS, hiking alone. I have also driven on 4WD trail and hiked further up in Dripping. There are other smaller dropoffs.

LOOP HIKE: I have combined Dripping C with Step for a long but very nice dayhike loop. This takes a certain amount of stamina, and I recommend parking at Dripping and hiking over to Step, then coming back out Dripping [bushwhacking and route-finding are easier when fresh than tired]. Of course with two vehicles this is easier. And if you cannot drive old Mormon Trail, you might want to multi-day hike it.

WATER: a usually reliable spring .8 mile upcanyon from ggulch, except possibly in dry years [such as 2002]. Other smaller springs upcanyon, also may disappear in dry years.

ATTRACTIONS: all these tributaries to ggulch are quiet, scenic, relatively easy hiking [compared to Shieks or upper Bullet]. I have come back after several months and never seen fresh footprints. Dripping C, Cow Tank C, and Step C all have nice rock art panels just up from ggulch.

* * *

12) COW TANK CANYON: is a *cr* [north] side canyon of ggulch @ 22.8, but it does not now go thru to ggulch [w/o a rope]. A short distance upcanyon from ggulch a pouroff years ago suffered a flashflood and now is about 30 feet high.

HIKING UPPER COW TANK CANYON: if coming

into upper Cow Tank C it is easy and shallow. It gradually deepens just before an impassable dropoff. Blackburn and others say that years ago this dropoff was much lower before a flood, and perhaps used as part of a cross-ggulch trail by horse thieves 100+ years ago.

WATER: a spring marked on TI map, .8 mile upcanyon from ggulch is now unreachable. There is a small spring below pouroff, usually reliable except probably in dry years.

ATTRACTIONS: there is a small rock art panel near ggulch.

* * *

13) POLLYS CANYON: is a *cl* [east] side canyon of ggulch at 26 miles approx. It is just upcanyon from Government Trail. Perhaps most hikers go up it to get water at its fine spring. It forks into two 1.5 mile branches and both do go.

MAPS: Pollys Pasture 7.5 covers it all. Use TI #706 also.

GETTING THERE: *Option A:* easiest is to drive to Govt. Trail parking lot and hike from there. Use Slickhorn road: @19.1mm, Hwy 261, turn west onto SJ245. One mile from hwy follow main road left. 2.6 miles from hwy, turn right [sign for Govt. Trail]. 5.5 miles from hwy, turn right at 'Y'. 7.4 miles from hwy is turnoff to Govt. Trail, turn north and drive to end. Road is 1.5 miles to end, and gets rough, requiring a medium clearance vehicle, or a good driver. Some hikers park before last .2 mi., as road gets very rocky, and ledgy. If you can see a stock pond w/cottonwoods, that is parking area.

Option B: follow above directions, except @4.6 miles from hwy turn north onto a faint road which is blocked off after 2 miles.

GETTING STARTED: from either option you can in/out either upper fork. Hiking over to north fork takes a bit longer from *Option A*, but is scenic. Hike due east until soon you get to Pollys. If it is too cliffy where you come to it, hike upcanyon. Just below a dropoff, where canyon is shallow, are two constructed horse trails *cl* that will get you into inner gorge.

Option B: follow road around and/or follow any gully that deepens and find a route. I have yet to hike this extreme upper end of north fork Pollys. If you want to head for north fork, walk a little further upcanyon until you find a way across. There is a guard tower ruin nearby.

HIKING POLLYS C: North [East] Fork Pollys: it is easy to get into where still shallow, harder downcanyon. Except for several boulder blocks, one of which you can sort of detour *cl* or slither around thru hiking is relatively easy. It is wider and less brushy than south fork.

South [West] Fork Pollys: there are a few brushy/ boulder detours in lower end near springs, only 2 small dropoffs at head [downcanyon one you can climb thru in 2 places]. After upper forks join hiking is quite easy with standard zigzags. It took me 2-3 hours to hike up Pollys and across to my vehicle using south fork, my first time including photo-op stops.

WATER: a usually reliable spring 1 mile upcanyon from ggulch; other smaller ones upcanyon in both forks may disappear in dry years.

ATTRACTIONS: there are a few sites, possibly some rock art. It may not be a faster access than Govt. Trail, undoubtedly it is more interesting. Then again, vues from flats along Govt. Trail are spectacular. I would recommend it as one half of a dayhike loop to Big Man panel; say hike down Pollys and up to Big Man panel, then back out govt. trail when you are tired and feel like an easy plod. This makes a long and very interesting dayhike.

PERSONAL EXPERIENCES: my first time in I hiked in govt. trail, up to Big Man panel, then back to Pollys C. I had no idea if it would go, and elected to take fork closest to parking lot. I shot a GPS location at my car before starting. I was pushing my envelope of daylite-remaining time as I headed upcanyon. One helpful clue was plenty of bighorn tracks and some one-way footprints ahead of me as I started into south fork. I was pleasantly surprised at how easy it went, and did not even mind two little stepups. When I topped out, using a horse trail, I walked over to a sandstone hump and pulled out my GPS. Faster than I could get a good 'goto', tho, I saw cottonwoods near parking lot. Barely 15 minutes got me there.

* * *

14) GOVERNMENT TRAIL: is a well constructed trail into ggulch across from Pollys Island @26.2 miles. Approach is a bit long across a now-closed road, and even tho Govt. Trail is old, it is in excellent condition. According to one source Butch Cassidy's gang used to cross ggulch near here, maybe using Collins C and Pollys C. Excellent for solo novice hikers, once you find trail, route-finding is not needed.

MAPS: Pollys Pasture 7.5 covers it all. Use TI #706 also.

GETTING THERE: use Slickhorn road: @19.1mm, Hwy 261, turn west onto SJ245. One mile from highway follow main road left. 2.6 miles from hwy, turn right [sign for Govt. Trail]. 5.5 miles from hwy, turn right at 'Y'. 7.4 miles from hwy is turnoff to Govt. Trail, turn north and drive to end. Road is 1.5 miles to parking lot, and gets rough, requiring a medium clearance vehicle, and a good driver. Some hikers park before last .2 mi., as road gets very rocky, and ledgy. If you can see a stock pond with cottonwoods, that is parking lot.

HIKING GOVT. TRAIL: is easy, tho you hike 3 miles over a now-closed road just to get to canyon. It is a well-maintained short descent into ggulch. Trail starts by crossing a dam for a stock pond near parking area.

WATER: None, except a stock pond at trailhead which is low or dry in some years. Some years there is water in ggulch just below where trail enters. Water upcanyon in Pollys C, about 1 mile. After a good rainstorm you may find slickrock pools near ggulch.

ATTRACTIONS: you can vue Pollys Island, hike upcanyon to Big Man panel, or downcanyon in ggulch. A quite popular entrance to ggulch. Can be combined with Deer C for a super dayhike loop, tho route-finding is necessary.

* * *

15) DEER CANYON: is a *cl* [east] side short side canyon of ggulch @31 miles. It has a good spring about .5 miles in, and perhaps this is as far as most hikers go. It does go; one way is easy, one a lot harder. If using a gully in/out it is moderately rugged, bottom is mildly bouldery and brushy. Not for solo novice hikers [as an in/out].

MAPS: Pollys Pasture 7.5 covers its eastern upper end; Red House Spring covers it at ggulch. It is labeled on TI map, not on topo. Use TI #706 also.

GETTING THERE: use Govt. Trail parking area; @19.1mm, Hwy 261, turn west onto SJ245, Slickhorn road. One mile from hwy follow main road left. 2.6 miles from hwy, turn right [sign for govt. trail]. 5.5 miles from hwy, turn right at 'Y'. 7.4 miles from hwy is turnoff [sign] to Govt. Trail. *Option A:* park at Govt. Trail parking lot.
Option B: continue for about 2 miles; I have parked near a gated fence.

HIKING DEER CANYON: Deer has two main forks with two arms of each. Two northern ones, #1 and #2, are easily reached from Govt. Trail. Neither goes w/o a rope. Two southern arms are close to Option B above. Both have dropoffs, #4 if counting from N, clockwise to S, ends in an impassable dropoff. Just upcanyon from this dropoff, in #3, is a *cl* slickrock slope which gets you into #3 below another dropoff. Below this is a steep boulder garden, and once out of it walking is somewhat easier.

BEST: in south fork, just upcanyon [south] from its confluence with north fork of Deer, is a *cr* gully with a boulder fall in it [east side of Deer C]. You can easily work up this boulder/talus slope, there is even a trail leading to it from below. At an upper dropoff, there is a talus/juniper slope about 20 foot *cr*. Actually it is easier to use a steep slickrock slope *cr* of this gully for part of route. I recently went back up this route in 20 minutes. To get to it, park at govt. trail parking lot, and hike west along a long ridge. When you get to Deer, scout around until you find this gully.

WATER: there is a usually reliable spring where Deer's two forks split, and one in each, below their respective pouroffs. In dry years these may all disappear, but I think North fork spring is more reliable.

ATTRACTIONS: is not overly difficult as an in/out to this section of ggulch, and charming enough by itself. There are a few sites in ggulch nearby. It makes one-half of a fine loop dayhike with Govt. Trail.

* * *

16) COLLINS TRAIL: Collins C is a *cr* [west] side canyon with a constructed horse trail thru it, @36 miles. *No dogs, horses or other pack animals allowed in ggulch below Collins C.* Actually, it is last easily accessible entrance to ggulch. Fewer hikers come to ggulch's lower end than upper, and some use Collins Trail as one end of a loop hike. It is fairly easy hiking, tho rugged, along an obvious trail. Fine for solo novice hikers, no particular route-finding needed Please close a flimsy wooden gate behind you to keep cattle out.

MAPS: Red House Spring 7.5 covers it all. Use TI #706 also.

GETTING THERE: @ 84.5mm Hwy 276 turn east at sign for Collins onto SJ260. Turn right at a 'y' about 2.3 miles from pavement, no sign there; left fork goes to a drillhole site. It is 6.5 miles from hwy to trailhead. Usually this road gets less rain/snow than ones higher up on Cedar Mesa.

HIKING COLLINS C: trail is well cairned, and was constructed with dynamite for livestock access. Supposedly it is 2 miles to ggulch. In one overhang, *cl*, there is remains of a long-used horse camp, with a large grain box. Generally it takes me 45 minutes to hike to ggulch. I have hiked up to Bannister Ruin in 2:30 hours from trailhead, with stops to photo-op.

WATER: sometimes there is water in streambed, and a large pool below one pouroff. In ggulch there is usually water at Narrows [it dried up in 2002].

ATTRACTIONS: fewer people come into lower ggulch, it is quiet, abounds in animal tracks, there is some water and it is scenic. There are a few scattered sites. Some people ride horses into ggulch thru Collins, then go upcanyon in ggulch. Bannister Ruin [see TI map] is nearby, upcanyon.

COMMENTS: Re a conversation with a BLM ranger, road past Collins was temporarily sort of open in 1999. That is, SJ county was fighting to open it up, and BLM was allowing some usage of it until, I guess, they decided what to do. I used it several times. In Dec, 2000 road was officially closed to motorized vehicles. There is now a locked gate. I suppose a mtn bike/hike combo is needed to access side canyons further down this road. See 'Redman-Wired C.' and 'Widow's Walk' paragraphs.

SIDE CANYONS: Late in Jan, '01 I hiked up a shallow side canyon just downcanyon, *cl*, from trailhead for about a mile, following cattle trails. Next, I hiked over a ridge into north fork of sidecanyon which enters Collins C. a little ways above ggulch. I saw no way down it w/o a rope, and hiked over into next fork. In this south fork there are two other terminal forks. Southern of these has 1 skimpy route down, tho my dogs were coaxed into it. Apparently others have used this, as I saw a faint trail. This route is about 100 feet *cl* of main drainage, drops down by a small tree, and you have to walk around a bulgy and slopey friction pitch, and jump down 2 or 3 feet. Going up would require trust in your vibram soles. Not for faint of heart, or beginners.

It did not take me long to thrash my way down into Collins C., where I took a short break. However, not done 'having fun', I immediately climbed into a little slickrocky gully, *cl*, maybe 200 yards downcanyon. It is barely shown on TI map. Getting into it was slightly more of a challenge than getting up it. Only one further stepup required a use of a rock pile and a modified 'mantle' technique; I contoured around into False Trail C.

I suppose False Trail C [next *cr* side canyon, of ggulch, upcanyon from Collins C] is named for hikers thinking it was really Collins C., tho there is no real comparison. I saw a definite route down False Trail C., tho above me it totally cliffs out. I contoured around further upcanyon, above ggulch, towards yet another slickrock gully. But, there is a 30 foot nasty and exposed traverse both hi and low to enter this canyon which with dogs was certainly impossible [may not be possible anyway]. I returned into False Trail C. and dropped down it into ggulch, then plodded back up Collins to my car. I saw no sites in any of these sidecanyons.

RIMWALK: Nov, 2002 I rimwalked from Collins parking area along Collins and ggulch as far as Water C confluence. Most of this walk is on a flat, wide ledge of slickrock and there are two parallel trails most of way. One is human formed, other is likely cattle formed. It is a super-easy and scenic hike, and only in a few places did I have to change ledges or dodge around huge boulder blocks. A few years ago some clown on a dirtbike had driven all over this country, trying to get down into ggulch, and his tracks are evident everywhere. This is main reason BLM has installed a locked gate on continuation of road past Collins parking area, and other areas.

When I came back, I crossed over to a shallow drainage which feeds into Red Man C, found a cow trail, and eventually came to a now-closed ranch road which comes into this drainage. I followed that road back to my pickup, taking only 1:20 to return. This loop hike took less than 5:30 hours. One could easily use this road to get to Redman or Rope Canyons, hike into ggulch, explore further downcanyon, and return via Collins C, thus making an interesting loop hike, and obviously a long dayhike.

* * *

17) SLIDEROCK CANYON: is a *cl* [east] side canyon @37.8 approx. It is short, moderately steep and goes with minor difficulties. It is first *cl* canyon down from Collins. A circled '38' designating Bannister Spring on TI map is next to its head. This is my unofficial name only, I have not seen it named on any maps. Not overly difficult, with caution, and not for solo novice hikers.

MAPS: Red House Spring 7.5 covers it all. Use TI #706 also.

GETTING THERE: on same road for Govt. Trail. At 19.1mm Hwy 261, go west on SJ245 [Slickhorn Rd]. One mile from pavement go left on main road. 2.6 miles from hwy turn right [sign for Govt. Trail]; 5.5 miles from hwy stay right. Follow almost to end 11.5 miles from hwy. I actually park where this road makes a sharp turn to south at a now-closed spur road, where there are [sometimes] several salt blocks for cattle, and a wand-type sign reads 'Closed to Motor Vehicles'.

HIKING SLIDEROCK: hike NW about 1.5 miles, using one of several cattle trails. For landmarks I use a little sandstone dome, then aim for some undercut cliffs. Sliderock is just west of these cliffs. There is another ridge west of these little cliffs which separates Sliderock C from Water C. When you finally get there try southern of two short upper forks. It is pleasantly easy to hike, mostly slickrock tho there is one small dropoff to detour, *cl* about 200 feet, several minor boulder falls, and two slideoffs. A name comes to mind, Sliderock Canyon, because unless you use detours at both slideoffs, you must slide down two very short convex chutes in slickrock.

One is only about 6' long, other a little less, but easier to go down than up. I have had to detour *cr* upper chute using a slab for handholds when tired and going upcanyon. Lower of two has a long *cr* detour using a sloping ledge system and, downcanyon, a talus/juniper slope. Recently I brought along a rope for assistance. With two people and about 10 feet of rope going up these slideoffs would be easy. If alone and wanting rope help when returning same way, use a 50 foot rope on upper slideoff, and about a 100 footer on lower [only because tie-downs are remote]. A thin handline rope [5mm] is fine, or use detours instead.

About 90% of Sliderock's length you walk on pretty clean slickrock, and mostly it slopes gently down to ggulch. Last .25 miles is flat and easier yet. There can be iced over water in winter, making hiking tricky or even impossible. Generally it takes about 1:30 to get to ggulch.

WATER: minimal, unless rain or snow meltoff. Sometimes I find some water below one slideoff in a small pool, where there is a skinny ledge you can use to skirt this pool. There is usually water in a spring just upcanyon from Water C, usually in Water C also.

ATTRACTIONS: it is a very nice little canyon and provides a relatively easy in/out to ggulch. Also it is quite fun to hike for its own sake. It is not very practical as part of a loop dayhike, multi-day is better--e.g. combine with Shangri La C.

* * *

18) SHORTCUT CANYON: is a *cr* [north] side canyon @39 miles approx.; it is first major *cr* side canyon downcanyon from Narrows. This is my unofficial name only, I have not seen it named on any maps. Rough, bouldery, brushy, several stepups to detour, not for solo novice hikers.

MAPS: Red House Spring 7.5 covers it all. Use TI #706 also.

GETTING THERE: you can no longer drive near its head; park at Collins C trailhead, either rimwalk *cr* Collins, or follow an old road past parking lot [closed by a gate] which cuts across country away from ggulch.

HIKING SHORTCUT: several times I have come out this short and steep side canyon rather than return up ggulch and Collins to my car. It starts out from ggulch a bit thrashy and a little bouldery but soon mellows and gets easy. A few stepups above cause you to route-find a bit. Above are very fine vues of ggulch, rincon behind Narrows and nearby under a sandstone hoodoo is a slabsided ruin, not much of which remains. To return to trailhead, merely rimwalk Collins upcanyon on one of several comfortable and wide ledges; a very scenic hike.

WATER: minimal, unless rain or meltoff, tho I have seen a small amount in some years.

ATTRACTIONS: scenic upper rims, provides a shortcut back to Collins C trailhead from ggulch.

*   *   *

19) WATER CANYON: is a *cl* side canyon of ggulch at 41.5 miles [approx]. It is a complex canyon system, moderately long, and is not an expedient in/out. It goes only two ways that I know of and I describe these below. Due to its remoteness and difficulty I recommend exploring its upper forks; only expert hikers should attempt its entire length. When I finally found a standard route thru it, it took me 2:15 hours to get to ggulch [including a break and route-finding]. It has several dropoffs and boulder gardens, not much trail, sections are easy, other sections are slow-going. It has a little rock art, and a very few rubbly ruins. I saw no signs of Anasazi Steps anywhere in Water C.

MAPS: Red House Spring 7.5 covers it all. Use TI map #706 also.

GETTING THERE: Relatively easy if roads dry. Use Slickhorn road: @19.1mm, Hwy 261, turn west onto SJ245. One mile from hwy follow main road left. 2.6 miles from hwy, turn right [sign for govt. trail]. 5.5 miles from hwy, stay right at 'Y'. 7.4 miles from hwy is turnoff to Gov. trail, stay straight [left] to its end at a drill hole site, 12.2 from hwy [near its end, main road goes west at a small fork].

HIKING WATER C: It has two main upper forks which divide, forming 4 distinct canyons, plus another further south [5 in all]. Most of these forks have multiple impassable dropoffs. I list two routes, without GPS data [one in #4, one in #5].

#4 WATER C ROUTE: From a capped drill hole site walk WSW towards an E pointing sidecanyon [of longest main canyon--#4 if counting clockwise from N--which points towards a '5403T' elevation on quad map] and there is now an obvious trail. If you get to a fork where you see a cairn near a dropoff and only way down is to jump onto a large boulder then scramble down, *do not proceed*, it is later impassable, instead climb up, head south over a low ridge to correct sidefork. There is a cairn in streambed.

Continue down this sidefork. You'll come to a little dropoff with a stack of rocks to step onto. Soon this sidefork joins main canyon [#4] at another dropoff. Go *cl* and use two stout leaning logs as ladder--I lowered my pack on a short rope. Further downc perhaps ½ mile is another dropoff. Walk down streambed past a *cr* cliff, then go across a *cr* slickrock ramp to top of a leaning attached tower and work downc of it--another log helps for last 4 feet. This area is hardest to get thru due to exposure--what I find helpful is to turn and face slickrock and carefully step down to a skinny ledge, then walk upright over to tower route--this would be impassable if icy.

Soon after you come to a sidecanyon, #3, and obvious deer-bighorn trails. When you get to next canyon-confluence, #1 & #2, it almost looks like you're in GG finally. Immediately downc is a boulder garden. A faint animal trail works thru colluvial boulders *cr* which I used then descended into streambed and got onto a flat ledge *cl*, followed for about 150 yards, then slid down two leaning trees to easy trails, it's only another 10 minutes or less to GG.

#5 WATER C ROUTE: First cl fork [when coming up from ggulch], has a barely do-able route [so I've heard]. At first dropoff, go *cr* up a talus slope, and across a ledge. Soon you come to another dropoff. Some hikers have leaned a log *cl* for a ladder. This leads to a further very steep slickrock slope to a ledge system. Reportedly you will encounter further difficulties above. I have not done this route, thus do not recommend it at all. In Dec, '01 I scouted it from above, except for a first topcliff-ledge break and I saw only one possible place for it but did not go close.

Mostly I have entered lower Water C from ggulch, hiking down from other in/outs. It was not until Feb, 2003 that I finally followed another hiker's footprints and figured out Water C for myself.

WATER: Most years there is water in lower end, near ggulch, and further upc.

ATTRACTIONS: Its upper forks are interesting until dropoffs, scenery is complex with many domes, hoodoos, balancing rocks, etc. There is probably year-round water in its lower end, and some rock art. Ann Zwinger, in "Wind in the Rock" writes about hiking into Water C on a guided hiking trip thru ggulch in 70's. They were looking for water, and had to hike further up to a second spring before finding any. Of course she doesn't mention it by name.

You can combine Water C with Shangri La C or

Sliderock C for interesting loop hikes; combine it with Rope C, Red Man C, or Shortcut C for a ggulch traverse, with two cars; there are several other interesting routes in that area not described in this book.

* * *

20) RED MAN CANYON: is a *cr* [west] short side canyon @42.3 mile ggulch and is labeled on TI map. Not for solo novice hikers.

MAPS: Red House Spring 7.5 covers it completely. Use TI #706 also.

GETTING THERE: you can no longer drive near its head, park at Collins C trailhead. A faint 4wd road leaves parking lot and continues south across open grazing land; it ends about a mile past Rope C. BLM has installed a locked gate to bar vehicular access to this road.

STARTING OUT: during winter of 1999-2000 this road was open. I drove on it twice, parked and hiked further. Now, you will have a long and not very exciting plod unless you either bring a mountain bike or do it as a multi-day. There is not much elevation gain/loss, road is sandy in spots, and biking may be a chore. In 2002 I hiked from near Red Man C to Collins C Trailhead in 1:20 hours.

HIKING REDMAN C: I scouted Redman from above, and it looked like it goes. A subsequent conversation with a BLM ranger indicates that it does go with some slithering down thru some boulders. I glanced up into its mouth while hiking by, and it looks only moderately choked with boulders. A rope and companion would come in handy.

WATER: minimal if any; I have yet to hike thru it.

ATTRACTIONS: mostly as a not-too-easy in/out to ggulch; could be used as one part of a loop hike. There is a red pictograph of an anthromorph [man] at its confluence with ggulch.

* * *

21) ROPE C: is next *cr* [west] short side canyon @ 42.7 mile, approx., and is not labeled on TI map, nor on 7.5 topos. It is remote and steep and probably more people hike up from ggulch than hike cross-country to Rope C. There is a 3-strand piece of electric wire tied to a tree at its major dropoff, but an alternative route exists. Not for solo novice hikers.

MAPS: Red House Spring 7.5 covers it completely. Use TI #706 also.

HIKING ROPE C: it is an easier access than Red Man C. I believe its name comes from first people to in/out it by tying a rope to a stout juniper and dropping down a not quite vertical dropoff. Now there is a 3 strand electrical wire with parts of its outer insulation frayed. Gloves would be handy, but I think BLM should remove this unsightly mess [it is coiled all over].

ALTERNATIVE: rather than testing strength of this wire, pick a ledge *cr* which is comfortable to rimwalk downcanyon; you will rimwalk to near its mouth.

Pass above 1 house size boulder which you cannot get to, another you can but cannot climb down without a log or rope, then 2 house size boulders, one of which leans cutely against other. Barely 150 feet past this is a break in cliff below you. Jump across a 3' gap [I brought along a 5' log on my return and left here] onto another boulder, and climb down to a wide ledge. Follow this ledge back under leaning boulders and back upcanyon towards 'wired falls'. It seems like you cannot continue, but dropping down onto a lower ledge, which narrows, leads you easily into streambed. Once there, it is an easy few minutes walk into ggulch.

Just upcanyon, *cr*, from where you enter ggulch is a small area with some few walls standing. It has been dug by pothunters, and my educated guess is that they made an obvious trail above, perhaps they strung electric wire to tree also.

WATER: minimal, only after rain or meltoffs, possibly below pouroff or in ggulch nearby.

ATTRACTIONS: scenic, short, possible to combine with Collins for a loop hike.

* * *

22) SHANGRI LA CANYON: is a *cl* [east] side canyon of ggulch @48.5 miles [approx.]. It is not marked on any map except perhaps in KGRS. It is last *cl* tributary of ggulch before San Juan river. It is remote, rarely visited, not easy to get to or into, and is a bit fancifully named for its reality. It is quiet and inhabited by deer and bighorn at times. Not for solo novice hikers [as access route].

MAPS: Slickhorn Canyon West 7.5 covers it all. Use TI #706 also.

GETTING THERE: not difficult to drive to if roads are dry [hiking to it is another story]. Use Slickhorn road: @19.1mm, Hwy 261, turn west onto SJ245. One mile from hwy follow main road left. 2.6 miles from hwy, turn right [sign for govt. trail]. 5.5 miles from hwy, stay right at 'Y'. 7.4 miles from hwy is turnoff to Govt. Trail, stay straight. Road does go thru some deep sand spots but none are very long. About 12 miles from hwy, road turns back to west, look for a small road going south. This is western end of SJ253a and tho not maintained it is ok for hi clearance 2wd for first mile, then degrades to 4wd. Park somewhere on slickrock about where this road turns east again. There are some nice camping spots thru here.

HIKING SHANGRI LA: orientation can be more of a problem than hiking upper Shangri La. Like Water C, which is just around to northwest, this whole area is broken by gullies, hills, domes, hoodoos, balancing rocks, etc. I have several times taken a wrong route and had to rethink where I was. North fork Shangri La is shallow and easy to hike, and quite similar to West branch of North Slickhorn. However it finally reaches an impassable dropoff [without a rope, gear, and experience]. A gps is handy for orienteering this corner of Cedar Mesa.

Shangri La, main, has basically only one entrance above as far as I know. If and when you find this canyon, you will notice it forms a large cliffed out bowl. There are two medium length upper forks of Shangri La [main]. At head of northern of these two [near '5017' elev. on map], just *cl* of its streambed a deer trail with cairns contours around and down next to a little balancing rock/dome. Below, it drops down a fault line which deer and/or bighorns have turned into a trail. There should be a few cairns. It is fairly straightforward if a little steep and overly efficient.

Once down, walking is extremely easy until near ggulch, as Shangri La is a wide flat canyon. Generally it is 1 hour hike down to ggulch, tho I did not hike last narrow and rockier 1/4 mile my first time. I would not count on finding springs in either fork in summer; only water I saw was runoff; later I found water in springs near ggulch, and at confluence w/ggulch.

REVISIT: in March, '02, I returned to Shangri La Canyon, having entered ggulch upcanyon. After a recent rain, there were plenty of temporary pools, and spring at mouth of S-La had water. When I turned into S-La I found more water, almost continuous upcanyon until somewhere downcanyon from main forks. Most of this will probably dry up in summer. I saw only one faint set of footprints, possibly mine, and lots of bighorn and deer tracks. Again I saw no sites. Lower S-La, above ggulch is bouldery and ledgy, but still easy hiking and this stretch is short. When going upcanyon, northern of two main forks looks merely like a minor sidecanyon, narrow; it does widen and has major animal trails.

WATER: minimal, except after rain or meltoffs, lower springs may be reliable most years.

ATTRACTIONS: Shangri La is quiet, rarely visited, remote and interesting in some ways. Could be combined with an upcanyon in/out for a multi-day loop hike.

SLICKHORN PASTURE ROAD: [SJ253a] here are milages based on coming off SJ245 onto SJ253a east of Govt. Trl. turnoff [driving west]. SJ253a [Slickhorn Pasture road] is maintained for 2.6 miles, then high clearance [real] 4wd. 3.7 miles is where I parked earlier to hike north Slickhorn C and an intersection. Main road goes left. 4.0 miles is another intersection, main road goes hard left [both spur roads go into Slickhorn Pasture gully]. 4.8 miles is a short spur left to a ruin under a 'hat rock' mushroom shaped sandstone mesa. Soon after road enters a sandy gully. A cow trail crosses and climbs gully right. Downgully where road climbs out is very sandy and washed out. I have come down this slope once but not again. Better is to drive downgully .1 or .2 mile where you can thrash over and thru sagebrush and rejoin road. 5.9 miles, if you get that far, is a dry stock pond. Road is difficult to see, but it is used by cattle as a trail west. 7.5 miles is where I parked for a hike [tho I would come in from other end], and you rejoin SJ245 after 8.4 miles. Hardest part is crossing Slickhorn Pasture gully [very sandy sides], and some minor slickrock steps near east end. Any hiker for Slickhorn North could park at end of maintained road, SJ253a. Any hiker for Shangri La can 2wd [with common sense] almost 1 mile from west end.

* * *

23) WIDOWS WALK CANYON: is a *cr* [west] short side canyon to ggulch @50.7 mi. [approx.], or 1 mile up from San Juan R. It can be used as an in/out to lower ggulch. It is not labeled on any map I have seen;that name comes from BLM sources. Ok for novice hikers with caution, if not alone; but it is extremely remote.

MAPS: Slickhorn West 7.5 min map covers it all, it is a very short canyon. Also TI map #706.

GETTING THERE: you never could drive to its head; park at Collins C trailhead [see above for directions]. A faint 4wd road leaves parking lot and continues south across open grazing land. BLM has installed a locked gate near parking lot. It is approx. 7 miles cross-country to head of Widows Walk, partly by road.

HIKING WIDOWS WALK: a little route finding is needed just to find it, as your approach is so long. Perhaps most interesting way is to rimwalk ggulch. Widows Walk is only major canyon in this lower part of ggulch on *cr* that goes. There is one other little canyon upcanyon about a mile which does not go. Once you find it, only fork which goes is southeast of 4644 elev. as marked on maps. There is a dropoff, but you can easily skirt it *cr*, and work under north fork dropoff. Downcanyon is a boulder garden in which some hikers have tried to cairn a route *cl* under cliffs to avoid boulders. Apparently bighorn sheep use this route also. Soon your route is easier and you are in ggulch. It took me 2 hours from farthest point I was able to drive [when road was open].

When I got to ggulch I had to check my map four times, and hike down to first sharp corner to be sure that I was in ggulch. I had hiked up to Shangri La C. from a San Juan river trip back in mid 80's but could not remember ggulch being so crappy. It is amazingly narrow, bouldery, overgrown, and there is barely a discernible trail. A small dropoff at confluence is skirted *cl*. Upcanyon, tho, I soon found more of a trail, and easier going. I hiked upcanyon a little ways past Shangri La C took a break, and returned. I saw no ruins, no rock art, tho I saw a few places where there could have been some art. There are a series of rincons, and at confluence of ggulch and Shangri La, there is one which can cause minor confusion as it seems there are canyons going every which way.

I got back to my pickup after 8 hours, just before dark.

Hiking along thru upper cattle country is only neat if you rimwalk by ggulch, otherwise it is bland blackbush and sand with a few small hills. Without extra part of Collins C. road being open, I never could have done this dayhike. Still, getting to Widows Walk this way is faster than trying to hike down ggulch; this would make an interesting multi-day loop. It is easier to access via Shangri La C.

WATER: minimal, I do not remember seeing any.

ATTRACTIONS: not very many due to remoteness. If one were able to drive that closed road it would be a nice in/out. It is a cute little canyon, tho very short. Probably most hikers in it come from SJ river trips.

CHAPTER 36
OTHER CEDAR MESA HIKES

SLICKHORN

Slickhorn has many side canyons, overall it is approximately 25 miles long, and is between GG and Johns Canyon. Only 6 sidecanyons are commonly used as access routes, and only 3 of those very often. Looking at a map, Slickhorn canyons are numbered clockwise starting at longest one, #1. #2 and #3 are two forks of next short, east side canyon. #4 is next longest fork. #5 is a short one between #4 and #6, next longest side canyon. #1, #4, and #6 are used most often. Slk. is narrow, entrenches dramatically, has limited water and sites, and is not as well-visited as GG. Access is via one road on east side, off Hwy 261. Fee for dayhiking and camping, *no dogs allowed.*

It probably served as a subsidiary residential area on Cedar Mesa. Many river runners come in from San Juan River to swim in a few fine granite pools near river. It does provide a restful solitude most times of year. Thruout, vegetation is sparse.

All forks of Slickhorn are rugged, some quite rough, bouldery, brushy, sometimes full of dropoffs, and not recommended for solo novice hikers. Route-finding skills necessary if doing loop hikes using two forks.

* * *

SLICKHORN #1: Long, remote and ruggedly kool canyon system. Not as popular or accessible as ggulch, nevertheless Slickhorn has its fan club. It is certainly more known by river runners for its campsites and lime-stone pools near San Juan river. This is true head of Slickhorn, and its longest arm.

MAPS: Slickhorn Canyon E 7.5 covers most of it; Pollys Pasture 7.5 remainder. Use TI #706 also.

GETTING THERE: Use Slickhorn road: @19.1mm, Hwy 261, turn west onto SJ245. One mile from hwy follow main road left. 2.6 miles from hwy, turn left onto SJ203 [sign points right to Govt. Trail]. First mile or more from hwy can be very bad if wet, but further down road gets sandier. 4.2 miles from hwy is another junction [no sign]. Turn right here for #1, road ends about 1/4 mile near a gully, a feed trough, and register box. Trailhead is in nearby gully.

HIKING SLICKHORN #1: interesting, rough, and then easier. It starts out shallow and moderately interesting for about 30 minutes. At an impassable dropoff, you detour up a slickrock ramp/hill *cl* about 15 feet, then get on a wide and flat ledge. >From a nearby promontory you can see your route around in next gully *cl*. Follow this ledge and cairns. Eventually you come to a long talus slope and zigzag down. Hiking below is much easier. Generally, it takes a little less than 2 hours to reach #2, without stops.

ATTRACTIONS: Depends on you. There are a few sites, some art, and more notably a well-publicized and well-maintained kiva ruin *cr* just below main dropoff. You can climb up from below if you can spot it. Another site downcanyon may have had a ruin but it has washed away, rock art is well above your head and consists of many handprints. It is *cr* and not far above #2.

WATER: upper #1 has small springs, there is water below main dropoff, probably some near #2 in good years.

COMMENTS: A big part of Slickhorn's charm is its remoteness, its ruggedness, its narrowness and that few people hike it [compared with ggulch or Fish/Owl]. Of course during spring break you may run into lots of hikers. I have hiked it many times in fall-to-spring seasons and never seen anyone, nor fresh footprints. In a Grand Canyon environment, trails are marked, maintained, populous, etc. In remoter canyons of Cedar Mesa, and Slickhorn is a prime example, route finding can get tedious, trails are often imaginary, rescue problematical, and perhaps a GPS is handy to find your way back to your car. This said, enjoy.

* * *

SLICKHORN #2 & #3: both these are really two forks of next canyon south of #1. #2 has remains of an old constructed horse trail.

MAPS: Slickhorn Canyon E 7.5 covers most of it; Pollys Pasture 7.5 remainder. Use TI #706 also.

GETTING THERE: Use Slickhorn road: @19.1mm, Hwy 261, turn west onto SJ245. One mile from hwy follow main road left. 2.6 miles from hwy, turn left onto SJ203 [sign points right to Govt. Trail]. First mile from hwy can be very bad if wet, but further down road gets sandier. 5 miles from hwy is a cairn in a shallow gully which may mark #2; 5.6 miles from hwy is a spur road to right [west] which may go to a drill hole and #3. I have always hiked in another arm and out these shorter arms then bushwhacked cross-country to my vehicle.

HIKING SLICKHORN #2 & #3: lower part of this canyon is easy walking. #2 has a rudimentary livestock trail and it climbs far up *cr* to avoid a boulder garden and stepup [dropoff]. At another stepup upcanyon, trail is more obvious *cr* with logs to shore it up, and a neat little ramp above. #3 is straightforward with one little stepup which you can skirt *cl.* #2 has one small ruin above.

WATER: small springs in upper ends, more water in lower parts in good seasons/years.

ATTRACTIONS: #2 has one small ruin above, there may be a little rock art, tho I have never seen any. They are both short, efficient exit routes, neither is well used, cairned, or has much of a trail. They are quiet, neat little canyons.

* * *

SLICKHORN #4: is one of 3 most popular tributaries of Slickhorn. It also may be easiest and I have combined it with #3 or with #5 in about 5 hours.

MAPS: Slickhorn Canyon E 7.5 covers it all. Use TI #706 also.

GETTING THERE: Use Slickhorn road: @19.1mm, Hwy 261, turn west onto SJ245. One mile from hwy follow main road left. 2.6 miles from hwy, turn left onto SJ203 [sign points right to Govt. Trail]. First mile or more from hwy can be very bad if wet, but further down road gets sandier. 7.1 miles from hwy you enter an obvious gully and drive down thru it for about 100 feet. This is #4, and there are camping/parking areas next to it.

HIKING SLICKHORN #4: This canyon is 'relatively' easy hiking, and none of its obstacles are difficult. Basically go *cl* at first 3 dropoffs, either way at another and *cr* at a boulder garden. At first major dropoff there is a 'hidden' [by trees] easy route about 50 feet *cl* from streambed. It becomes obvious as you start down.

WATER: there are small springs scattered thruout in good seasons/years.

ATTRACTIONS: there are a few small sites *cr* in upper canyon with some rock art. It is a scenic, popular, and well traveled canyon, tho many more people hike ggulch. There may be a few more rock art panels than some other Slickhorn canyons.

* * *

SLICKHORN #6 & #5: #6 is last accessible major tributary of Slickhorn, #5 is a short tributary just north of it. TI map #706 has #6 marked but not #5.

MAPS: Slickhorn Canyon E 7.5 covers it all. Use TI #706 also.

GETTING THERE: Use Slickhorn road: @19.1mm, Hwy 261, turn west onto SJ245. One mile from hwy follow main road left. 2.6 miles from hwy, turn left onto SJ203 [sign points right to Govt. Trail]. First mile or more from hwy can be very bad if wet, but further down road gets sandier. 8.3 miles from hwy is a corral west of road. Park by this corral, and follow a nearby gully.

HIKING SLICKHORN #6/#5: #6, aka. Trail Canyon, is not as easy to hike as some, and has two dropoffs and a boulder garden to skirt on *cl*. It is easier to find than #5; I usually go in #6 and out #5 then bushwhack back. There is a well used trail and cairns to follow in #6.

#5 is about 15 minutes hike upcanyon from #6, alternates brushy/slickrock stretches, climbs fast, is mostly easy, and has some water. It is rarely hiked, so do not expect a trail or cairns. Eventually you come to a real stepup, which you can skirt *cl*. Immediately you see another, and a headwall where this canyon begins. Easiest way is up a short side canyon which points north here; it is a *cr* fork. There are several stepups with little detours *cr*. Later, just below last stepup, climb a small slope *cl* and walk thru *cl* side up a slickrock chute with a minor 2' step. You can also climb up a talus/ledge *cr* just upcanyon from this side canyon, and work back into it. Either way, soon you can get back into open valley of #5 and get out several ways.

WATER: there are a few springs in upper end, possible water lower down in good seasons/years.

ATTRACTIONS: near lower of main dropoffs is a nice ruin, which most books mention, called 'Big Ledge Ruin', and a horse trail at end of detour. It is generally about 2 hours hike down to main Slickhorn canyon, not counting stops. From #6, it is about 30 minutes hike to #7 [a no-go].

* * *

SLICKHORN NORTH: is remote, rarely visited, and is actually west of parts of Slickhorn. It has two main, long forks which meet just above an impassable dropoff.

MAPS: Slickhorn Canyon E 7.5 covers it all except its upper 'breaks'. For this use Pollys Pasture 7.5. TI #706 also covers it.

GETTING THERE: Not easy, a 4wd vehicle or long walk is needed. Use Slickhorn road: @19.1mm, Hwy 261, turn west onto SJ245. One mile from hwy follow main road left. 2.6 miles from hwy, turn right [sign for govt. trail]. 5.5 miles from hwy, turn left at 'Y' onto SJ253a. This road is maintained for a few miles then almost disappears as it turns rough 4wd. It is marked on 7.5 maps but not on TI #706 [1997 version]. You can also walk down this road and turn south after it gets out of rocky part. This road continues over to drill hole used for Water C access. [see its page] but is rough, hard to follow, and crosses one wash where you will have to find a detour.

HIKING SLICKHORN N: western fork is shallow, bland, and used by cattle. I saw one ruin trashed by cattle using a small alcove for shade. After several hours of hiking this fork deepens quickly. A dropoff can be skirted *cr* about 150 yards down an easy sloping slickrock ramp which can barely be seen from dropoff. Below this are minor obstacles and an impassable dropoff. A cottonwood log jammed in streambed could be used to rope down, but another dropoff is below.

Another main fork, from just above this dropoff also has a dropoff. You can climb up *cl* downcanyon within sight of it, then work across a wide ledge. Upcanyon, hiking is much easier, and there are several springs. I have only been in west fork of this canyon where it splits upcanyon. When I reached a tiny granary *cr*, I climbed out and hiked back to my pickup. To get out here, I started up a gully with white/red/white bands of sandstone downcanyon from this granary. Someone had stacked rocks up to a small cliff and used a log ladder. Instead, I contoured downcanyon around a corner, perhaps 250 yards and found a very easy way out.

WATER: I remember seeing water pools/springs thruout, intermittently.

ATTRACTIONS: fork closest to main Slickhorn canyons of these two is more interesting and deeper. There seem to be very few sites. Upper Hat Flat 'breaks' are an interestingly complex area, where you could spend many days if so motivated. It is also cattle country.

* * *

POINT LOOKOUT

Is an area of Cedar Mesa between Slickhorn and Johns Canyons. There are numerous short canyons relatively unknown to most hikers. Rough, rugged, remote, not for solo novice hikers.

MAPS: Slickhorn East 7.5 covers it all. Also use TI #706.

GETTING THERE: Drive on past #6 Slickhorn Canyon trailhead to end of road. Use Slickhorn road: @ 19.1mm, Hwy 261, turn west onto SJ245. One mile from hwy follow main road left. 2.6 miles from hwy, turn left at 'Y'. Stay on main road until it 'ends' about 10 miles from hwy. There is a large patch of slickrock, a red pickup bed used as a feeder, and further along a stock pond. Canyon west of this road is commonly known as 'Point and Look Canyon' but not labeled on maps. Road does sort of continue another few miles, but is hard to see.

HIKING POINT AND LOOK: from slickrock parking lot you can enter fork nearest you, however it is perhaps easier to rimwalk over to next fork south. Once below these upper forks you soon encounter boulder gardens and other problems. Downcanyon, hiking is easier. I have come back out first fork *cr* which is about 1.5 miles down tho it was very tricky and not recommended; I did not have my dogs with me. I have also tried to come up this canyon from below where it joins Johns-Slickrock trail. I did not succeed as it is bouldery, brushy, steep-sided, and very narrow.

BEYOND P&L: road deteriorates but does continue on about 2 miles to near Point Lookout. This area is about as remote and seldom visited as any on Cedar Mesa.

WATER: upper P&L Canyon has several springs scattered for about 3 miles or more. Lower P&L is dry.

ATTRACTIONS: quiet, solitude and interesting canyons well describes this area. Plus potentially fantastic vues if you get over to Johns. This area was probably on fringe of Anasazi habitation on Cedar Mesa, but there are a few sites.

PERSONAL EXPERIENCES: There are 4 other small canyons here, PL #1, #2, #3, #4 east to west. Mar, '00 I drove in a 2wd [front] SUV with high clearance 2.6 mi. past a stock pond at head of P&L. Road is mostly clay, seldom used, and a bit high centered tho mostly level [years ago I could not find this road, now it was easy]. In about .5 mi. I passed other upper fork for P&L. Eventually I came to a 'y' and took a .2 mi. short right spur which humps over sage and ends at a campsite. I hiked into nearest gully which w/i .25 mi. turns into a canyon [#1]. I easily found a way down thru minor dropoffs and soon to canyon bottom. This is nearest '6171' elev. cairn.

I hiked downcanyon almost to S28,29,32,33. After passing multiple skirtable dropoffs, I elected to climb a cliffy and crappy route out *cr* rather than go further. This canyon loses its charm, and descends thru basic moencrapola rock layers, and going is tougher. After goofing around sightseeing and photo-oping I think it took me about 3 hours to get about .25 mi. above last small fork above bench where Johns-Slickhorn road is. I climbed up onto a nice ridge between two forks of this canyon and followed it up. It took me about 1:30 to climb up completely onto juniper flats. I rimwalked around various forks and back to my car, which I could see thru a small telescope [before buying Swarovski binocs] from 2 miles away.

Continuation of access road ends in .2 mile above rims of Johns C. I could see where some drivers had driven off closer to rim, but I did not follow their 'road'.

* * *

JOHNS CANYON

Is a western Cedar Mesa moderately long canyon system with easy access. Parts of it are very popular with large groups, others with locals. Most hikers explore its upper short forks. Fine for solo novice hikers with some orienteering knowledge but there are many impassable dropoffs.

MAPS: Slickhorn Canyon E 7.5 covers its lower third; Cedar Mesa S 7.5 covers its upper 2/3's. Use TI #706 also.

GETTING THERE: it is surrounded closely on three sides by roads.

UPPER: @ 17.3mm Hwy 261 turn west onto SJ221a. *Option A*: park near first gully. *Option B*: .6 miles from hwy is a drill hole road to south. *Option C*: 1.7 miles from hwy, a very rough 1 mile long road to south. *Option D*: 2.4 miles from hwy, woodcutters road to south, turn left at immediate 'Y', 1.1 miles to end.

EAST: 7.5 map shows an old road which skirts east side of Johns. Whether this is still drivable I cannot say. There are numerous short roads from Hwy 261 going east to Johns.

LOWER: same as if going to Honaker Trail. Just north of Mexican Hat turn up Hwy 261, go north .8mi, turn left towards Gooseneck Overlook and go .5mi to first dirt road to right [west]. This is fine for 2wd if dry and maintained by county to Johns. CAUTION: surface is clay and can be extremely dangerous if very wet, as you drive just above sheer cliffs for parts of way, and 4wd is required. It is 14.5 miles to Johns C streambed. Road splits before this, stay left. Road splits after streambed, right goes upcanyon a ways. Left at 'Y' goes on over towards Slickhorn, continues for about 7 or 8 miles, and immediately after streambed deteriorates into hi-clearance 4wd with some washed out spots. You can hike from road's end over to Slickhorn along original road [now a trail] some oil drillers built. They tried to haul a rig over and drill for oil. Parts of rig and engine are below cliffs where river runners camp. There is some very interesting rock art along this road.

HIKING JOHNS CANYON: there are many upper forks and they all have dropoffs. Western forks mostly have impassable dropoffs. I have never tried to hike completely down Johns. Hiking in from lower Johns takes a long time to get interesting, tho cliffs above you are kool. There are remnants of an old horse road, and Jimmy Palmer may have built it perhaps 150 years ago. Reputedly he "borrowed horses from Bluff locals and forgot to return them". His road was used to get these horses up onto Cedar Mesa. Some books describe a route from Johns-Slickhorn road down to San Juan River, I have never tried this as Honaker trail is much easier.

WATER: springs scattered thruout Johns Canyon, with an intermittent stream in lower end.

ATTRACTIONS: it is a scenic canyon, upper and lower. There are some sites scattered around and plenty of places to hike with varying degrees of difficulty.

* * *

ARCH CANYON

Is in far northeast section of Cedar Mesa, if indeed it is still considered Cedar Mesa. BLM charges no fees in Arch C. It drains south Elk Ridge and drains into upper Comb Wash, all north of Hwy 95. Very easy hiking in lower 10 miles, then more rugged. Fine for solo novice hikers.

MAPS: Kigalia Point 7.5 covers upper ends of all 3 main forks, Butts, Texas, and Arch. Hotel Rock 7.5 covers remainder. Use TI #703 for full coverage, or TI #706 for partial coverage.

GETTING THERE: Drive north of Hwy 95 on Upper Comb Wash road, SJ205, [at bottom of hill west of deep Comb Ridge road cut] which can get slimy if wet. After 2.5 mi., you will go thru a closed gate, with corrals nearby. Turn upcanyon immediately after, driving thru a closed off picnic area [signs everywhere proclaim it Ute land, no trespassing] cross a cattle guard and you will see a BLM sign/register [no fee]. Either park here or continue upcanyon. This 4wd trail is slow-going, very rough in places, and requires a hi-clearance vehicle with an intermediate experience driver and ends in about 10 miles. You could also park along Arch C overlook up on South Elk Ridge and hike down all of Arch, perhaps leaving a vehicle at Arch's mouth beforehand.

HIKING ARCH CANYON: very easy, just follow road or a sometimes faint trail, or hike in streambed. Main arches are where 4wd road ends, one more is further up Arch C, tho few hikers go that far. Most visitors either come to see ruins in Arch's mouth or ATV up and picnic. Texas Canyon is not well-visited and a bit harder to hike than Arch. Butts has suffered a forest fire and has a few stepups to negotiate, also not well-visited. You can also get to both rims. For south rim access, follow directions for Mule upper forks, and continue on SJ263. There is an overlook 6 miles from hwy, tho a short but real 4wd hill intervenes. A set of stairs gets you out on a little promontory just below Texas C. For north rims follow directions on driving to Hotel Rock.

Both lower *cl* forks go, tho not easily. Upcanyon one is much harder requiring patience and route-finding skills. Downcanyon one cliffs out, but can be skirted or [as I have done] climbed *cl* to a top cliff break in another gully. Both are half NMF hiking.

WATER: there is water all thru Arch Canyon, more in wet years, much less in dry years. Most perennial springs are upcanyon, or at heads of side canyons.

ATTRACTIONS: many, a very scenic canyon. Most people drive it, but they may miss its best attractions.

* * *

MULE CANYON

Is a moderately long and deep canyon in NE quarter of

Cedar Mesa. It starts north of Hwy 95 and ends at Comb Wash. South of Hwy 95 it deepens dramatically to form a classic Cedar Mesa canyon. Above hwy 95 forks are relatively easy, below it is rough then gets very easy near Comb Wash. Parts are fine for solo novice hikers.

MAPS: South Long Point 7.5 covers its upper forks, Bluff NW 7.5 covers its middle, and Hotel Rock 7.5 covers its eastern end. Use TI #706 also.

GETTING THERE

UPPER MAIN: @ 102mm Hwy 95, turn north onto SJ263, aka. Texas Flat road. Road immediately drops down into a gully over a low dam. Either park on this dam, or just past it in some camping spots. Trailhead for main upper fork of Mule is upcanyon by a register box and sign.

UPPER N FORK: follow directions for main upper Mule and drive northwest on Texas Flat road approx. 1 mile from hwy. There is a new bridge across this fork. Park in large open area south of bridge. Trailhead starts *cr* near this parking lot, and is easier if you stay out of N Fork Mule for awhile, tho some hike thru it anyway.

HWY 95: @ 102.5mm Hwy 95, turn south onto a small dirt road [it will be first one west of bridge over Mule]. It is ok for hi clearance 2wd vehicles if dry, but gets bumpy soon. It is probably less than half mile from pavement to end.

LOWER FORKS: @ 103.7mm Hwy 95, turn south onto a ranchers road which ends in .8 mile.

LOWER END: turn south off Hwy 95 onto SJ235 [Comb Wash Rd] which is next to Comb Wash and just west of Comb Ridge. Just after you cross creek bed first time, turn west onto an obvious dirt road exactly one mile from hwy. Most people park in a wide open area, some few drive on upcanyon tho road is blocked off soon anyway and rough 4wd.

HIKING MULE CANYON

UPPER MAIN: starts out bland and shallow, seems to not make sense why you are there. Gets better soon and becomes a nice canyon, with sloping, forested south wall and cliffy north wall. It is not difficult and there is enough of a trail for a few miles, then few people go further. Some scenic sites above on north wall. There are some 'sneak' routes from Hwy 95 near 98-99mm, tho not easy. Some hikers cross overland to combine these two forks [which would take a full day]. Hiking Time: about 3-5 hours round-trip if only going upcanyon where most people go.

UPPER N FORK: it also starts bland, and narrower than main upper fork. It stays narrow, has some sites, and is not as popular as Main Fork upper Mule. What trail there is ends soon, beyond going is slow but interesting. Hiking Time: about 3-5 hours round-trip if only hiking where most people go.

HWY 95: you actually are in western short fork just downcanyon from hwy. Probably most people come to see a few Hovenweep like ruins [there is a popular name for this short sidecanyon of Mule]. There is a trail down into this sidecanyon which starts *cl* of a drainage channel, near where you park, near one of rimtop ruins. Look for a ramp to a 2 foot step, then a trail slanting down. Just downcanyon is a boulder garden which is short, and after a mile or so hiking is much easier, tho not as scenic as Arch canyon. Hiking Time: depends on how much you goofaround.

LOWER FORKS: there are two short *cl* forks near mouth of Mule. Western [upcanyon] fork is definitely NMF hiking, being thrashy, cliffy, etc. NOT RECOMMENDED! Other fork takes more walking to get to and some route finding. I scouted this from above and do not think it would be difficult to get into where it deepens about 1 mile from Mule. I saw no sites from above. Its bottom is flat and wide. There is a relatively easy and steep deer trail just downcanyon of a promontory between these two sidecanyons of Mule which I hiked up. Hiking Time: both these forks are short, figure about 1 to 1:30 hours, a loop in about 4 hours if you goof around in Mule.

LOWER END: hiking is easy, with standard zigzags across stream. Most people come into mouth of Mule to see obvious ruins there, which are similar to those in lower Arch. Not that many people hike thru lower Mule up to hwy, tho it is a nice hike. It would be easy to leave a vehicle at both ends for a one-way hike. Hiking Time: I have hiked from Comb Wash to within sight of hwy 95 dropoffs and back in about 5-6 hours, with stops.

WATER: both upper forks usually have plenty of water, even for dogs. Mule and its sidecanyon just below hwy 95 have small springs. Lower Mule, above Comb Wash, also has intermittent water up to hwy 95. Purify/filter all water, or bring your own.

ATTRACTIONS: it has many parts, some sites, is certainly scenic and easy to get to.

* * *

FISH CANYON

May be longest canyon on east side of Cedar Mesa, Arch C is not much shorter. It starts near Salvation Knoll, just south of Hwy 95, and drains into Comb Wash. Owl C. is basically a side canyon of Fish and they are commonly combined as a fine multi-day loop hike. Fish and Owl are second only to Ggulch in popularity, with perhaps Mule C a close runner-up. McLoyds C is also basically a sidecanyon of Fish. Parts of it is moderately rugged, but overall it is fine for solo novice hikers. *First-timers please read my orienteering caution below.*

MAPS: South Long Point 7.5 covers its northwestern upper end; Snow Flat Spring Cave 7.5 covers its middle; Bluff NW 7.5 covers its lower end at Comb Wash. Use TI #706 also.

GETTING THERE: Hwy 95 skirts its head [beginning] on

north, Comb Wash road skirts its mouth [end] on east, and another road off Hwy 261 goes to main trailhead. @ 27.5mm on Hwy 261, turn east onto SJ 253, a.k.a. Owl Creek road. Park at deadend 5 miles from hwy. See sections below for further directions.

HIKING FISH CANYON:

UPPER: I have scouted upper Fish a bit and not found a good route with dogs. I did find one further around *cl* downcanyon, but I saw one car parked at 96mm on Hwy 95 so assume there is a route there.

Option A: turn south of Hwy 95 @ 97.5mm [just east of Salvation Knoll] onto a dirt road which is part of old Mormon trail and may have no SJ number. Soon it turns east and starts down to a lower level. Walk south on a small dirt road above this drop, as recently I noticed it is closed by BLM. It ends on a patch of slickrock. Hike south to a short *cl* gully which has '6000' elev. printed on TI map.

Do not expect cairns, bring machete for manzanita. This is a rough, steep, but doable route. Start in gully head, preferably *cl*. Very soon, get out of gully before it deepens much, and follow sandstone slopes around to *cl* [south]. Look carefully and you will find a break off small cliff below, which leads to several parallel talus/juniper/boulder ridges. Pick one, further to your left and work to it. Once along streambed hiking is easy. I have made it in 2 hours down to main part of Fish. There are a few nice pools.

Middle [main]: from parking lot, go north to Fish, or east down a slickrock gully to Owl. It is about 1.5 miles to an in/out with a small cliff [maybe 10' high, but there is an intermediate step 1/3 of height and it is not 100% vertical], which I have done w/dogs [had to catch and lower them] even in winter with some snow on ground. This section is described in many hiking books as most hikers combine Fish and Owl as a multi-day loop.

Basically, this in/out is a steep and brushy talus slope.

Hiking is slow until you get down to main canyon due to a few small dropoffs, then stays easy. There is one high arch you can see if you are alert, a few ruins if you can see them from below.

ORIENTEERING CAUTION: If you are coming up Fish from downcanyon, and are new to this area, exit canyon out of Fish is on west side of Fish, right where it makes a sharp 90 degree turn to north [after trending west or northwest for miles] and there is usually a large pool of water at confluence--do not expect cairns, but a trail will soon be obvious. This is first major *cl* sidecanyon of Fish, upcanyon from Owl C. You hike up this western sidecanyon not quite a mile and look for cairns on south side, and a trail skirting a stepup.

At this stepup, a steep trail goes south up to a cliff crack which you climb up and cross about 1.5 miles of mesa top along an obvious trail with cairns. Last part of this trail follows a gully, then turns south out of it a short distance to a parking lot [gully is wider and flatter near parking lot]. If you pass by this parking lot and get to Owl, turnaround and go upgully about 1/4 mile, look on your left for a flat area above you, with or without cars; there is a sign and register. In 2001-2002 a couple got lost in Fish and had to use a cellphone to call for help from BLM--I assume they just missed exit sidecanyon--as there is really no other place to get lost.

South Fork: NMF hiking! Upper S Fork Fish is slow going, very much like upper forks of Mule, narrow, overgrown, but with lots of water. Lower down where it joins Fish it is only slightly easier to hike. It is still narrow, with continual boulder gardens, little signs of a trail, steep and overgrown. There are more people who come into S Fk. Fish from main fork Fish than hike upper end, as I saw no trail at all. I used a road at 95mm on Hwy 95, then walked across a large chained area, relying on a compass for orientation. Anasazi did not use canyon bottom of S Fk. Fish as a route, a much better alternative route is nearby. Thus, I discourage anyone from attempting it.

Lower: there are several ways to get into mouth of Fish. Easiest way is off Comb Wash road. Near 4630 elev. at intersection of S18,19, there are two roads which lead to same drillhole site. Northern road is 8.8 miles from hwy 95 and in 2002 suffered some new erosion. Southern road may be in better shape and has a large BLM sign; they join at Comb Wash. There are beaver ponds and numerous small ruins. Canyon is shallow, but interesting. About 3 hours will get you to McLoyds Canyon, and 1 to 2 hours more to Owl. Before McLoyds, Fish gets deeper and more defined. You will share trail with cattle sometimes, and this part of canyon is typically defined by steep juniper/talus/ boulder slopes. *A road into mouth of Fish, shown on older quad maps, is no longer usable.*

Another, not as easy access has gained some popularity among locals. It is similar to that described in Twist Hikes. From Comb Wash road, take southern of two roads described above, 9 miles south of hwy 95 on Comb Wash road. After these two roads join is a difficult 4wd stretch.

NEW IN 2002: crossing Comb Wash, drivers have made a minor detour [due to new arroyo cutting] thru a small gully just north of 'old' road, but I made it up out of Comb wash after several tries. Several miles further, near first drillhole site, a new arroyo has cut across this road, a short detour goes around, to north. This road may now require 4wd, at any rate it requires a high clearance vehicle. Soon original road joins from south [shown on maps], it is washed out where it enters Fish tho dirtbikers still use it somewhat. Continue to end or as far as you can, last drill hole is about 4 miles, road ends about .8 mile further. There are picnic/camping sites and you will be on a small, steep-sided mesa with a valley between you and bigger cliffs to west.

On map this is 1/4 mi. west of 5086 elev. drillhole site.

Easiest route off is on extreme south end of mesa, down a small barely defined drainage. Below is a substantial side canyon, and you will work your way around above it to west and then south, *cr*.

After heading two short forks of this sidecanyon to Fish, come back to cliff edge [small trail thru here]. Just south of fork which points to 5234 elev. on map are several breaks. Best for dogs and people is down a small drainage, thru a tree, down a stepped 6' drop, then thru broken off slabs. It is visible from above, and my dogs have done it several times with minimal help. Just below this is a bench which you can follow around easily to a ridge which points into Fish. Drop off it anywhere and head up Fish. If you know this route you can save time vs. coming in at mouth of Fish.

ALTERNATIVE: 8 Dec, '01 I found another route off this small mesa. From last of two drill holes onto top of this mesa may require a 4wd vehicle. But, from NW corner I found an easy trail with multiple cairns. It drops off north side of this mesa, and curves around into drainage to meet up with above mentioned route, and is easier but longer. I used part of it to climb up onto mesa between Fish and Dry Wash; I used a talus gully and saw one faint set of footprints. A probably now-closed road ends nearby on this 'Island in the Sky.'

2002 REVISIT: in early November I returned to this mesa and used NW route at beginning of hike, south route at end. Overall, I think south route is better and shorter to access this sidecanyon of Fish. There are confusing trails connecting NW route, and SW route is easier to see/do. I finally scouted an alternative route down into this sidecanyon, which is barely 100 feet from my usual route. It goes, but my route [thru a juniper tree] is easier with dogs. An obvious trail leads across rims towards Fish, but from scouting while hiking up Fish, I saw no other good breaks into Fish for miles.

It took my dogs and I about 40 minutes, going long way, to get down to Fish [regular trail]. It took another 50 minutes to get to McLoyds/Fish confluence, and another hour to get up McLoyds to Graham Spur [major sidecanyon]/McLoyds confluence 2:30 total]. Going back to my pickup took only 2:15 hours.

WATER: in upper Fish only in wet years except intermittent pools/springs in its forks. At confluence of S. Fork and main, reliable springs intermittently downcanyon to about 1.5 miles upcanyon from Fish/Owl confluence. Exit side canyon has water in wet years. Lower Fish, above Comb Wash, has water usually. Just upcanyon from McLoyds/Fish confluence is probably reliable water. In lower, northern sidecanyon that is accessed via drillhole road, I have only found water in slickrock pools above its rim. Fish seems to be single best watered canyon on all of Cedar Mesa.

ATTRACTIONS: Upper ends of Fish and Owl are perhaps more interesting than where they join. Both are very popular, usually done as a loop, multi-day backpack. An alternative multi-day loop hike is to hike into McLoyds C, go downcanyon to Fish, then upcanyon and out either Owl C or Fish C. Use two cars, or a very long circuitous cross-country hike is involved to return to your vehicle.

* * *

OWL CANYON

Is a long southern tributary of Fish Canyon, on east half of Cedar Mesa and between McLoyds and Fish. Most hikers combine it with Fish for a multi-day loop, and it is deservedly very popular. It is much rougher than Fish, but is a good introductory hike for a solo novice hiker as trail is obvious.

MAPS: Snow Flat Spring Cave 7.5 covers most of it; Bluff NW 7.5 covers remainder. Use TI #706 also.

GETTING THERE

Upper: @ 26.6mm Hwy 261 turn east onto a small hi-clearance track. It is more or less ok for 2wds for several miles, then degrades into nasty 4wd and/or is impassable

Main: 27.5mm on Hwy 261 turn east onto SJ253, 'Owl Creek'. This is first main east sideroad, along hwy 261, south of KGRS. Road fine if dry for 2wds, deadends in 5 miles at parking lot.

GETTING STARTED

Main: Owl and Fish trailheads leave from this parking lot. For Fish, find a trail going north. For Owl, follow a nearby gully downstream.

HIKING OWL CANYON

MAIN: most hikers make a standard loop of Fish and Owl. I usually climb out a side canyon and return via rim above to get a multiple vue of Owl. Owl in character is a bit rough at first with rock gardens, detours, dropoffs, etc. Start *cl* close to drainage channel, and follow cairns down a talus slope. Soon after reaching canyon bottom, you detour *cr* around a dropoff, usually there are cairns. Downcanyon, at highest dropoff, trail goes north into a major sidecanyon detour about .25 miles long. Below is a fine and popular campsite. After last main dropoff, Owl opens and gets easier. Generally it takes 3 hours to get to Nevill's Arch.

UPPER: when road skirts Owl Creek where it deepens in white sandstone cliffs is benchmark 6350. There is a seldom used brushy entrance, and few hikers ever come up here. Hiking is fairly easy for about two miles. Then it gets brushy and difficult until it is joined by another branch coming from '6167' benchmark to west.

It is 'NMF' hiking. Canyon bottom is narrow, overgrown, has many pools to skirt, boulder [big] gardens to clamber thru, two dropoffs to skirt *cr* [I went left at first and had to backtrack], etc. Later there is a faint trail from animals/hikers, tho it is also NMF. Perhaps a half mile short of Owl I have climbed out *cr* up a steep talus/slickrock slope, tho it is definitely NMF.

Better yet, upcanyon is a distinctive faulted zigzag in canyon. *CR*, below is a very easy exit gully [better than one I used earlier]. *CL*, above is also an easy exit gully. It goes right on up thru top cliff with no particular difficulties. I have scouted midfork of Owl from above, it seems to have a faint trail, but also might be NMF.

There is a rimwalk trail which leaves Fish-Owl parking area, and winds around to head of Owl's middle upper fork, then thins out. Perhaps some people hike this fork. It looks NMF from above.

WATER: there is water thruout upper Owl, but it may get scarce in dry seasons/years below Nevills Arch.

ATTRACTIONS: mostly popular as part of Fish-Owl loop hike. There are some sites, and probably largest arch on Cedar Mesa.

* * *

McLOYDS CANYON

Is a very popular canyon which is actually a south fork of Fish Canyon, tho there is a named "South Fork" further upcanyon. It is between Owl and Snow Flat Spring Canyon. Mention Moonhouse or Moon Kiva, tho, and most people know where you are talking about. CAUTION: THIS CANYON HAS SOME IMPASSABLE DROPOFFS! ANY ROUTES DESCRIBED BELOW, EXCEPT #3 CAN BE EXTREMELY DANGEROUS FOR NOVICE HIKERS!

MAPS: Snow Flat Spring Cave 7.5 covers most of it, Bluff NW 7.5 remainder. Use TI #706 also.

GETTING THERE: @ 22.5mm Hwy 261 go east 8.3 miles east on Snow Flat road, SJ237, look for a parking area on south side [short road goes to a drillhole site]. Either park here or drive north to rimtop parking lot. See 'Comments' below.

HIKING McLOYDS

Access 1: park along Snow Flat road 6 or 7 miles from hwy 261 and hike north into upper McLoyds.

Access 2: first time I entered McLoyds, I rimwalked upcanyon from #3 and entered next side canyon, *cr* [#2]. When I did this, at first dropoff I scrambled down *cl*. Since then, I see there is another route with Anasazi steps, not much easier. You can also contour downcanyon and drop down near Moonhouse.

Access 3: main, is where most people go, mainly to see Moonhouse [aka. Moon Kiva], is north of parking lot along SF road. Use a now reopened road which goes to rim of McLoyd C. Walk out to rim for a fine vue of Moonhouse. Trail [some cairns] starts *cl* of a small gully just north of rim area parking lot. Start *cl*, look for cairns, then work back to 'streambed' and down a 3 foot drop, then back *cl* along a long ledge to top of a talus slope which you follow down. Go under 2 large boulders and into streambed. To continue downcanyon, you detour a dropoff immediately downcanyon *cl* then follow trail.

Access 4: there is another sidecanyon a little ways downcanyon from access #3, *cr*; mostly I have used it to get out. Hiking downcanyon from #4 you soon come to an impassable dropoff. There is a vue trail *cl* which soon ends on some scary ledges. NOVICE HIKERS SHOULD NOT CONTINUE DOWNCANYON AT THIS DROPOFF!! There are only 2 ways to continue downcanyon from here.

Option 1: backtrack upcanyon to a *cr* saddle and climb up to its upcanyon side using a talus/juniper slope. Cross it and immediately descend a zigzag course to a 15-20 foot rudimentary log ladder. NOT RECOMMENDED! Anyone using this will want a rope and companion, maybe a trampoline to land on. This 'ladder' is pretty flaky. Recently I hiked in from Graham Spur and back out, going up this ladder. It is not safe, and needs to be rebuilt or removed.

Option 2: ALSO NOT FOR NOVICE HIKERS! [best] after crossing same saddle, descend just a ledge or two until you can work around south to a nearby promontory with a large leaning boulder. When at this promontory, look around corner. You must now decide which ledge you choose to follow around into Graham Spur [see Comments below]. Higher is narrow but goes and later on you still need to drop off of it.

Lower requires friction moves or a jump to get to, is also narrow and scary, but widens further on. Both ledges are extremely exposed, and you should use caution. At last promontory which splits McLoyds and Graham Spur, you must get onto only ledge which 'goes' further. This ledge is narrow, and in places a bulge tries to force you outwards. A technique I use is to trail a hand along underside of overhang as I walk along, in case I stumble a bit. For more info, see Access #5. My dogs have been along both these ledges, over into Graham Spur, and along single ledge which 'goes'. Once around corner where ledge widens, you still must find breaks down to a ledge which will get you below Access #5.

Access 5: NOT FOR NOVICE HIKERS! Graham Spur [my name only] is longest *cr* side canyon and is in middle of S2 on TI map. Do not start at its head, but downcanyon *cr* just above its biggest dropoff is a long talus/juniper slope. It gets you down to just above main dropoff, and on down below this dropoff. From there it is a short walk down to McLoyds.

Upcanyon from Graham Spur confluence, in McLoyds, there is another impassable stepup. A narrow ledge, which you can do standing up, starts *cr* at McLoyds/Graham Spur junction, and around a corner you climb up to a higher ledge with a faint trail but easy walking upcanyon from this dropoff. This climb up is only about 10-12 feet in a wide, sloping crack with some footholds and is only moderately difficult for EXPERT HIKERS ONLY!!. Downcanyon from Graham Spur is a wide trail to Fish, not quite 2 miles further. A hiker died in Graham Spur, according to BLM, a year or so back; a BLM ranger told me he took one step he shouldn't have, due to tiredness and lack of attention.

DOWNCANYON FROM GRAHAM SPUR C: is very easy walking along an obvious trail, there can be some water in slickrock pools for first 1/2 mile, and I found water under a house-sized boulder in streambed about 1/3 way down to Fish C. It took me 45 minutes to 1 hour to do this lower end, depending on site-seeing and breaks.

WATER: there are springs thruout McLoyds and Graham Spur, but lower McLoyds may be dry. Fish Canyon has intermittent pools thruout, even in 2002 [a very dry year].

ATTRACTIONS: Most people come to see Moonhouse [Moon Kiva]. So many that BLM has posted a sign asking people to stay out. This seems not to work very well, perhaps a fence or total closure is next. There are other sites, some art, some of which are also well visited.

COMMENTS: McLoyds is named for one of two early pothunters introduced to this area by R. Wetherill [or perhaps vice versa]. His name is spelled McCloyd sometimes, but according to a laminated brochure at Moonhouse, he signed as McLoyd. 'Graham Spur' [not official], is named by me after C.C. Graham. Bullet C. used to be called Graham C., and although Graham and McLoyd were possibly worse pothunters than Wetherills [certainly open to argument, many archaeologist/historians label Wetherills as 'Crude Excavators'] Graham was an important catalyst to ggulch's initial popularity, thus I name this otherwise nameless sidecanyon after him.

NOTE: whether you enjoy now reopened road from Snow Flat road to McLoyd rim, or passionately hate SJ County or BLM for reopening it, please take my advice. Do not block this road with logs, rocks, interfere with vehicles parked at trailhead, argue with hikers using road, or in any other way childishly act out your opinions. Instead write or call BLM and/or SJ County and vent. This road requires a hi clearance, narrow vehicle, with experienced driver and should not be attempted when wet, and that should keep most drivers out anyway [it is not main-tained, and starts thru a little gully].

Due to immense popularity of Moonhouse and heavy visitation you are asked to treat it as a national treasure. Just as you would handle with care any artifact you found. Help keep others out, photo from below or across canyon. Buy books with photos of it. Or look at a few photos in my website. I believe one option BLM could consider is to post a larger sign with thorough pictures of its insides, hoping this might suffice. Another option is, of course, total fencing off. Moonhouse's future is up to every person who goes to see it.

If I seem to be over-emphasizing difficulties in using some of detours I describe above, there is good reason. McLoyds is a very popular canyon, or at least part of it, but overall it is quite hazardous. Graham Spur is a viable alternative to accessing McLoyds' lower end, and its long talus slope is merely strenuous, dangerous if not paying attention. Upper McLoyds C is also interesting, but has smaller dropoffs. When in doubt about your hiking abilities/strengths in any area of Cedar Mesa, a fine alternative exists--rimwalking. There is plenty to see, walking is usually very easy, many times there is water in small pools, and usually a faint trail to follow [thus avoiding cryptogramic soils].

* * *

ROAD CANYON

It is moderately easy, with some difficult spots, has three main forks, and is quite popular. It is on east side of Cedar

Mesa and drains into Comb Wash. Lower Road C is fine for solo novice hikers.

MAPS: Snow Flat Spring Cave 7.5 [main], Bluff SW 7.5 [lower] and Cedar Mesa N 7.5 [upper] cover it all. Use TI #706 also.

GETTING THERE: *North Fork*: use Snow Flat Road, SJ237, aka. 'Emigrant Trail' @ 22.5mm Hwy 261, or about 1 mile west of Comb Ridge on Hwy 163. *Main and South Forks*: use Cigarette Springs Road, SJ239 @ 19.1mm Hwy 261.

HIKING ROAD C

NORTH FORK

Access 1: about 4.5 miles east on SJ237 from hwy [left at first 'Y' close to pavement] park where you can and hike south. I have yet to do this.

Access 2: park at Moonhouse trailhead parking lot on south side of SJ237, 8.3 miles from hwy 261. Hike south and find one of many breaks into Road [I found one thru a small gully here just below upper two forks]. There are other ways in/out I have spotted from below between #2 and #3, one is south of 5562 bm in a gully to east.

Access 3: from 'Twist' [see its page] and realize an alternative route is to contour from Twist up into this North Fork and find a break down [my first route in]. Or, hike in from mouth of Road C. This fork is fairly flat and easy hiking.

MAIN FORK

Access 1: 3.4 miles east of hwy 261 on SJ239, and about 100 yards east of a road shown on maps which goes around head of Lime C, park in a camping area on north side. Follow a trail north which heads around one little upper fork, goes down thru some logs and gets onto slickrock. Immediately you encounter a rock garden which does not take long to get around. Road C gets interesting w/i first 30 minutes from your car, and is fairly easy walking.

Upcanyon from 'main' entrance are 3 dropoffs. First is easy to detour, second you can go either way although *cl* is perhaps safer [easier]. Third, unless you swim thru a pool, only realistically goes *cr*, and it is a long walk around before you can descend. *Option 1*: descend just opposite of a small ruin you will see, it goes although it may not look like it from above, and you drop down 3 feet near a small tree. *Option 2*: continue along another several hundred yards before you can get down, and this last has several cairns marking it at canyon bottom.

It is just about 5 minutes further downcanyon to 'main' entrance, and another 20 to 7 kiva ruin. STAY OFF KIVA ROOFS! This ruin is quite visible from below; pick which route you use into it carefully to minimize erosion. I think very soon BLM will have to barricade parts of 7 Kiva Ruin as it has others in ggulch to protect it from careless visitors.

Access 2 [main]: 5.6 mi. from hwy 261 on SJ 239 is a short spur road [closed]. .4 further, 6 miles from hwy, turn north on a bumpy hi-clearance, ok-for-2wd-if-dry, 1 mi. 'road' to parking area. This 'road' is 4wd if at all wet. Route is in a gully east of this parking lot. You can go NW to a little spur of this gully, then back east to skirt dropoff, and follow cairns down talus/juniper slope *cr*. An alternative route further *cl* in this gully is more visible from below, but is not a shortcut. Just before you reach main canyon a cairned detour goes *cr*, but you can as easily stay in streambed of this route if not too wet/icy. There is a visible trail downcanyon.

Access 3: park in or near first major gully crossing east of #2 turnoff on main road about 6.3 miles from hwy 261. Follow shallow gully, there is now an obvious trail as this route is gaining in popularity. There are 3 dropoffs downcanyon, and some minor boulder gardens. It might be possible to stay *cl* at all dropoffs, as I could see where some people had stacked rocks at one ledge, but *cr* for first two is better. At last dropoff a trail *cl* goes across alluvium down to Road. Years ago, I stayed *cr* for all of it, and never saw other footprints. Look around for cairns, etc.

Access 4: NOT RECOMMENDED just north of S23, 24,25,26 intersection is a short side canyon into Road. Follow SJ239 to its end and hike north. I actually came out this access, but it is steep, brushy and I do not think I would use it again. At its lower end I mistakenly tried to go up inner gorge [someone has made a little campsite here], but came to a dropoff. Returning to main trail I went upcanyon and saw a side trail steeply going up a slope. It has some cairns which I lost soon. I hiked up onto benches above inner gorge, detouring around north fork of this side canyon [which looked barely doable] and walked over to and up a steep talus slope *cr* up south fork. Dusty [one of my slickrock dogs] found us a faint animal trail up but when we got under top cliffs on a skinny sloping and overgrown ledge we thrashed until we found a way up and out [took us an hour total]. *Access 5*: at Twist [see its page].

Access 6 and 7: near elev. 4990 in S33 [not labeled] it is easy to enter a shallow inner gorge. You can also enter lower Road where Snow Flat road crosses it in S1 near 4491 bm, or near 4850 bm further west. There are of course other possible ways in/out along entire length of Road.

SOUTH FORK

Access 1: follow SJ239 to its end at a camping area. There are two short forks, separated by 1/4 mile. It could be possible to make a loop of both, contouring along lower ledges. I have explored this upper area but not hiked downcanyon.

Access 2: hike in further downcanyon in Road.

WATER: there are numerous springs thruout all of Road C, but carry water anyway and definitely filter/purify as needed.

ATTRACTIONS: Road C is a very interesting place,

relatively easy to hike in and is gaining in popularity everyday. There are a number of sites of all kinds, you only have to look around and ENJOY.

* * *

LIME CANYON

It is a medium length, moderately popular, canyon on east side of Cedar Mesa. It starts very near Hwy 261 and flows thru VOG and down to SJ river. Basically hiking is easy in its mid-stretch. In/out routes are rough, bottom is fairly easy hiking. Ok for solo novice hikers, with caution.

MAPS: Cedar Mesa N 7.5 covers its head; Cigarette Spring 7.5 covers lower part. Cedar Mesa S 7.5 covers West Lime Creek Canyons. Use TI #706 also.

GETTING THERE

MAIN UPPER: just north of 16mm Hwy 261 turn northeast on an unmarked dirt road. About 1.2 miles later, look for a 4wd rd branching left [this road goes around head of Lime, over to Cigarette Springs road and is shown on TI map] and nearby a small sandstone mesa with '6424' elev. shown on TI map. On main road [past this side road] you soon come to a barbed-wire fence. Park here somewhere. Not shown on TI map, this 4wd road continues several miles onto a ridge between Lime and West Lime.

LOWER: drive in thru VOG [see its page] and some route finding is needed. You will not be able to drive closer than wide valleys where Lime opens out.

W FORK: anywhere between 14-16mm east side of Hwy 261 are roads leading over to its many forks. Use VOG roads for lower W Lime access.

HIKING LIME CANYON:

MAIN UPPER: follow barbed-wire fence north and use a small gully just east of it. Or, back towards hwy, take a 4wd road shown on TI map around to head of Lime. Or, continue on 'main' road southeast where several side canyons go, more or less reluctantly. Hiking in Lime is relatively easy, there are some sites, and plenty of water tho maybe not in summer.

LOWER: starts out thru cattle country in VOG and is pretty bland/blah. Gradually you enter a canyon and soon reach various impassable stepups. However, when rimwalking above VOG there are several possible Anasazi routes visible below.

HIKING W LIME CANYON: mostly interesting for many canyons and ridges areas with fine vues. W Lime has a major dropoff which may be skirtable with difficulty *cl.* Below it is easy, flat and in cattle country.

WATER: intermittent small springs thruout all forks, less in lower parts. Purify/filter all water.

ATTRACTIONS: it is quiet, seldom visited, scenic, has a few sites, water for dogs, no fee is charged as of last time I was there.

* * *

COMB RIDGE

Is a prominent long ridge which abuts against Abajos and ends near Kayenta, AZ. I cover only Comb Ridge north of Hwy 163. It has impassable cliffs on west side, and sloping slickrock juniper/canyons on east side. Great for solo novice hikers.

MAPS: from N to S: Hotel Rock 7.5, Bluff NW 7.5, Bluff SW 7.5, Boundary Butte 7.5. Use TI #706 also.

GETTING THERE: SJ river and Hwy 163 cut thru it on south end, Butler Wash road is next to it on east, Comb Wash road is next to it on west, Hwy 95 cuts thru it further north, and several other small roads cross it south of Whiskers Draw. Some of these roads change SJ county numbers, so study a map closely.

HIKING COMB R: is a highly overlooked gem of SE Utah hiking. A few popular sites draw people for short hikes. Cliffy west side is impassable, except for several breaks north of Hwy 95, and further south a few very worn out sets of Anasazi steps [aka Moki Steps].CAUTION: these steps are shallow, eroded, very steep and dangerous. Of course, it would be fun to top-rope them with a companion, and they are very scenic from below.

East side is easy hiking, whether you choose many little canyons which sometimes cliff out or intermediate slickrock slopes. It is fun to hike up to west rim and walk north or south, having to route-find your way along edge. Usually, when driving up Butler Wash road if you see a turnout there is something interesting nearby. There is even one washed out 4wd road up to top.

WATER: almost every little canyon has water in wetter years, many have water even in dry years. A few have large pools next to popular ruins.

ATTRACTIONS: Comb R combines easy hiking with superb vues, plenty of water holes for dogs, no fees, few other hikers, and plenty of complex little 'problems' of route finding to solve. There are also many fine camping spots, sheltered from an ever-present wind. Hiking is mostly on slickrock.

* * *

DRY WASH

Is a truly named short canyon on east side of Cedar Mesa which drains into Comb Wash between Mule and Fish canyons. One fork has a good spring, and a Hovenweep-like mesa top ruin.

MAPS: Bluff NW 7.5 covers it all. Use TI #706 also.

GETTING THERE: Turn south off Hwy 95 just east of 101mm onto SJ236, Balleys Lower rd [may not be a sign]. There will be one or two branch roads turning right in first 2 miles, but stay on main road. You will skirt a fenced section of land on your left; stay on main road for about 6 miles, slimy if wet, until you come to a capped drill hole where road narrows and forks. Turn right, pass by another capped well, and follow as it winds thru trees less than a mile. Road ends next to a small canyon. Picket fork may be accessed from one fork of this road. You can also in/out lower Dry Wash from Comb Wash road, tho it is a long hike on cattle trails to see anything. I am probably one of few hikers to do this.

HIKING DRY WASH: most people come here to picnic and/or see Balleys Towers. I have hiked down from near a spring and around into main Dry Wash, upcanyon a few miles then up, out and back to my pickup. It is well-named and has very little streambed [dry]. Far down this valley is a small hilltop ruin with a spring nearby. If you know where to look, you can see it from Balleys Towers.

WATER: may be some near ruins in wet years. Smaller hilltop ruin downcanyon has a spring nearby.

ATTRACTIONS: mostly small ruins and vues.

COMMENTS: there may be some confusion about proper spelling of Balleys. TI map claims "Little Baullie Mesa" where Hotel Rock is. An ancient SJ County sign at drill hole reads "Balleys Lower". TI map lists a 'Baullies' just west of Mule C. Either whoever made sign can't spell or when making up map someone guessed. I use local spelling until I see evidence other is correct.

* * *

HOTEL ROCK

Is a distinctive little sandstone mesa between Arch canyon and Comb wash; it is on juniper flats at same level as Texas Flats, and below Milk Ranch Point. Hiking to it is easier than driving.

MAPS: Hotel Rock 7.5 covers it all. Use TI #706 or #703 also.

GETTING THERE: you can drive to it most months except winter with 4wd hi-clearance vehicle; drive up onto South Elk Ridge [connects Abajos with Dark C. plateau]. Turn north off Hwy 95 onto Hwy 275 as if going into NBNM; just off hwy turn north onto SJ228, aka FR088.

Soon after going between Bears Ears, follow FR088 east thru an intersection and around above heads of Arch and Butts canyons. Turn south onto FR182; several miles further, go right at a 'Y'. Road goes downhill soon and immediately becomes 4wd, hi-clearance. I have not driven this road yet, but walked most of it. TI map #703 incorrectly shows that this road continues on as 2wd alongside Arch and down to Comb wash. ROAD IS SEVERELY PRIMITIVE 4WD SE OF HOTEL ROCK, and there is one spot where only very narrow vehicles can go.

HIKING HOTEL ROCK

Option A: follow directions for Arch canyon on its page. About .3 mile past Arch canyon's mouth along Comb Wash road is bottom of this 4wd road, to west. Hike up it, thus scouting it also.

Option B: drive on up Comb Wash for about 1 mile further and park somewhere that looks interesting. Hike west up any slickrock slope, or up any shallow canyon. As soon as you top out above, you can see Hotel Rock and hike over to it.

Option C: hike up into Arch Canyon to first *cl* sidecanyon, up to its head, and climb out [not easy] then hike over to Hotel Rock, and back along 4wd road next to Arch Canyon, back to your vehicle. See 'Arch Canyon' page for more details.

WATER: bring your own, as there are no springs or creeks, and only if it rained would there be slickrock pools.

ATTRACTIONS: it is very scenic, you can hike up around on top [bring your camera], and there are some sites all around it, tho none are big or particularly well-preserved. You can also rimwalk along Arch canyon or its nearby forks. There are other small canyons on west slopes of Comb Wash north of Hotel Rock.

* * *

TWIST

Is an appropriately named section of Snow Flat road aka SJ237 where road switches up a short sandstone cliffed incline. This is very obvious as road downhill [east] of Twist is easy if dry and climbs slowly. Twist is 4wd going up, rough for a 2wd [hi-clearance only] coming down. All hikes described here are easier from slickrock flats halfway up Twist. Some areas are easy, some rough. Ok for novice hikers.

MAPS: Bluff NW 7.5, Snow Flat Spring Cave 7.5, and Bluff SW 7.5 plus TI #706 maps cover this area. It takes so many because Twist is in extreme lower left corner of Bluff NW 7.5. There are also 15 min. maps which cover this area, if still available.

GETTING THERE: moderately easy if roads dry. Snow Flat road [aka Mormon Trail or Emigrant Trail] joins Hwy 261 @ 22.5mm [approx.]. Just east of this SF road forks, north fork is main road, south fork goes to private land at Brushy Flat [acquired via homestead act years ago]. Down south, SF road joins Hwy 163 about 1 mile NW of Comb Ridge roadcut. SF road can get impassable when very wet. You will know when you get to Twist as it is roughest stretch of this otherwise 2wd road.

HIKING TWIST

North: from an obvious parking area below, and north of SF road you can hike into Snow Flat Spring Cave Canyon [my name only] easily. Just scout below you for a route. SFSC Canyon can be reached from above via a short now-reopened road off SF road. I have also hiked across country from Twist to lower Fish C tho this is easier from north of Fish [see Fish C]. There are several ways down into Fish which I have found, tho they are difficult to scout from above. One has a few small sites nearby.

South: I have also hiked into Road C from Twist merely to access midway parts of lower end. Thru trial and error I have found only one good route into Road C w/o having to contour upcanyon for miles. From SE flats just below nasty section of Twist, hike south along a little ridge. Look for cairns and there is a way down on west side of this ridge. You can see this from below easier. Final climb down [which I have come up w/dogs] is in a small gully break in inner gorge, just to right of '4800' contour on TI map, and just south of '5226' elev. marker. Careful scouting should reveal this from above. Downcanyon from this break may be other breaks.

WATER: none unless it has rained recently. Both Fish C, Road C, and SFSC C have some water. Packing your own water is always best.

ATTRACTIONS: Whether or not you hike very far north or south, it is an interesting area. You can also goof-along ledges, bask in sun, or just picnic with a vue. Access to Road is closer than Fish, and could be done as a loop with another vehicle up or down Road C.

* * *

HONAKER TRAIL

Descends inner gorge of San Juan river near Goosenecks overlook. A great place to hike in winter, when snow or mud keeps you off Cedar Mesa or just for its own sake. Great for solo novice hikers.

MAPS: Goosenecks 7.5 covers it. Use TI #706 also.

GETTING THERE: Just north of Mexican Hat turn onto Hwy 261, go north ..8mi, turn west towards Gooseneck Overlook and go .5mi to first dirt road north [Johns Canyon road, no sign]. Follow for 2.5 miles, turn left at a 'Y' near a steel water tank, there is a small steel sign reading "Honaker Trail". Follow this road for 1.6 miles; [small hill @ 1.1 mile can be 4wd coming back, as everyone chews it up with their 2wds] road is mixed sand and clay and rocky stretches. At a 'T', just before San Juan River, go left on a limestone/sand bench [road to right ends after .5 mile approx.]. After ..3 mi.

look for a small road going right to edge of canyon. Most people park here, as road is only .1 mi. long and has a 4wd bump. If you continue, main road ends after 1.3 on a windy, private 'Goosenecks Overlook'.

HIKING HONAKER TRAIL: look for a 3 foot hi cairn next to cliffs. Trail starts there, and was constructed by miners hoping to strike it rich. They did not, but you benefit from this fine trail, since maintained by BLM. A few places can be a bit washed out or fallen off, but overall it is in excellent shape. Generally you can get to river in just over an hour, tho stopping on a distinctive promontory is a must. From there you can look straight down on a river runners' camping beach. Trail switches back and forth in long legs and is about 2-2.5 miles long.

You can stroll along up or down river as far as you want [or until you are cliffed out]. If you go up river about a mile to mile and a half trail pinches out but if you backtrack a bit and look up you can follow a kool ledge with cairns and deer tracks and keep going. Around corner is a fine vue up river. Look closely for miners ruins both up and down from river runners' camps where Honaker meets river.

WATER: none until you get to San Juan river, unless it has rained recently.

ATTRACTIONS: Great for dogs. No BLM fee. Great place to hike in winter, as usually there is little precipitation [snow] and it usually melts off fast. Plus, tho dry, there is a whole river for dogs to swim in and drink at bottom. Super scenic, reminds me of many Grand Canyon hikes. Gradient is mellow, except in a few cliff bands and near river. Boy Scout groups hike here often.

* * *

VALLEY OF GODS

Is an open valley walled in on one side by Cedar Mesa's cliffs. It is similar in some ways to Monument Valley, and about 10-12 miles north of Mexican Hat. Some come just to drive thru, some to climb its spires, some to hike. There is a classic overlook along 'Moki Dugway' a lovely section of Hwy 261, and another at Muley Point, just west of where Dugway tops out. A Bed and Breakfast is near its NW side, very visible from above.

MAPS: Cigarette Spring Cave 7.5, Cedar Mesa South 7.5 and Goosenecks 7.5 maps cover most of it. TI map #706 also covers it all.

GETTING THERE: easy, sometimes more difficult to drive thru it [when roads wet]. About 4.5 miles NE of Hwy 163's intersection with Hwy 261, in a sharp bend, SJ242 leaves Hwy 163. It winds around thru VOG and comes out on Hwy 261 just south of Moki Dugway. Another road, SJ226, leaves Hwy 163 at top of long hill [Lime R] west of Comb R. There is a corral and stock pond north of Hwy 163. This road joins SJ242 west of Lime Creek and is used mostly by local ranchers.

HIKING VOG: there is nothing particularly difficult in hiking in VOG unless you use it to access lower parts of Lime Creek. I have been into both main forks of Lime. To get there, you have to study your maps well and hike long ways thru cattle country. Both do cliff out in large stepups, tho there are other ways to get up. Above you along rims are widely scattered sites which take persistence to find.

In VOG there is at least one arch, and it is difficult to spot until later in day. It is north of Franklin Butte, almost exactly where S16 is printed on TI map. If you elect to rimwalk above VOG [from hwy 261], realize that any dirt road [works for John's Canyon too] which actually leads somewhere will have ruts [needing high clearance car] and wood-cutters roads usually have sagebrush growing in middle, with almost no ruts [has to do with years of use].

WATER: most of Lime Creek's forks have water, otherwise along rims and in VOG you will only find water in slickrock pools or cattle tanks.

ATTRACTIONS: Several years ago, I spent many consecutive dayhikes rimwalking VOG. I returned 20 Jan, '01 during balloon festival. I used a rutted, snow covered, almost 4wd ranch/woodcutters road and repeated a route done before. I found a small ruin I thot very difficult to access [and did not], not even my old footprints, saw almost no evidence of visitation, nor anyone. I even repeated exactly a little section which I remembered, where I had to jump up a little ledge to avoid an overgrown juniper. These rims are cliffy, and often I had to hike around to find some break doable with dogs.

Once out 'on point' vues are fantastic. VOG rims are similar to Comb R in their understated complexity, a fact you may not discover until halfway lost. Landmarks seem ubiquitous, and a route taken down [difficult to scout] may be missed on your return, thus leading [as in my case] to minor confusion at trying to find your vehicle. Any rewards, of course, seem complete. Canyon hiking, while ever popular, seldom gives you great vues.

CHAPTER 37
OTHER AREA HIKES

BLANDING

Westwater Canyon and Big Canyon are two canyons just west of Blanding, Utah. Use TI #703, Manti-La Sal Nat'l Forest map. If you drive west on Hwy 95, within a mile of leaving 'Shirttail Junction', where a gas station and junction of Hwy 95/Hwy 191 is, you descend into Westwater Canyon.

Westwater Canyon is a tributary of South Cottonwood Creek. And a short ways upcanyon from Hwy 95, Big Canyon splits off. After driving thru Westwater Canyon, Hwy 95 climbs its west side. Immediately after, turn north on SJ288 a.k.a. Warren Allen road, which is just a rutted clay road. About .75 mile north, ignoring many turnouts, is a 'Y' with a survey marker nearby. Turn right and drive barely .2 mile and park where Blanding teens party. Just below you is 'Spirit Cave', as it is known locally, which is a partly trashed out multi-room ruin under a kool overhang in streambed.

Over in Westwater Canyon, and reachable by paved road, is another ruin. Take Ruin Road, SJ232, a paved road west of Hwy 191, which is just south of an old Drive In Theater screen [still visible] on south side of town. There is a sign reading 'Scenic View'. Across canyon where this road turns back to south is a small barely visible arch [similar to Gold Bar arch near Moab], and where it deadends is a ruin.

* * *

DARK CANYON

Is a remote Wilderness Area which starts on western side of Abajos and drains into Lake Powell. It is about 40 to 45 miles long, ranges from sagebrush-bland to full-blown kool and rugged canyon. Not for solo novice hikers.

MAPS: I do not have these maps, but I think these cover most of it: Indian Head Pass 7.5, Black Steer Canyon 7.5, Warren Canyon 7.5, Poison Canyon 7.5, Woodenshoe Buttes 7.5 and Kigalia Point 7.5. Use TI #703 also.

GETTING THERE

MAIN: turn north off Hwy 95 onto UT 275 [NBNM.], drive .6mi, turn right onto SJ228 [aka FR088], 7.7mi turn right at 'Y' and stay on FR088 thru several intersections, passing heads of Arch C and Hammond C. Eventually you come to head of Dark C, called 'Notch' and sign at trailhead.

WOODENSHOE C: follow directions above, but at a 'Y' 7.7 miles from hwy, turn left onto SJ256 [aka FR108], you will pass Peavine trailhead at 2mi, and a 'Y' for Woodenshoe at 3.6mi. There is a sign, road is maintained, but could get slimy if wet. There is some gravel on steep parts of SJ228 above NBNM, but on top of Dark C. Plateau, there is very little. Anyway, after leaving SJ256, it is 1mi north to trailhead, which has a new outhouse and parking lot.

SUNDANCE TRAIL: there is a little map with directions on TI map #703. There are many other side trail entrances not as well known. Study maps.

HIKING DARK C: it starts out at Notch shallow and sagebrushy, and takes a lot of miles before it deepens. Woodenshoe, my favorite side canyon also starts out foresty bland for several miles before getting down to slick-rock. For more info, please see one of many hiking guide books available.

PERSONAL EXPERIENCES: I have hiked parts of Woodenshoe. In last few years there is little water until you get to Cherry C. I have been up Cherry Canyon to its first creek split. I have driven down Peavine in 4wd and hiked down from Rig Canyon to Trail Canyon which except for one arch is really bland. And I have hiked once down Sundance almost to river. Sundance is an almost insane route [not really much of a trail] into lower Dark, but is used enough to be almost obvious. Among certain crowds, lower Dark is popular. I recommend you go with someone on this remote lower trail, and stay several days exploring.

WATER: Dark Canyon has springs in good years all thru it. Woodenshoe has several springs, one has dried in recent years, but at Cherry C confluence that spring should be reliable.

ATTRACTIONS: parts of Dark Canyon are very scenic, it is remote, not a lot of people go there and it is quiet. There are a few scattered sites, at least one arch.

*   *   *

HORSESHOE CANYON

Is a detached part of Canyonlands Nat'l Park on west side of Green River and north of Maze. No camping is allowed, but its rock art panels are within easy walking distance anyway. Fine for solo novice hikers. It is growing in popularity.

MAPS: Use TI #246.

GETTING THERE: Easiest access is off Hwy 24, which joins Hwy 95 in Hanksville and goes north to I-70 just west of Green River, Utah, just south of Goblin Valley paved turnoff on east side. There is a sign for Hans Flat Ranger Station but it does not mention Horseshoe Canyon. Stay on main road and after awhile significant forks are signed with directions to Horseshoe. It is a good road if dry, and only last 2 miles has a few rough spots. DeLorme's Utah Atlas shows route in but overcomplicates it with many side roads, which are a lot less obvious as you go in.

Overall this road entices one to zip along, be aware of

some sharp corners, however, and there are some nice vues. You can also get to it from further north, but I have not driven this way.

HIKING HORSESHOE CANYON: Once you finally reach parking lot, trail is well cairned and follows an old [now closed] ranch road down into canyon. Hiking along stream is easier than ggulch, as it is a wide, mostly flat canyon bottom. Main attraction is 4 main areas of Anasazi art on canyon walls, and if you can find them, dinosaur tracks. Further upcanyon, I climbed partway up Deadman Trail for a vue. This is a possible in/out and is described in most hiking books with a chapter on Horseshoe, but road leading to it is remote and rough, it starts at Hans Flat RS. I have not explored up or downcanyon from central area. Most books about rock art mention Barrier Canyon [Style], which is older name for Horseshoe Canyon.

WATER: when I hiked there was some runoff/springs which may dry up in hotter months and drier years.

ATTRACTIONS: mostly 4 very nice Barrier Canyon Style rock art panels. As stated earlier, original name for Horseshoe Canyon was Barrier Canyon, thus these panels are archetypes for similar panels found wherever Fremont [contemporary but culturally different from Anasazi] roamed. No doubt mapmakers and BLM have changed its name to minimize visitation. Other notable BCS rock artpanels can be found on Capitol Reef and San Rafael Swell, along Fremont River, in Thompson Canyon near I-70, and in Nine Mile Canyon just north of Wellington Utah, to name a few [also around Moab].

* * *

HOVENWEEP

Is a large open canyon-valley between Blanding and Cortez. It is a Nat'l Park and has several clusters of tower ruins, combined with small cliffdwellings. All of these clusters are near water, most in nondescript short side canyons on top of level ground above Hovenweep Canyon. None of trails are very long or difficult. You can now buy a pass from NPS which gives you unlimited access to Arches, Canyonlands, NBNM and Hovenweep for a year for $25.

MAPS: probably best maps would be highway maps of Utah and Colorado, as it straddles UT/CO state line. Topos are not really necessary.

GETTING THERE: there are several ways.

From West: on Hwy 191 in Utah, about 36mm, turn east onto Hwy 262 and follow signs for about 20 miles.

From Cortez, CO: just south of Cortez on Hwy 666, at new traffic lite where M and M truck stop is, turn west onto McElmo road. Stay on it and follow signs for 35 or 40 miles.

From North: on Hwy 666, northwest of Cortez, CO, and near town of Pleasant View, turn west at signs for Hovenweep and you will eventually pass some of its isolated northern ruin groups of Hovenweep. CAUTION: this road is not a very good 'all weather road' and it can easily become slimy 4wd in winter.

WATER: bring your own, as most hikes are very short, but there is some seep/spring water near most main ruin groups. Water probably also at Visitor's Center.

ATTRACTIONS: many easily accessible tower ruins, in clusters.

* * *

SAND AND EAST ROCK

Are one of many tributary canyons to McElmo Creek which is west of Cortez, Co. Many people drive thru McElmo on way to Hovenweep NP, and this whole part of Four Corners has thousands of sites scattered around. Sand and East Rock have become so popular sometimes you might think you are in a city park on a Sunday. At other times you will see nobody.

MAPS: Battle Rock 7.5 and Woods Canyon 7.5, both in

Colorado cover most of this area.

GETTING THERE: Very easy.

Bottom end: south of Cortez, on Hwy 666, turn west at a new traffic lite where M and M truck stop is onto McElmo road which soon passes airport. Stay on pavement 12.5 miles. About 1/2 mile after crossing a creek, a large slickrock area with a little rock tower is on right. Park here and hike up past signs around north side of a rock tower.

Upper end: drive north of Cortez on Hwy 666 about 3 miles after road squeezes back to two lane. Turn west on 'P' county road which is a well used intersection. Continue on west and eventually road makes a wide detour north then joins a north-south road [about 4 or 5 miles from hwy]. Go south less than a mile back to 'P' road and continue west. As soon as practical, go south one mile to 'N' road and continue west. Sand Canyon pueblo which is undergoing an official dig by Crow Canyon Archaeological Center [in Cortez] is very obvious and south of road. Trailhead starts in midst of pueblo, which is believed to be one of largest in this area. There may now be signs marking route.

STARTING OUT [bottom end]: trail goes around left of sandstone mesa [west side] and is well cairned. Trail splits just before small cliffs after a sloping slickrock patch. BLM has put up new trail signs, one is here. If you continue straight, you enter Sand Canyon. If you follow trail west below these cliffs, after a few miles you enter East Rock Canyon. Later, you can hike between these two for a nice loop.

EAST ROCK CANYON: starting as described above, hike west below cliffs and there are numerous ruins above you. Soon trail turns SW and you can see a guard tower ruin above. It rounds a promontory, and turns north again. Now you can see East Rock which heads north for several miles. Your trail soon drops down a little and follows an old roadway. There is an arch north of you which hugs closely largest cliffs between canyon inner gorge and a promontory which actually separates East Rock from Sand.

Two easy options offer: either continue on this roadway until you get to large cliffs to north or find one of several ways down into inner gorge of East Rock and hike upcanyon until you see a small sandstone tower *cr* with a ruin on top. Behind this about a hundred yards to west are more ruins and Anasazi rock art on small cliffs. You can hike on upcanyon a little ways further. There is a horse trail which leads from head of E. Rock back around west side of East Rock and south or back east across a ridge between East Rock and Sand. It is easy to hike across and over to Sand, passing a small adit [mine hole]. There are probably signs now.

ROCK CANYON: You can also hike over into main canyon of Rock C. There is a short section of lovely slickrock narrows which is fairly easy to hike thru, and beyond it seems to get bland and go forever.

SAND CANYON: Soon after leaving slickrock at trailhead, trail levels off and winds around upcanyon on this broad bench. There are numerous obvious ruins. There is a sandy gully on left of trail with a small trail near it which leads over to saddle and East Rock. [Marker post here now.] A small rock house ruin is above this gully and probably was a ranch cabin. Soon after passing this route over to East Rock, Sand C. trail switches down a short hill. There is a nice overlook which looks down into several more ruins.

Eventually, trail enters inner gorge and seems to cliff out. Just back downcanyon trail climbs *cr*. BLM extended main trail up steep switches and further north to Sand Canyon Pueblo far above.

Just where trail enters inner gorge, a faint horse trail crosses to east side of Sand C and continues around for miles.

Both these canyons are perfect for winter dayhikes, as

they rarely have much snow in them for long. East Rock is more exposed to winter sun. While living in Durango, I used to drive over thruout winter for dayhikes in Sand/East Rock. There are other nearby canyons/valleys with ruins and art. Sand/East Rock are merely easiest to access, and by far most popular. A very fine area for dayhikes!

WATER: there is water in both canyons, but cattle graze here, so I would bring my own. Usually there is a pool near trail, in Sand, just south of switchbacks. Most of trail is above inner gorge, so water is remote. Usually there is some water for dogs, and many people bring them along on their hikes, also horses and llamas.

ATTRACTIONS: in Nov, '00 for lack of a better idea, I returned to Sand with 2 dogs for a snow hike after an eventful absence of almost 4 years. Some new facets that I found and liked are new 4" by 4" signposts marking junctions of trails and one at 'Alcove Ruin'. Also, at 'Alcove Ruin' BLM has built a trail against cliff to keep visitors off midden pile, probably wishing nobody climbed into it but bowing to inevitable. Also, while hiking out and not paying attention, I followed a short spur trail and literally stumbled into a ruin I had probably passed 20 times and never seen. There is a similar ruin less than 10' from trail very near marker post for East Rock and Sand trail junction. Basically Sand and East Rock are easy hiking, full of sites easy to see, and relatively warm in winter.

PARKING LOT

CHAPTER 38
ANASAZI WAY

Following is not intended as a definitive treatise on Anasazi, merely a discussion.

Anasazi is a Navajo word meaning "Enemy Ancestors" or "Ancient Enemy" and has been accepted thru common usage to represent prehistoric Puebloan residents of Four Corners area of North America. Hopi [descended from Anasazi and other nearby cultural traditions] tribe prefers everyone use "Hisatsinom" which means 'old ones' in their language. Also according to Adler[1] Hopi prefer archaeologists stop writing about 'abandonment' of Four Corners [more later] but as I am not Hopi, nor do I know any, I will use 'Anasazi.'

'Puebloan', as used by Adler and others seems easier than "Pre-historic Puebloans". Term 'Pueblo' is Spanish and means walled city; when first Spanish explorers came into Southwest that is what they called mud-walled or stone-walled towns where indigents lived. Some call them [nowadays] 'Indians' or 'Native Americans.' 'Anasazi,' however derived suggests to most people those people who lived in 4 Corners area of geographical USA, before and during time they lived in pueblos. Before living in pueblos they lived in scattered pithouse structures, sometimes aggregated closely, and later in cliff dwellings.

Most popular interest is in their cliff dwelling period of habitation. Some of more spectacular Anasazi town sites, such as Chaco Canyon, were large towns with multiple story, thickly walled rooms all contiguous and connected, sometimes stacked 3 stories hi, and with enclosed plazas [or partially enclosed] and 'kivas.' These people were not really defined by their house or town styles, nor by any single aspect of their culture and since Navajo gave them name "Anasazi" I will use it. I do wonder if "Enemy Ancestors" suggests one reason for 'regional abandonment,' that Anasazi were in way of Navajo progress/migration, or at least they and Navajo did not see "eye to eye."

Anasazi predecessors either came across a *land bridge*[2] from Siberia/East Asia thru present day Canada and Alaska [highly probable], or rowed/sailed across on boats [highly unlikely, although barely possible in some cases], and spread out into North America. Anasazi predecessors were just one of many 'tribes' of Asians [or Europeans?] who migrated across. Some eventually migrated down to Central and South America, some to California, some to eastern USA. These disparate tribes probably came across at different times, there may have even been a much earlier migration before 11,000 [approx.] years ago. According to archaeologists, these emigrants spread fairly fast perhaps as quickly as 900 years.

Anasazi may not have immediately settled in Four Corners, they may have reverse-migrated from northern Mexico. Whatever exactly happened on these migrations, Anasazi as a cultural phenomena probably evolved from earlier Archaic man, who himself evolved from Paleo-Indian man. There are widely scattered sites representative of Archaic Man and some is known of his culture, but Paleo-Indian man is less well known archaeologically.

Jared Diamond[3] discusses world conquest history and claims reason Europeans went on to conquer our world is because they progressed to an Iron Age [and beyond] level of technology plus they developed ships capable of traveling around our world. Mayans, Inca, even Anasazi never progressed much beyond Stone Age technologies and certainly never had any ships with potential to cross oceans.

Anasazi descendants, Puebloans, were kicked into other technologies and cultural levels when conquered first by Spanish conquistadors and later by advancing tides of settlers from eastern US [more Europeans].

Backing up a bit in time, Anasazi moved in after Archaic, who in turn moved in after Paleo-Indian [Ferguson argues against direct evolution[4]]. They probably migrated thru, or traveled into for hunting-gathering trips, Four Corners area long before actually settling here. Archaic presence, archaeologically speaking, is scarce; early Anasazi presence more prevalent. Later on, possibly as climate and better cultigens allowed, population numbers increased and Anasazi building sites became ubiquitous to greater Four Corners area.

Archaeologists, in 1927 [thanks mostly to Kidder at his first Pecos Conference], began to separate Anasazi history into time/culture periods. There was originally a Basketmaker 1, 2, and 3, followed by a Pueblo 1 thru 5 with 'P5' being historic Puebloans. Basketmaker 1 [BM1] remains archaeologically non-existent, mostly replaced with 'Archaic' and archaeologists start with BM2. According to Cordell[5] diagnostic traits for each culture stage are: [I paraphrase from her book].

BM1, no longer used, basically it was pre-agricultural.

BM2, no pottery, agriculture is known, atlatl is used.

BM3, lived in pithouses or slab houses, pottery is made/used and not decorated, no cranial deformation.

P1, cranial deformation [caused by being strapped to cradle boards as infants], cooking vessels [pots] have banded necks, villages are above ground and composed of contiguous rectangular rooms of masonry [pueblos].

P2, cooking pots are exteriorly corrugated, small villages spread over large geographic area.

P3, very large communities [i.e. Chaco], and artistic elaboration and specialization in crafts.

P4, regional abandonment, little artistic elaboration, pottery devolves into plain ware.

P5, AD 1600 to present Pueblo history [i.e. casinos].

Actual calendrical dates applied to these stages are highly variable, depending on individ archaeologists. Ortiz[6] provides following chronology.

6000BC [approx.] to 200 BC Archaic

200BC to 400 AD BM2

400AD to 700 AD BM3

700 AD to 900 AD P1

900 AD to 1100 AD P2

1100AD to 1300AD P3

1300AD to 1600AD P4

1600AD to PRESENT P5

Adler dates P3 from 1150AD to 1350 AD. At any rate, these stages are somewhat arbitrary, although dated scientifically by carbon-dating; these stages are archaeologically determined as Anasazi probably did not have historians as such, nor did they see their progress in such a chopped-time manner. Archaeologists have since figured out that similar but different cultural stage classification schemes are applicable to nearby indigent populations; what seems to work to describe Anasazi may not work for Mimbres for example About all that remains of Anasazi 'history' are a few Pueblo migration and origin myths, at least as is known to ethnologists.

An increased sedentism and reliance on agriculture possibly also coincided with or started early stages of increased population aggregation. When corn, beans and squash cultivation over most of Anasazi area became a more important source of food than reliance on hunting and gathering, not only were more people needed to maintain and plant these crops, but population probably grew with increased stability of food supply.

Recent studies by archaeologists have shown that a shift to agriculture as main food source did not guarantee better nutrition or health. Possibly sedentism brought more disease thru contamination of a locale or water supplies. Hunter-gatherers seemingly had a better protein source in red meat. One question I have not seen answered by archaeologists, however, is "What if Anasazi elected to become sedentary, to evolve into Puebloans, for reasons we cannot now fathom?" Such as that they wanted to settle down, and a hunting-gathering lifeway is not compatible with a fixed residence--you tend to deplete local resources rapidly--of course sedentism leads to resource depletion as well. There may have been many factors leading them to this decision. Perhaps their leaders sensed that some beneficial effects would accrue from choosing to live in one locale. Perhaps they grew tired of constantly moving around, perhaps love of place drew them to certain locales. These kinds of questions are hard to ascertain from archaeological data alone, often ethnologists may provide clues.

A shift towards agriculture worldwide was an extremely important 'watershed' event, and for Anasazi it probably started their rise to P3 expansions and higher levels of populations. Possibly due to decreased moisture deposition and encroachments of territory by invaders, Anasazi culture/civilization began to decline as regionally large abandonments occurred. Consolidation into Hopi, Zuni and Rio Grande Pueblos happened only several hundred years before invasion by Spanish explorers.

Anasazi shared greater Southwest with other cultural traditions, notably Hohokam, Mogollon, Mimbres, and to a lesser extent Patayan. Some technologies were shared, some were not. Hohokam, for instance, are well known for their desert adaptability and extensive use of irrigation. Anasazi rarely used irrigation in riverine settings, however they did practice *akchin*[7] crop-watering. Whenever possible, such as on Cedar Mesa, they built small dams across streambeds to trap water, probably using pots or baskets to carry water to their plants, which is highly labor-intensive but may have been expedient given landscapes. Some irrigation was practiced on Mesa Verde and at Chaco, but never to full extent of Hohokam canals.

Agriculturally speaking, one more startling 'invention' whether by Anasazi or some other nearby cultural tradition was planting of corn in sand dunes. Water is retained deep under sand, and when planted below ground, corn tends to dig deep roots to tap this source, later bursting above ground to grow to a seemingly stunted height but providing corn. Some Navajo and Hopi continue this practice today.

Life expectancy of Anasazi was rarely more than up to low 30's, with a few exceptions of individs living into 40's or more. Infant mortality was probably high, due to nutritional supply and disease. Almost all adults suffered dental problems caused by practice of stone-grinding their grains in mano/metates; stone chips were a portion of their food.

Questions About Anasazi.

1. Why did they leave [abandon] 4 Corners area about 1276AD?

2. Where did they come from?

3. Who were they?

4. If Paleo-Indian man domesticated horses, what would have been different?

5. Why did they gradually switch from a hunter gatherer to a sedentary-agricultural lifeway?

6. Did endemic health/nutrition problems sap their mental outlook on life, or were these tribulations merely accepted as part of life?

7. What use did they make of kivas or Great Houses?

8. How much did certain centers of population/'power'

such as Chaco Canyon really influence smaller and more dispersed settlements?

9. Why did they build defensive structures, or in defensive locales late in their occupation?

10. Were they peaceful farmer-traders or warlike, sometimes resorting to cannibalism?

* * *

1. *Why did they leave [abandon] 4 Corners area in late 13th century?*

There are two main theories plus other minor ones. Environment, i.e. drought and uncertain growing conditions [over-population]. Warfare, or imminent threat therein either by less well-off Anasazi, or invading newcomers such as Utes or Navajos. Or, of course, a combination of these.

Many people are not aware that Anasazi never lived in one place very long, not even Mesa Verde. Most individ houses were probably only occupied for 15-40 years before becoming so dilapidated that it was easier to build anew than repair. A lifespan of most Anasazi was much less than anglos today, perhaps 30-40 years was a norm. Some individs may have lived much longer, many infants never survived one year.

There were many other hiatuses from certain areas, some lasting tens of years, some hundreds of years. Some areas were abandoned, with a few possible hangers-on, never to be returned to [Dolores, CO]. Cedar Mesa saw habitation in several cycles, interrupted by long hiatuses. Therefore, abandonment of an area or house was a regular pattern of lifeway for Anasazi, and their reasons are mostly obscured by time and lack of physical clues.

Nobody really knows, except possibly a few current Pueblo individs, why Anasazi seemingly all at once abandoned 4 Corners area. There is a persistent 'mystery' revolving around "where did they go [i.e. disappear] to." Currently this question is answered by understanding that they out-migrated to other centers of Puebloan population, such as Hopi villages, Rio Grande villages, Zuni villages, and others. Probably their reasons for a 'sudden' withdrawal revolve around at least one aspect of their lifeway. That is, they probably had some social interconnectedness, self-reliance and paradoxically a mutual support system, and when some families started to out-migrate, this system fell apart, thus necessitating a wide-spread migration elsewhere.

In other words, "when it is time to go, there is no use hesitating."

Also, a big part of this so-called mystery revolves around a human need to explain enigmas anyway they can. I have seen how some people borrow their easiest and favorite myth, some sort of science fiction and try to shape it to find some facts they read somewhere about Anasazi. Science fiction, obviously, is far from an appropriate truth. Joseph Campbell probably has commented on this phenomena before. At any rate, it is a durable myth--a sudden disappearance.

2. *Where did they come from?* Basically, Anasazi infiltrated 4 Corners area from somewhere else, perhaps from West, perhaps from South, maybe from further north. More than likely, tho, they came up from South--in northern Mexico or Central America. Of course I refer to a time just before Archaic or Paleo-Indian lived in southern fringes of 4 Corners, previously they also came across a land bridge from Asia.

3. *Who were they?* Genetic and language studies have shown that Puebloans came out of certain areas of Asia. Some tribes came from different places, such as Utes, Athabaskans, etc. Perhaps Anasazi ancestors came from one corner of Asia different than later-in-time indigents.

4. *If Paleo-Indian man domesticated horses, what would have been different?* What a fundamentally interesting question and how different their lives would have been. If

early on Paleo-Indian man had learned to ride and breed horses, anglo invaders would have had a much harder time surviving here. Just as certain Plains tribes 'ruled their universe,' so would have Anasazi, Hohokam, Mimbres, Fremont, Uto-Aztecans, etc have ruled 4 Corners. How different our landscape would appear.

There were certain technological achievements unavailable to a populace who moved continually, having to carry everything they owned on their own backs since they had no beasts of burdens. Jared Diamond writes of this aspect of humanity--of how cultures with beasts of burden advanced, those with none usually foundered.

5. *Why did they gradually switch from a hunter-gatherer to a sedentary-agricultural lifeway?* I have read articles which argue that a sedentary-horticultural lifeway was not any, or much, better than a hunter-gatherer lifeway and that actually latter were healthier. But, one thing perhaps these archaeologists seem to miss--what if Anasazi and others chose to switch out of love of place? Or more correctly, out of a desire to stay in one place, any place, rather than move around continually.

This is, of course, not a sufficient answer because even Anasazi never lived continuously in one place for very long. But their migrations were probably more severely limited than hunter-gatherers. Also, there must have been real benefits from a greater chance for a ready food supply [after putting more energy into agriculture] than merely wandering around hoping to find something to eat. Knowing that you planted scattered fields on dryland hoping some would be harvestable, and that you had small fields near a streambed with readily available water even tho some would be flooded, gave you a kind of certainty that you would be able to eat tomorrow. This shift to agriculture, plus building granaries and storing food surpluses for drier years must have given Anasazi and others a feeling of some security.

6. *Did endemic health/nutrition problems sap their mental outlook on life, or were these tribulations merely accepted as part of life?* I think we will never know for sure, but it does not hurt to speculate. When I look at how much Anasazi achieved, with their spread of habitations and farms, at how they built massive towns and houses under rock shelters, or on open mesas, how they built some road sections, how they spread into almost every habitable corner of this vast Greater 4 Corners area, I doubt that a few illnesses, genetic disorders, or endemic diseases caused by aggregation "got them down" much. I think they were an extremely tough and hardy people, and probably accepted "good aspects of life along with tougher aspects." I have seen many rock art panels which suggest to me a love of life, and a love of many animals they shared this land with. I see very few rock art elements which suggest an overwhelming dread, fear, hatred, or general malaise in their artists. And usually, a people's art represents their spiritual side--but usually not divorced from their more physical and immediate side.

7. *What use did they make of kivas or Great Houses?* Steven Lekson[8] argues that a kiva was not always a kiva, or as most anthropologists or archaeologists think of it. In some or most cases, he argues, a kiva was a communal living place, a more modern replacement for a pithouse. Whether it was living and gathering quarters for bachelors, while married couples had separate rooms, or not, is open to discussion. My intuition is that Lekson is correct. I think different styles of kiva interior decoration or architecture developed because these were their shared spaces. Individ houses may have been decorated or not, depending on who lived in them. But, perhaps, a kiva was also a kind of receiving room for guests and therefore murals reflected a communal personality or character of who lived in each

village. A kind of "putting on a good show for visitors".

Most archaeologists seem to agree that Great Houses, of which Chaco Canyon has classic examples served as some kind of trading center, or gathering center for ceremonies [or both]. Great Kivas, with classic examples open for vue near Aztec or Bloomfield, NM and Chaco C., seem by their very nature to suggest ceremonial uses, alternatively as meeting-halls.

8. *How much did certain centers of population/'power' such as Chaco Canyon really influence smaller and more dispersed settlements?* For a period of time and for those villages relatively close to Chaco/Aztec there was some influence in architecture, trade goods desired, lifeways, and perhaps religious ceremonies. But as Jeffrey S. Dean[9] (1996) and E. Charles Adams[10] (1996) argue for Kayenta and Hopi respectively, Chaco was peripheral to their development, and may have had little or no effect, specially for Hopi as Adams argues. Their proof lies in lack of similar architecture, in lack of certain trade goods, and in other artifacts representative of individ lifeways.

As others argue, Chaco and Aztec were temporary and unique phenomena for 4 Corners, and most Anasazi, Hohokam, Mimbres, Fremont, etc. but more specifically Anasazi lived in dispersed and smaller villages or isolated households [unit pueblos]. Generally speaking, Chaco/Aztec influence seems to wane east of Kayenta, east of Hopi area, north of San Juan river, and east of Chimney Rock, and just north, perhaps, of Mt Taylor. Chaco's local environment either never was, or changed to never be, able to handle large populations for long. But, as others argue, perhaps most of Chaco never was inhabited, with most rooms open for visitors at certain ceremonies.

Perhaps Chaco/Aztec was a kind of fad, a temporary change of attitudes, and perhaps there were certain personages of 'power' or influence at Chaco who awed other populaces, 'country hicks' [in modern parlance] and they sought to emulate 'big city folkways.' Perhaps not, perhaps it is a fascinating topic destined to be discussed forever. There are a great many articles written about what Chaco was, and how it influenced a "Greater Anasazi World."

9. *Why did they build defensive structures, or in defensive locales late in their occupation?* Several theories abound, one that they fought each other, or threatened to over limited resources [i.e. food], or that some invaders, perhaps Athabaskans [Apache and Navajo] actually threatened and fought to evict pre-Puebloans, or even just kept raiding so much that locals had to leave for safer grounds after trying defensive architecture and tactics. Perhaps we will never know. Personally, my intuition is that a bit of both, with an emphasis on latter theory, of invaders--actual or eminent.

10. *Were they peaceful farmer-traders or warlike, sometimes resorting to cannibalism?* According to ChristyTurner[11] and others, some Anasazi resorted to cannibalism as conditions worsened due to climatic changes and over-population. Some writers feel that cannibalism was a tool of certain shamans/medicine men to "steal power from their enemies." Personally I think anyone who thinks that has watched too many late-nite low-budget movies on tv. One theory I have not seen forwarded is that some people resorted to cooking their dead to feed their dogs, which makes more sense to me since I have never read that pre-Puebloans ever ate their domesticated dogs as Asians now do.

Or perhaps they cooked their dead to make some kind of glue for some unknown reason, or paste for paint. Eating your own dead is a fairly dramatic and strange phenomena, and for a people who often buried their dead under their own floors, and in their trash middens near their houses it makes no sense for them to turn around and start cooking stews of their parents. Coprolitic evidence of human consumption of other humans is scarce, and leads me to think there was some other explanation extant that we cannot or have yet to see--perhaps a few pathological individs.

Otherwise there is no particular abundance of evidence to support any theories of long-term warfare amongst tribes. Most defensive architecture has been shown to be in later stages, i.e. PIII, of habitation, and not earlier. Cliff houses could be argued to be defensive in nature, and some were so constructed, but over most of their period of habitation pre-Puebloans lived in pithouse communities which were hard to defend. This does not quite mean that Anasazi were always cheerful and peaceful as some New-Age believers would have them. There was probably as much evident violence in individ cases as Man has always shown, whether caused by jealousy, greed, lust, hatred, religion, etc.

* * *

GENERAL DISCUSSION

William Ferguson, in "Anasazi Ruins of the Southwest in Color" and "The Anasazi of Mesa Verde and the Four Corners" provides a fair introduction to Anasazi lifeways and both books have many photos of ruins, and some rock art. His text is not geared for those with advanced knowledge of archaeology or anthropology, but informative anyway. There are many other books that I revue in my website, but these I recommend for beginners.

There are many sources of information about Cedar Mesa and William Lipe has written some of most interesting articles about Cedar Mesa. Some of his articles, and others, are listed in my web site. "Archaeology of the Southwest," by Linda Cordell is an excellent all-around source for info about Anasazi. "Cowboys and Cave Dwellers," by Fred Blackburn and Ray Williamson, for history buffs, covers early 'pre-scientific excavators' such as Wetherills, McLoyd and Graham.

Polly Schaafsma and Sally Cole have both written several informative books about rock art, although not specifically for Cedar Mesa. Kenneth Castleton's two volume book about rock art is quite popular, also.

David Roberts has popularized Anasazi thru several venues, notably "In Search of the Old Ones," and several magazine articles.

Mesa Verde, Hovenweep, Chaco Canyon, Aztec and Bloomfield NM, Navajo Nat'l. Monument and Canyon de Chelley in NE Arizona, Anasazi Heritage Center near Dolores CO, Natural Bridges National Monument, Ute Mountain Tribal Park, Yellowjacket and Lowry ruins NW of Cortez CO, Sand Island rock art panel near Bluff UT, 9 Mile Canyon rock art panels near Wellington UT, Petrified Forest near Holbrook AZ, all provide easier ways to see sites than on Cedar Mesa.

Only a very few sites are marked on maps of Cedar Mesa; most notably Big Man Panel, Bannister ruin, Jailhouse ruin, Perfect Kiva, Turkey Pen and Split Level ruins are labeled on Trails Illustrated map #706. Some old topo maps have ruins marked but not labeled, and you will notice that most of these are eliminated on newer versions.

This is due to CRMs requests. Peter Tassoni, in his book "Hiking Guide to Cedar Mesa" [and Grand Gulch], gives directions to many sites that BLM wish he did not. However, many of these are already in "public domain" of knowledge; they just had not been so blatantly published before.

For any visitor new to this area and wanting to see sites on Cedar Mesa, Grand Gulch offers easiest means. It is relatively easier hiking, offers more sites, and is easiest to get to. A very good introductory hike is from KGRS down to and out Bullet Canyon. Or hike all thru Grand Gulch as a week-long backpack, and keep your eyes open.

As stated elsewhere, no ruins on Cedar Mesa are very large, usually only a handful of rooms. Moonhouse is perhaps largest in terms of a well-maintained 'village' and may be most photogenic on Cedar Mesa. It can be photographed easily from opposite side of its canyon, with a short hike from an access road.

Basically, anyone wanting to see what Cedar Mesa has to offer will have to get out there and hike, as there are no easy drive-up sites as in Mesa Verde.

CHAPTER 39
THOTS

I came to this land to explore, and I did. I did not find what I expected, but not less. I am no longer same person who started this hiking, this journey.

I took along some paper maps, I used a few tools. I got lost a few times.

There is only a small portion of what I learned, of what I came to understand that I can ever communicate. And in an ongoing way, I ask that readers use these passages as waypoints, as markers for your own lifeway, for your own enlargement.

Think of yourself as a pseudo-Anasazi, and ask yourself "why would I live here, what would I think of this place, this figure of a small bighorn family, drawn with love, or this wall of rooms perched on a hi mesa, lost in time but not in space?"

How would I get into my home carrying a load of water, corn, or mud for my walls? Could my children live here in joy, could we find enough food for them, and would our winter be beneficial but mild?

I may have helped you a little, in finding your way on Cedar Mesa. I could give you a map, but I cannot lead you by your hand; I cannot think your thots for you. I may only show you a way, it is up to you to choose your path.

Here you have read my way, how my path lead me towards an understanding of a landscape and a people. I may not have shown you all, only portions. Perhaps this picture is incomplete. I think I gave you all you need, if you are ready. And if you can ask yourself, "What is it I want to find here." Perhaps you will come to love this land, and work for its preservation. Perhaps someday we will meet on a route I have come to love, perhaps not.

* * *

I stood at a parting of trails, and pointed, saying, "I have been that way, it is very beautiful." And you did go that way, it shows on your being. You may have come back, to find what you missed when you were another sort of person. You found what you did not know you sought.

I once found a small panel of art and saw myself there, and did not wonder how that came to be. I once found a fallen down wall, and knew how I helped build it. I once knew where to find a pool of water, without looking. I feel no sorrow on returning after so many years gone, because I have never been here before. But I have known all along I would be back.

One time I met a woman crying, "what is it?" I asked. "it is just so beautiful," she spoke into her hands, "I love it so here." But I could not help her, she had not come to understand, yet. She could not quite know my grin, when I step onto sandstone.

Once I came across a group of hikers who wanted to hike from here to there and back. I had to tell them they could not do that, as they had not quite gotten to where they thot they were. And if you are not aware you are lost, you certainly cannot get to there from here, not ever.

One hike I met no-one, but I could tell they had been here not long ago. I wondered if they found beauty, or even looked. There was no sign, either way. I often think I leave confusing footprints on sand, as it seems I seldom use trails anymore. I tried looking for a path, but found that I had to climb out first, and where I wanted to go only Anasazi had agreed. This seemed to be confirmation that I was not lost. When I find coyote scat, or Anasazi steps, I know I am on my path, for these interpret my way.

I have known for a long time I was not an Anasazi, and yet I can see their trails before me, not quite covered by sand today. They lead straight to water, it seems, and my dogs are happy to follow.

We have tried hiking in a snowstorm, but feel that we are not making sense. So much warmer to sit in front of a fallen down house and watch flakes drift down. Only after they have piled up outside, do we venture out and continue our way.

And my way, with dogs to scout to sides, leads straight for a place I call home, even tho it was built by someone else. Along my way are zigs and zags, and stops as if to reflect. Sometimes I cross a rabbit's hop and skip, sometimes I follow where only deer go, often times I seem lost; but always it is my path, I shaped it and was shaped by it, and I followed it as much as it lead me, and I know it as well as it knows me, for we are one and same.

My path is my dream, or perhaps my path merely dreamed me up. Somewhere on some rock face is a drawing, and this is where I came from.

And as I leave, I know I will have to come back.

AFTERWORD

There are many places in SE Utah I did not cover, such as White Canyon, Moqui Canyon, fringes of Canyonlands [i.e. Beef Basin or Fable Valley], Indian Creek, around Moab, Butler Wash, Cottonwood Wash, Montezuma Canyon, Hammond Canyon and others. Some of these places are covered by other authors, some not. Mostly this is due to exigencies of time or limitations of my interest for whatever reason. In other words some places fascinate me, some draw me for indiscernible reasons, some do not. There are many details, places, or sites I deliberately did not discuss for their protection.

My use of terms such as Heuristic Way, Enemy Way, Sandstone Way, Mountain Way, Anasazi Way etc. are merely convenient labels and do not indicate that I am a New Ager, that I am a Navajo-wannabe, or that I think all Puebloans or Navajos are kool [some are].

For a list of relevant/interesting articles and more books than I list below, go to *www. anasazis.com.*

This book was not professionally edited, thus all errors, omissions, oddities of syntax, mistakes, repeats and boring paragraphs are solely my responsibility. I do feel, though, that many books professionally edited lose an ambient charm and tend to read similarly as if pressed from same mold.

I am not any kind of expert on Anasazi, their lifeways, or anthropology. I do know Cedar Mesa fairly well, though, and where many Anasazi sites are. I am self-educated, thus any opinions expressed here are purely my own--nobody else is to blame.

APPENDIX

SLICKROCK DICTIONARY

Alcove: an open faced cave, usually in sandstone on Cedar Mesa and most of 4 Corners. These sometimes flat floored caves are caused by water soaked rock spalling off their ceilings when undergoing freeze-thaw cycles or horizontal cracking due to inherent weaknesses in their ceilings. Some are full of ceiling rubble, some are full of sand and rubble, some have hard rock floors, some are large and deep, some more shallow and low-ceilinged. Anasazi used many of these alcoves for building sites, using either ledges, hammering steps in sandstone, or building ladders and/or towers for access.

Alcoves directly below a mesa-top cliff are usually damp with springs and vegetation. Those further down into a canyon are usually drier. In some places, Anasazi used both types.

Arroyo: a water cut gully thru clay/soils/rubble, along a watercourse, usually caused by an intermittent stream--e.g. from flashflooding. In archaeological texts, as relates to Anasazi, it is understood that cycles of aggradation and degradation of soils, gravel, and rocks sometimes left flat plains along canyon bottoms with meandering streams [e.g. alluvial flats]--excellent for farming except for limited sunlight. At other times other factors led to arroyo-cutting [such as lowering of a water table due to drought, over-grazing, clear-cutting, aquifer pumping, etc], as is currently evident everywhere on Cedar Mesa. For example, when hiking Ggulch in its streambed, you would be below a higher alluvium level, in an arroyo, and perhaps Anasazi would not have seen this deep arroyo and farmed above where you walk.

Crack: this is any failure in sandstone's integrity or self-adherence, usually in a vertical dimension, and I don't usually differentiate whether caused by a geologic fault, large top-cliff block spalling, or water. Most that are usable are caused by faults, tho. A prime example is a fine in/out route from upper Shangri La Canyon, pioneered by bighorns and deer which is a geologic fault and can be seen plainly from a distance.

Crossbedded Sandstone: as it applies to hiking Cedar Mesa provides little sloping ramps usually no wider than one's feet and assists in ascending or descending. Technically, I suppose it is caused when sand was laid down as dunes and then formed sandstone.

Dams: many small streamcourses across Cedar Mesa were dammed up by Anasazi to impound water for irrigation or household use. In some places you can still see rocks piled up oddly nearby watercourses, most of these dams have long ago been washed out by flashflooding. Anasazi also deliberately impounded water in slickrock pools near canyon rims knowing that it would eventually trickle down thru sandstone and reappear in first ledge springs [even tho Cedar Mesa sandstone is mostly continuous, there are harder layers or sometimes limestone beds which are impermeable and form springs].

Desert Varnish: see *patination.*

First, second, and third ledges: starting from rimtop as [ground] zero, going downhill. Cedar Mesa's canyons commonly have relatively wide and flat ledges, usually on sides facing sun [south-facing]. Below third ledge these canyon frequently steepen into cliffs. Sometimes there are up to 6 ledge systems along a canyon. Rarely do these three ledge systems continue uninterrupted for miles, but it does happen. They are often connected intermittently by colluvial deposits and talus/jp slopes, sometimes by slick rock ramps, sometimes they merge.

Gully: I use it mostly to label minor erosional cuts, either on sandstone flats, slopes, or along either side of a canyon wall. For example, when walking along a Cedar Mesa canyon's ledge, often a sandstone gully entrenches up to an impassable cliff, either causing you to detour, jump across, or retreat depending on its progress. I use it interchangeably as a canyon-to-be, e.g. sidegully which provides an in/out for a canyon, but it is not entrenched enuf to be a true sidecanyon.

Hoodoo: a mushroom shaped dome or mesita of sandstone caused by erosion of a softer underlying layer of sandstone which supports a harder dome [or roof] of sandstone. On Cedar Mesa they are easily found near Government Trail, downcanyon from Collins C trail, across ggulch near Hat Rock, or anywhere near Water Canyon. Hoodoos are usually found up high along canyon rims, sometimes on projecting promontories somewhat lower than mesa-top levels. Often they form semi-caves which were seldom, but sometimes, used by Archaic and later Anasazi, due to nature of their often discontinuous and leaky 'roofs'. Sometimes these hoodoos are very large, but usually less than 300 feet in diameter.

Patination: staining by minerals on sandstone, i.e. *desert varnish*. Commonly seen most plainly in alcoves as dark streaks. Manganese, iron, sodium and potassium salts usually form these stains. Any recently fallen boulder will show differing quantities of patination. Many rock art panels were etched thru desert varnish and have since had fresh layers of patination added. Archaeologists can guess-timate relative ages of rock art by how much new patination has been added. There are a few rock art panels on Cedar Mesa almost completely covered by desert varnish.

Sandstone: my dictionary states "A sedimentary rock

formed by the consolidation and compaction of sand and held together by a natural cement, such as silica." In geologic terminology there are many types of sandstones, differentiated by their mineral makeup. Typically this translates to shades of color, whether a particular sandstone forms cliffs, how these cliffs hold together, how parts spall off, how cracks form, or how it erodes, how it was laid down, whether it is cross-bedded or not. For example along Indian Creek, going towards Needles District of Canyonlands, rock climbers love Wingate Sandstone, for its tall cliffs with nice cracks, corners, chimneys etc. Most of Cedar Mesa is thin layers of loess or sand [as dunes] on mesa top levels, and Cedar Mesa sandstone many hundreds of feet deep, underneath. Canyons on Cedar Mesa mostly are formed when water cuts an entrenching course down thru these underlying layers, assisted in places by faulting and to a limited extent wind.

According to some diagrams in one of Michael Kelsey's books [top to bottom] are Kayenta formation, Wingate Sandstone, Chinle formation, Moss Back, Moenkopi Formation, [sometimes Organ Rock Shale], Cedar Mesa Sandstone, [sometimes Halgaito Formation], Upper Cutler Formation etc. Sometimes these strata continue underneath for miles [horizontally], sometimes they are interrupted or thin and thick. White Canyon and Ggulch are in Cedar Mesa Sandstone.

On Cedar Mesa this variety represents itself as either continuous cliffs, steep slopes of talus, ledge/cliff/ledge/cliff, slickrock ramps, bulges, domes, promontories, etc. Hiking is very often interrupted by boulder fall, by abrupt ends to ledges; or helped by joining ledges, boulder fall. There are very few 'slot canyons' on Cedar Mesa, tho White Canyon has a few.

For example, along one side of Grand Gulch are steep cliffs interspersed with ledges. Along opposite side are often steep slopes with cliff bands, boulder fall, talus buildup, and jp's. Kane Gulch's trail follows its streamcourse, and thru biggest cliff band a long-ago constructed livestock trail is used today by hikers. Government Trail descends on east side of ggulch, some dynamite was used, and trail construction by building up rock ramps is evident today [built by CCC workers in Gr. Depression era]. Collins Canyon trail was constructed for livestock, with dynamite in places, and is somewhat washed out but quite popular.

About half of Cedar Mesa's in/out routes are via sidecanyons or gully-slopes [e.g. canyons-to-be in some distant future], about half are directly down steep slopes whether on sunnyside or shadowy-side [north or south]. Fish Canyon's upper in/out trail uses talus-jp slopes interspersed with slickrock ramps.

Comb Ridge is an uplifted sandstone ridge which starts at Abajos and ends near Kayenta, Arizona. It is broken only in a few places: by nature notably at San Juan River, by modern man by dynamite, by Anasazi at a few places with Moki Steps hammered out while clinging precariously to its cliffy western side. When you drive along Comb Wash you can see its layers, when you hike its eastern side you climb up a mostly uniform layer of Cedar Mesa sandstone cut by many deep but short canyons.

Sandstonicity: very similar to serendipity except as refers to hiking or finding my way on slickrock/sandstone. Serendipity often refers to coincidences which seem to assist in one's path thru life. Sandstonicity more specifically to coincidences of landscape/ terrain, in how an area or feature lends itself to housing an Anasazi ruin, where there is water nearby and a route onto mesatop. Also to many quirks of slickrock which allow sometimes easy travel across or thru it. May also be seen as a home-forming process, Sandstone Way may be seen as a pathway leading to acceptance of, and adherence to, sandstonicity. One is a material given, other is a system of knowledge, e.g. 'Way'.

Slickrock: most dictionaries don't even list 'slickrock' as it may be mostly a colloquial term used by residents of 4 Corners area of Southwestern US. Perhaps it started with jeep-drivers who love to drive on sandstone: when wet or when surface grit loosens it becomes slick [slippery]. Now it is widely used instead of 'sandstone'. Some writers claim slickrock is sloping sandstone, others don't differentiate. I use it interchangeably with sandstone, perhaps based more on "how it sounds" than any specific inherent meaning.

Tinaja: a pool formed in rock by water, usually along a watercourse. Tinajas can be found in many types of rock formations, most common are perhaps granite and sandstone. See *Waterpocket* also, but I often use 'tinaja' to refer to any slickrock pool, even if on an open slickrock flat out of any clear watercourse.

Waterpocket: supposedly a pool formed in between fins of sandstone, as in Waterpocket Fold area, in Arches NP, and other areas in SE Utah; or a pool formed on slickrock flats by erosional forces [water-wind] and not necessarily located in a watercourse. I have also noticed that in a shallow depression a top layer of sandstone absorbs water, later in winter it can freeze and crack up forming flattish rocks--I think a long continuation of this cycle forms many of these slickrock pools. I mostly use term 'tinaja.'

NOTES

ABBREVIATIONS

BCS: Barrier Canyon Style [rock art]
BLM: Bureau of Land Management
cl: creek [canyon] left, facing downstream
CM: Cedar Mesa
cr: creek [canyon] right, facing downstream
CRM: Cultural Resource Manager
GG: Grand Gulch
ggulch: grand gulch
grcanyon: Grand Canyon
jp: juniper/pinyon [jp's: plural form]
KGRS: Kane Gulch Ranger Station
mm: mile marker
NBNM: Natural Bridges National Monument
NMF: Not Much Fun [hiking]
NPS: National Park Service
USFS: United States Forest Service
VOG: Valley of Gods

* * *

CEDAR MESA: there are actually no cedar trees on Cedar Mesa, only junipers, pinyon pine, cottonwoods, and other varieties.

CHAPTER 4: Fine Art of Reading This Land

1. *White Man's Way*: a smug and arrogant conviction that our modern lifeways are better, cleaner, saner, healthier, higher quality than those of "primitive man," whether Anasazi, Andean farmer, or Easter Islander, and a failure to see how prehistoric man could have found happiness, joy, love, or how he could have felt "love of place." I admit I am

a white man, but I don't always think as such. I try to see beauty in an Anasazi house site, or farm patch, and realize that not all ruins are as spectacular as large cliff dwellings in Mesa Verde canyons. Most are small, falling apart, no more than piles of rubble. But, it is also where they are located, what kind of vue is around, how much exposure to sunlite, where is nearest water, how hard is an approach ledge, etc that can suggest much.

Visiting a museum such as Anasazi Heritage Center helps fill in a mental image, but unless someone goes out there and restores every pre-historic ruin all over 4 Corners, I have to use my imagination--I prefer seeing artifacts, rock art, and building ruins in place and think of how it was for those who lived there, not how I am just a temporary visitor with modern conveniences and a home to return to.

CHAPTER 7: Solo Hiking

1. Whether kivas are always specifically for ceremonial purposes. See "*The Idea of the Kiva in Anasazi Archaeology*" by Stephen H. Lekson, KIVA, Vol. 53, No. 3, 1988.

CHAPTER 8: Getting To Know You

1. *Behind and beyond*: an ineffable quality which perhaps swallowed Everett Ruess--giving him what he desired most to embrace and become--one with nature [or so some fans would have us believe]. My argument with putting Ruess on some sort of pedestal, as hero, as example, or enigma is A) there is zero guarantee of survival in his imagined actions, except in minds of groupies, B) perhaps he was actually killed by someone, C) perhaps he just had a fatal accident with no real significance other than simple disappearance, D) mysteries only have value if never solved, but science always resolves to explain away enigmatic phenomena, and too many people prefer a mystery over a solution, E) despite former discussion I do not care very much, one way or another about Ruess [or another guy immortalized by J.

Krakauer]. Some people put this into simple mantras, e.g. "Back of Beyond."

My intent is merely to express a certain *je ne sais quoi* that others have noticed and commented on. It is out there, it is felt, but nobody can quite "put a finger on it."

See also Craig Childs, "*Soul of Nowhere*" possibly in 'Passage' chapter, he writes of a desire in some people to jump into Grand Canyon--indeed some do commit suicide at GC overlooks. He writes of how even Anasazi perhaps built houses into rock shelters as a similar desire--to be swallowed up by a landscape, to become one with.

CHAPTER 9: Hozho or Why I Hike

1. Maria Mitchell was an astronomer in late 1800's (1818-1889). Once when traveling by railroad across country to observe an eclipse, she wrote [later] of a stitch in her progress caused by feuding railroad companies.

"We learned that there was a war between the two railroads which unite at Pueblo, and war, no matter where or when it occurs, means ignorance and stupidity.

"The unit of measure of value, which the railroad man believes in is entirely different from that in which the scientist rests his faith.

"A war between two railroads seemed very small compared with two minutes forty seconds of observation of a total eclipse. One was terrestrial, the other cosmic."

From "Growing Up Female in America."

CHAPTER 14: Trepidation Blues

1. "*Why, they have got everything here they need. There is water, there is farmland, there is a lovely view, the climate is well, it is so unlike other major population concentrations, or at least other highly reported places such as Chaco Canyon and the Maya land where there are anomalies, where there does not appear to be an adequate supply of one of these basic resources.*"

Art Rohn writing about an outsider archaeologist used to

working in Mesoamerica, when taken to some sites in SW Colorado. Pg. 179, "Proceedings of Anasazi Symposium, 1981."

CHAPTER 16: Enemy Way

1. Flexic: a kind of alternate-logic, e.g. why people do things that seem illogical but true by their standards of either that moment or of their lifeway-to-date. "His flexic wasn't obvious to friends, and they agreed perhaps they didn't know him all that well." Also: a way of waiting for clues to reveal themselves in an ongoing process of life, "She's got a flexic outlook towards her current problems." Alternately: a philosophy of life unconnected with standard dogmas, religions, politics or even current paradigm. "Their flexics are visible in every decision they make, how they live their lives, in their ethics, morals, and how they treat their children."

CHAPTER 23: Walking Lightly

1. *Landality*: when a person has specific characteristics and ambiances I think of personality; when a landscape has specific characteristics and ambiances I think *landality.*

2. "*Book of Answers*": forthcoming.

CHAPTER 24: Water

1. Craig Childs: "The Secret Knowledge of Water".

CHAPTER 27: Hiking

1. Ferguson: "The Anasazi of Mesa Verde and the Four Corners".

2. Ferguson: ibid.

CHAPTER 30: Honaker Trail Thots

1. This chapter, and most material that follows in THIRD LEDGE, originally appeared on my website, *www.anasazihikes.com*, now *www.anasazis.com*, circa 1999-2000.

CHAPTER 34: Arch Canyon

1. Limited Activity Sites, sometimes abbreviated as "l.a.s"

are prehistoric sites such as a kiln area, where Anasazi shaped arrowheads [a lithic scatter signifies these], where Anasazi processed food near their fields, where they may have camped while tending their crops, where they perhaps gathered minerals for pigments, where they built a dam to collect water, where they drew rock art but did not live nearby, or for many other reasons used an area only occasionally.

2. AWUF, Architecture With Unknown Functions, e.g. "cultural features that are not well described or do not fit easily into descriptive categories" quoted from pg. 90, Adler: "The Prehistoric Pueblo World AD 1150-1350." These features could be: earthworks, low stone walls or stone alignments, cliff edge plazas enclosed by room blocks and low stone walls, stone circles, rectangular stone boxes, and possible defensive circular stone walls around cliff top cracks at cliff-top sites. [paraphrased from same source].

CHAPTER 35: Hiking Cedar Mesa

1. See notes, Chapter 29, 1.

CHAPTER 38: Anasazi Way

1. Adler, Michael A.: notes Chapter 33, 2.

2. *Land Bridge*: sometime during an Ice Age, when world seas were lowered due to massive glaciers containing much of this planet's water, a temporary land bridge spanned gap between Siberia and Alaska. Approximately 11,000 years BP [before present], this land bridge would have provided an avenue for migrants seeking new lands to settle or a way to escape population pressures and enemies.

Concurrently, a separation in glacial icepack thru upper Canada/Alaska would have helped. Early crossers would probably have sent 'runners' back to spread word of their success.

3. Diamond, Jared: *Guns, Germs, and Steel* [and ships I would add].

4. Ferguson, William: *The Anasazi of Mesa Verde and the*

Four Corners.

5. Cordell, Linda: *Archaeology of the Southwest.*

6. Ortiz, "*Handbook of North American Indians,*" Vol. 9 page 29.

7. *Akchin*: arroyo mouth irrigation, using periodic flood waters from rainstorms and/or spring-time runoff.

8. Lekson, Steven: notes Chapter 7, 1.

9. Dean (1996) "*Kayenta Anasazi Settlement Transformations In NE AZ: AD 1150 to 1350*" in Adler, notes Chapter 33, 2.

10. Adams (1996) "*The Pueblo III-Pueblo IV Transition in the Hopi Area, AZ*", Adler, ibid.

11. Turner, Christy: "*Man Corn...*"

SUGGESTED READING

For more go to www.anasazis.com, or your Library.

GENERAL

Anasazi Ruins of the Southwest in Color, William Ferguson

Desert Solitaire, Edward Abbey

In Search of the Old Ones, David Roberts

The Anasazi of Mesa Verde and the 4 Corners, William Ferguson

The Delight Makers, Adolf Bandelier

The Secret Knowledge of Water, Craig Childs

Wind in the Rocks, Ann Zwinger

HISTORICAL

Anasazi Basketmaker...1990 Symposium, Atkins, Blackburn, et. al. [Cultural Resource Series No. 24 BLM--Utah]

Cowboys and Cave Dwellers, Fred Blackburn and Ray Williamson

Richard Wetherill: Anasazi, Frank McNitt

The Cliff Dwellers of the Mesa Verde, Gustav Nordenskiold

Traders to the Navajo, Frances Gillmor

The Wetherills of the Mesa Verde, Maurine Fletcher

ROCK ART

Indian Rock Art of the Southwest, Polly Schaafsma

Legacy on Stone, Sally Cole

Petroglyphs and Pictographs of Utah, Vol. 1 and 2, Kenneth Castleton

Rock Art Symbols of the Greater Southwest, Alex Patterson

The Rock Art of Utah, Polly Schaafsma

ARCHAEOLOGY/ANTHROPOLOGY

Archaeology of the Southwest, Linda Cordell

Colorado Prehistory: A Context for the Southern Colorado River Basin, ed. by William Lipe et. al.

Cultural Diversity and Adaptation..., Lori and Paul Reed editors

Guns, Germs, and Steel, Jared Diamond

Handbook of North American Indians, Vol. 9, ed. Alfonso Ortiz

Man Corn..., Christy Turner

Origins of the State and Civilization, Elman R. Service

People of the Mesa, Shirley Powell and George Gumerman

Sacred Land, Sacred View, Robert McPherson

The Architecture of Social Integration in Prehistoric Pueblos, ed. by W. Lipe and Michelle Hegmon

The Chaco Meridian, Stephen Lekson

Themes for Southwestern Prehistory, George Gumerman

The Origins of Southwestern Agriculture, R.G. Matson

Theory of Culture Change, Julian Steward

The Prehistoric Pueblo World AD 1150-1350, ed. Michael Adler

Time, Space, And Transition in Anasazi Prehistory, Michael Berry

HIKING

A Hiking Guide to Cedar Mesa, Peter Tassoni

Colorado Plateau Hiking Guides [various ones], Michael Kelsey

ABOUT THIS AUTHOR

Since 1973, I have lived in Arizona, Colorado, and then Utah, with a two year hiatus to Wyoming [oil field job] in late 70's. I have worked in a wide assortment of jobs, ranging from ski lift attendant, bus driver, truck driver, carpenter and raft guide after 1973. In 1997 I moved to SE Utah from Durango, Colorado, and began hiking more intensively on Cedar Mesa. My website, originally anasazihikes.com, now anasazis.com, first went online in 1999.

When not consulting with BLM as a Rattlesnake Psychologist on Cedar Mesa, I manage an 11 acre Jackrabbit and Sagebrush Ranch in SE Utah. Three dogs allow me to live in their doghouse, they do let me buy my own food, as theirs is 'special', and they tolerate me when I write of them as 'mine'. Two of these dogs let me go with them on many slickrock hikes, letting me drive their pickup.

There is no map for where you are going, there are no signs along your path, nor will I show you a way. There is no understanding without turning corners, and sometimes only after you have become lost can you find yourself. What you do with yourself afterwards, and with whom you share is up to you.

Printed in the United States
18126LVS00004B/118-120

9 781589 393585